Sharing the Word of Hope with the World

Compartiendo la Palabra de la Esperanza en el Mundo

Das Wort der Hoffnung mit der Welt teilen

*Journal of the European Society of Women
in Theological Research*

*Anuario de la asociación europea de mujeres
para la investigación teológica*

*Jahrbuch der Europäischen Gesellschaft
für theologische Forschung von Frauen*

Volume 24

**Bibliographical information and books for review
in the Journal should be sent to:**
*Sigridur Gudmarsdottir, PhD.,
Skolegata 2, 8900 Brønnøysund, Norway*

**Articles for consideration for the Journal
should be sent to:**
*Sigridur Gudmarsdottir, PhD.,
Skolegata 2, 8900 Brønnøysund, Norway*

Sharing the Word of Hope with the World

*Compartiendo la Palabra de la Esperanza
en el Mundo*

Das Wort der Hoffnung mit der Welt teilen

Editors:
Sabine Dievenkorn, Teresa Toldy

PEETERS
LEUVEN – PARIS – BRISTOL, CT
2016

Journal of the European Society of Women
in Theological Research, 24

© 2016, Peeters Publishers, Leuven / Belgium
ISBN 978-90-429-3426-9
ISSN 1783-2454
eISSN 1783-2446
D/2016/0602/116
Cover design by Margret Omlin-Küchler

CONTENTS – INHALT – ÍNDICE

Journal of the European Society of Women in Theological Research 24 (2016) 1-11.
doi: 10.2143/ESWTR.24.0.3170022

Sabine Dievenkorn, Dimitra Koukoura, Teresa Toldy

Das Wort der Hoffnung mit der Welt teilen – Sharing the Word of Hope with the World – Voces de mujeres en tiempo de crisis: 16th International ESWTR Conference, 17-21 August 2015 Kolymbari, Greece

Das Wort der Hoffnung mit der Welt teilen

Der historische Augenblick ist aus Sicht der in Theologie forschenden Frauen unübersehbar durch politische und soziale Schwierigkeiten determiniert. Hautsächlich handelt es sich dabei um Herausforderungen, die sich vor allem aus den ökonomischen und monetären Grundentscheidungen der Europäischen Union herleiten lassen. Daher ist es nicht die feministische Grundlagenforschung der Theologie, die den vorliegenden Band des ESWTR Jahrbuches so spannend macht. Der konkrete Tagungsort war Kreta in Griechenland. Die konkrete Tagungszeit war August 2015, ein Höhepunkt der politischen und sozialen griechischen Finanz- und Bankenkrise.

Eine nicht zu unterschätzende konkrete Auswirkung dieser Krise war es, dass auf Anraten des Auswärtigen Amtes in Deutschland, von Reisen nach Griechenland abgeraten wurde. Auch wenn vom deutschen Außenministrium keine direkte so genannte Reisewarnung herausgegeben wurde, weil „Griechenland aufgrund unklarer sicherheitspolitischer Verhältnisse und damit einhergehender Versorgungsengpässe kein sicheres Urlaubsland mehr sei", wurde diese in den deutschen Medien aber nicht ohne Nachhaltigkeit immer wieder diskutiert und in Frage gestellt.[1] Die griechischen Geldautomaten waren für Bankabhebungen von mehr als 60,- € pro Tag geschlossen. Mit Kreditkarten konnte nirgends bezahlt werden. Jeglicher Finanzfluss war schwierig. Was hier wie eine Beschreibung touristischer Umstände erscheint, ist ein Spiegelbild tiefer Verunsicherungen. Ökonomisch. Sozial. Politisch. In der Geschichte

---

[1] http://www.welt.de/reise/nah/article143643682/Noch-gilt-Griechenland-als-sicheres-Urlaubs-land.html, 1 Juni 2016.

Europas hat sich signifikant in der Zunahme konservativer ideolgischer Strö-
mungen gezeigt.

Die feministische und feminine Stimme erhebt sich gegen gegen wachsende
reaktionäre Ideologien und aktuelle politische Entscheidungen. Die vorliegenden Artikel in Forum und Hauptteil sind Ausdruck dessen. Theologische Wissenschaftlerinnen reflektieren die politischen Herausforderungen und erheben
ihre Stimme im Chor sozialer Akteure, der Gesellschaft und Wissenschaft
zur Kenntnis. Es ist zu allererst die aktuelle Beschreibung der politischen
Umstände, durch die die europäische Gegenwart bestimmt wird und in denen
die Situationen von Frauen empörender Weise immer noch und immer wieder
eine untergeordnete Rolle spielt.

Das öffentliche und akademische Gespräch und der politische und popu-
listische Diskurs über die so genannte Flüchtlingsfrage haben in der Zeit zwischen dem Stattfinden der Konfrenz und der Herausgabe des vorliegenden
Bandes eine noch dramatischere Gestalt angenommen. Zwischen offenen und
zu schließenden Grenzen in dem eigentlich vereinten Europa, brechen wert-
konservative Vorstellungen auf, die in ihrer Macht des Faktischen feministische
Grundpositionen neu in Frage stellen und als Ideologie brandmarken. Die
modernen rückwärts gewandten Kräfte Europas finden sich schnell zusammen.
Sprachliche, kulturelle und historische Unterschiede spielen von Russland bis
Ungarn, von Finnland bis Bosnien-Herzegowina eine scheinbar so untergeordnete Rolle, dass frauenspezifische Werte und Wahrnehmungen nicht länger
relevant zu sein scheinen.

Doch sie müssen zu Gehör gebracht werden. Feministische Anliegen und
feministisch motivierte Positionen dürfen in der aktuellen Debatte nicht dem
gewaltigen Rechtsruck, der sich global und regional, öffentlich und privat so
laut und gestenreich positioniert, zum Opfer fallen. Institutionell und familiär
werden Tendenzen der Zensur und Selbstzensur sichtbar, denen es entgegenzu-
treten gilt. Von den Bemühungen der lateinamerikanischen Befreiungstheolgie
konnte die Europäische Theologie und Wissenschaft lernen, dass die geografische
Verortung von Lehre und Forschung ergebnisrelevant ist. Eine Ortsbeschrei-
bung ist die Basis auf der sich Gedanken- und Reflexionsgebäude errichten
lassen. Die Frage nach dem Wo? ist für die Antworten auf ein Was? Wie? und
Wer? ausschlaggebend. Diese Einsicht verlangt ein genaues Hinsehen, eine
genaue Beschreibung, die noch vor jeder thetischen Verallgemeinerung an
einer gemeinsamen Wahrnehmung von Phänomenen interessiert ist.

Das ist einer der unschätzbaren Werte der Europäischen Gesellschaft für
Frauen in theologischer Forschung: dass Wissenschaftlerinnen neben ihren

Forschungsergebnissen auch ihre Forschungsbeobachtungen teilen, dass Solidarität nicht nur Empathie ermöglicht, sondern auch eine gemeinsame kritische Perspektive, dessen Basis nicht selten eine geteilte Diskriminierungserfahrung einschließt.

Theologische Antworten auf politisch soziale Fragen sind ebenso nötig wie gefährlich. Gefährlich, weil in Kombination mit religiösen Institutionen und Autoritäten, Antworten aus dem Bereich des Unverfügbaren verfügbar gemacht zu werden drohen. Die als unüberschreitbar definierte Grenze zwischen Glauben und Wissen gerät ins Wanken. Notwendige Verallgemeinerungen lassen nicht immer den hinreichenden Raum für individuelle, regionale oder auch antidiskriminatorische Sichtweisen und Entscheidungen. So wird auch die Gender-Perspektive politisch schnell zu einer sozial unerheblichen und Entscheidungsprozesse verkomplizierenden sozialen Kategorie. Sie kommt im Zug wichtiger Entscheidungen einfach nicht mehr vor und wird faktisch irrelevant

Ein Beispiel dafür ist die aktuelle Übereinkunft in Ungarn, die es den jüdischen Gemeinden nicht ermöglicht, sich selbst als eine eigene Bevölkerungsgruppe zu betrachten. Judentum, so der politische Beschluss, ist eine Religion, wie das Christentum, der Islam oder andere. Der anthropologisch und theologisch herausfordernde Umstand , dass im Judentum entsprechend dem eigenen religiösen und demokratischen Selbstverständnis, Religion und Zugehörigkeit zu einem Volk ineinanderfallen, wird nicht berücksichtigt. Wie können angesichts solcher Schwierigkeiten jetzt auch noch zusätzlich Debatten über patrilinear vererbbares Judentum berücksichtigt werden?! Wen interessiert es schon, dass die Religionszugehörigkeit sich nach dem Gesetz der Halacha ausschließlich über die jüdische Mutter definiert. Wer weiss denn schon, dass das jüdische Ehebett, wenn es den Normen der Halacha entspricht, aus einem beweglichen und einem festen, so zu sagen unverrückbaren Teil besteht, da das Verbringen gemeinsamer Nächte intimer Zweisamkeit sich im streng religösen Judentum besonderen religösen Vorschriften beugt. Wer wollte, wenn die Aufassung über das Judentum als Volk oder als Glaubensgemeinschaft diskutiert wird, über Kindererziehung und Ehebetten reden? Frauenfragen stehen schnell hinten an, wenn es um das Große und Ganze geht.

Betrachtet man dieses Phänomen des Reduzierens in einem größeren Kontext, ist mindestens im westlichen Europa zu beobachten, wie sehr die Stimme der christlichen Kirchen relativiert wird. Ob dies nun durch Zensur oder aber auch durch vorauseilende Selbstzensur erfolgt, kann hier nicht geklärt, sondern nur gefragt werden. Klar scheint aber, dass es den Ruf nach stärkerer Visualisierung der Religionen im Prozess der Solidarisierung mit denen gibt, die nicht auf der Sonnenseite des Lebens und der Nordhalbkugel der Erde leben, gibt. Das betrifft auch den in der Flüchtlingskrise in Deutschland stärker werdenden Wunsch nach klaren Worten islamischer Gemeinden und Geistlicher, wenn theologisch und politisch zu fordern ist, dass Terrorakte laut und vernehmbar verurteilt werden.

Sabine DIEVENKORN

Sharing the Word of Hope with the World

The sublime voice of the Armenian soprano of the Vienna Opera, Hasmig Babyan, came from the depths of her soul. Her facial expression followed the meaning of the lyrics and her lips, whenever they uttered the refrain "Cilicia"[2], revealed the deep pain of the Armenians for their genocide. At the same time, however, they assured their firm resolve to stand up and continue their course in life.

On the evening of 19 July 2015, high up on the rock of Bikfaya, in the outskirts of Beirut, the concert was dedicated to the 100th anniversary of the Turkish massacre of 1.5 million Armenians. That bright night, the soprano's sublime voice took many different shades and, when it masterfully elevated, the blowing breeze lifted it higher and seemed to carry it on to neighbouring Syria: to the ruins of destroyed cities by the relentless bombing and to the countless refugee camps. The velvet voice of joy and sorrow seemed to embrace the grief and despair of Syrian women among the debris of the bombing, and the throng of crowded refugee camps. There is neither joy nor a drop of hope, only Rachel's inconsolable crying for her children which no longer exist.

In Europe itself, in its southeast end, a similar women's lament endures for nearly half a century. Since the Turkish invasion of Cyprus in July 1974, black-dressed women seek some 1,500 missing captives. They hold the photos of their loved ones to their chest, and drowned in tears, they ask: What happened to our people? Where are they? Are they alive, have they been killed, have they died from their hardships? Can they even find enough of their bones to bury them, to pacify their soul and their dead?

For many decades, pain and sorrow do not know any end. Recently, the impoverished voices of refugees arriving at European coasts of the Mediterranean spread even into our own continent.

---

[2]   The Armenian Kingdom of Cilicia was an independent principality formed during the High Middle Ages by Armenian refugees fleeing the Seljuk invasion of Armenia. It was centered in the Cilicia region northwest of the Gulf of Alexandretta.

In extreme forms of crisis, the cry of despair in face of devastation is very strong; and it has no gender characteristic. It comes from the deepest part of the human existence to scatter everywhere a shocking "why"? Why so much hatred and so much absurdity? Why so much analgesia to human life and so much disrespect for human cultural creation?

Woman's anguish, however, is indescribable and unique. Especially when a mother is asked to bury her children, children who lively jumped within in her womb and were raised in her embrace. Even if they survive the bloodshed, they consequently try to live in the caravans of refugees and in the unsafe boats of smugglers.

Undoubtedly, prolonged deadly conflicts and the multiple disasters that follow create serious crises, as is currently happening in our Southeast borders. Crisis, of a different form but not any less serious, exists also in the very Europe where the good of peace has been established for seven decades after the deadly Second World War – with the sole exception of some local armed conflicts that accompanied in some cases the collapse of totalitarian regimes in the beginning of the last decade of the 20th century and today in Ukraine.

The banking crisis that erupted in 2008 in the USA and quickly took proportions of a global financial crisis mainly challenged the Southern (European) countries, where weak economies did not have enough antibodies to resist it. Some of the painful consequences we are experiencing today are unemployment, reduced benefits, increased direct and indirect taxes, the high cost of life, and over-indebted households.

For this reason, in recent years crowds of citizens in Southern Europe often speak up indignantly. They seek a fairer distribution of wealth and a more human face to economic development.

Within the general outcry in face of the failure of the financial plans of the powerful, an anthropocentric orientation of the economy is the solution proposed for a more just economic-political system. As compensation for the excessive profits of businesses at the expense of weaker the Corporate Social Responsibility is proposed. Businesses should show respect to culture, to human dignity, they should grant equal opportunities and improve the quality of life, and should especially aim to preserve the natural environment.[3]

Furthermore, in the European Union the Social Economy, which ensures smooth and fair coexistence for all, is systematically promoted, without social

---

[3] http://www.eop.org.gr/news/109-2011-11-14-12-19-13.html

and economic exclusion, targeting collective benefit[4] and general social interest. In this way, the following are integrated into economic and social life: a) vulnerable population groups, and b) specific disadvantaged population groups finding it difficult to integrate smoothly into the labour market. This shift of the economy towards the collective good is encouraging, because it limits the unsaturated gain of the few and powerful, while simultaneously strengthening the sense of social justice in the distribution of goods.

The economic and moral crisis in Europe is interlinked: one feeds the other. Morality, however, comes first; it touches all European countries, adversely affects the choices of citizens, and threatens the cohesion of society. The moral crisis is linked to disrespect for human values, which constitute a society and ensure the balance between the individual and the collective good. These principles, convictions, and beliefs that shape people's character from birth and with every step regulate their decisions, dictating what is right and what is wrong, are taught by family, school, spiritual leaders, friends, and the wider society. Human values fit in human nature itself and for this reason most are found in all cultures, despite their diversity. Honesty, reliability, discipline, solidarity, respect for the environment and monuments of culture, peace, justice, care for the common good, and love are found in myths, proverbs, literature, art, philosophy, and above all, in the sacred texts of most peoples of the earth.

In order that these precious values germinate and bear fruit, they require fertile soil, oxygen and light, which are offered by religious faith. Otherwise they wither; they languish and finally drown in the wild vegetation of falsehood imposed as truth, and in individualism displayed as the criterion of everything.

Selfishness, the love of money, indifference to suffering, fraud, the breakdown of family and friendship, disrespect for human dignity and life itself, xenophobia, ecological threat, and the withering of religious faith are some worrying symptoms of the contemporary moral crisis. It is noticed in European societies to a lesser or greater degree, but nevertheless in its entirety, which makes it particularly worrying.

The treatment of this crisis is linked with the awakening and mobilisation of various factors, by definition contributing to culture and creating a similar ethos for the members of society. Family, spiritual leaders – both men and women, educators, and religious believers are all called upon to rise from oblivion and lead this mobilisation.

---

[4]   http://www.keko.gr/el/Pages/page2

Today's Europe is multicultural. If we consider that religion is still an important element in portraying culture, then we may accurately say that it is multi-religious. The rapid development of technology in communication and transport has led to the globalisation of economy and facilitated the movement of cultural elements, isolated individuals. and also mass populations to all countries of the world. For a variety of reasons, of which the most painful is polemical conflicts and political persecution, crowds of refugees arrived with numerous economic migrants to European countries as well. Modern European societies are therefore basically multicultural and tolerant to otherness.

Religion belongs both to the indisputable human rights protected by the principles of democracy and to the personal sphere. While most European countries are not considered anymore to be purely Christian, one cannot deny the role Christianity had played for two millennia in the formation of European civilisation, with Roman law and ancient Greek culture at its base. The current role of the Christian faith is the fight against the moral crisis. Within the framework of the free movement of ideas, the same applies to all religious traditions as well as schools of thought inspired by humanism. What is important is to revitalise moral values to form the basis of life for modern members of our society.

The role of Christians cannot be ignored. However, it must be initiated. Furthermore, Christians themselves undergo a crisis, as their congregations are constantly thinning, churches are being sold as historic buildings for various uses, and Christ ceases to serve as a source of hope and strength.

Revitalising the Christian tradition appears to be necessary in all European Christian Churches at the dawn of the third millennium: Re-evangelisation, that is, the evangelisation of the younger generations of traditionally Christian Europeans, who have not preserved something that resembles the faith of their ancestors, and seem either to ignore the Gospel or to be prejudiced or indifferent towards it.

Therefore, the well-known question of St. Paul is timely, as is the answer he gives: How can they believe in the One about whom they have not heard? And how can they hear if no one preaches to them? (Rom. 10:14-15). How will they be convinced if no one explains to them, and especially, if no one demonstrates to them how the unforced faith in the person of Jesus Christ gives meaning to life and creates moral freedom and responsibility?

Christ is clear. The criterion of human behaviour stems from one crystal principle: Treat others as you would have them treat you (Mt. 7:12, Tobit 4:15), a golden rule for human behaviour which follows in the footsteps of pre-Christian thinking.[5] However, the possibility of its implementation is not always guaranteed: it depends on whether the source of inspiration is convincing.

Christ calls believers to follow in His footsteps (Mt. 16:24): to renounce selfishness, to love everyone without distinction, to forgive even their enemies, to care for His lesser, marginalised brothers and sisters, to be peacemakers, to perform the works of light. Christ himself fulfilled what he taught and paid the full price of His consequences with the horrible witness of His voluntary death on the Cross. However, He resurrected on the third day and released the corruptible and mortal human nature from death, set it free to share the unending glory. This certainty of the resurrection of the dead is the good news that shapes the ethos of Christians and makes them worthy accomplices in spreading the kingdom of God (Col. 4:11).

In which way can Christians bear witness to the Light, so that all people through them might believe (Jn. 1:7)? They can by uttering words of truth, peace, and reconciliation, by engaging in social and educational initiatives, by alleviating human suffering, by respecting human dignity, by being consistent with their teaching and becoming servants of the traces of Christ. By raising a prophetic voice against the hypocrisy of the powerful, by fighting for understanding and solidarity with the weakest, by denouncing the cruelty of the powerful.

The Myrrh-bearing women first learnt the joyful message of the resurrection of the dead, and they were first dazzled by the light of the risen glory of Jesus (Mar. 16:1-8). With thoughts radiating the same light and with the experience of the risen Christ in their lives, Christian women can carry it today not only to those hiding from fear but also to those who do not know it.

The cross and ressurectional morals of Christians are the fertile soil for moral values to bear fruit and persist. Women, by way of their increased contemporary roles have the opportunity to transmit these values to multiple recipients: their children, their students, their relatives, their co-workers, their colleagues, their friends, their interlocutors in the mass media and social media. One undeniable spiritual experience, if accepted, may bring about valuable personal and social results. Christian women's voice is a hymn of enduring joy, optimism, and hope that permeates all levels of society, penetrates all layers of human existence, and provides convincing answers about the meaning of life.

Dimitra KOUKOURA

---

[5] ὅ σύ μισεῖς ἑτέρῳ μή ποιήσεις (Κλεόβουλος ο Ρόδιος): Don't do to others what you don't want them to do to you (Cleobulus of Rhodes , 6th century B.C.).

Voces de mujeres en tiempo de crisis

Las crisis son momentos de encrucijada. La presente hace que en Europa, aunque no solo en ella, vuelva a sembrarse de nuevo una cuestión que ha atravesado su historia y que con frecuencia reaparece. Se trata de la búsqueda de chivos expiatorios que "expíen" la incapacidad de los seres humanos para encontrar soluciones ante los fracasos de sus modelos sociales.

Esta búsqueda se presenta hoy bajo la forma de rechazo ante las personas extranjeras, cristianas y no-cristianas, del islam, de lo queer y de buena parte de Europa que sigue comprendiéndose como un "peso muerto".

En este sentido, todas las personas y más aún las cristianas hemos de preguntarnos cuál es el papel que debemos asumir en este proceso de "clasificación". A lo largo de la historia, el mecanismo del "chivo expiatorio", descrito con maestría por René Girard[6], se acompaña de una dinámica perversa de "des-humanización" del otro/a. Estos procesos han sido típicos en los totalitarismos donde las excluidas no son seres humanos como nosotras, sino seres infra-humanos.

Consisten en una forma de "desagraviar" los crímenes cometidos contra ellas al afirmar que "no son como nosotras". En ellos se afirma que no se trata de eliminar seres humanos, sino de "liberar a la sociedad del peligro que resulta la presencia de elementos que desestabilizan nuestra buena organización social". Los genocidios ha sido fruto de esta mentalidad. Al igual sucede con las mujeres víctimas de violencias, sean estas del tipo que sean, pues son comprendidas como "no-hombres", es decir como seres humanos de una clase inferior.

En este momento de la historia de Europa vuelve a ser pertinente la pregunta de Judith Butler ¿qué hace que una vida merezca ser llorada?[7]. Hasta el momento no han reaparecido en la Europa que llamamos comunitaria formas de totalitarismo, pero es muy preocupante el aumento de votantes que apoyan proyectos extremistas. Además en muchas ocasiones manipulan las religiones para legitimar su posiciones xenófobas. Ante este panorama la pregunta de Butler adquiere todo el sentido y hace que nos cuestionemos qué seres humanos son dignos de nuestras lágrimas, de nuestro clamor en contra de las injusticias, y cuál es el papel de las mujeres en medio de estos

El presente número de la revista de la ESWTR muestra experiencias, reflexiones teológicas y pastorales que nos recuerdan que muchas mujeres en situaciones de extrema violencia, explotación, negación de su autonomía para

---

[6] René Girard, *Le bouc émissaire* (Éditions Grasset Fasquelle: Paris 1982).
[7] Judith Butler, *Precarious Life: The Powers of Mourning and Violence* [*Vida precaria. El poder del duelo y de la violencia*] (Verso: London 2004), 20.

decidir son de hecho heroínas, como dice JR en su documental "Women are Heroes" [Las mujeres son héroes]. Ellas, al igual que la mujer de la parábola toman la levadura y la mezclan con tres medidas de harina (Mt 13, 33) hasta que todo queda dispuesto? Ellas crían, inventan, se esfuerzan por un mundo mejor aunque siempre es algo difícil, pero no imposible.

Y su grito por la igualdad, por la justicia, por la humanización del mundo en tiempos sombríos nos recuerda la herencia universal de la fe. No supone retomar malos sueños, perdidos ya, con los que se pretendía imponer el cristianismo, sino afirmar el diálogo inter-religioso basado en la creencia de que no hay fe que no constituya la afirmación innegociable de la humanidad para todo ser humano.

Teresa TOLDY

Inmitten der europäischen Finanz- und Bankenkrise in Griechenland und der beginnenden Herausforderung durch Flüchtende vor allem aus Syrien fand im Spaetsommer die 16. Konferenz der ESWTR statt. Sie stand unter dem Titel „Das Wort der Hoffnung mit der Welt teilen". Das kein spezifisch feministisch theologisch oder feministisch pädagogisch geprägtes Motto leitend war, spiegelt sehr klar die aktuelle akademische wie politsche Situation von Frauen in Forschung und Gesellschaft. Angesichts der ökonomischen und gesellschaftlichen Herausforderungen, scheinen spezifisch feministische Themen und konstruktive Gender-orientierte Debatten zu aus dem öffentlichen Raum zu verschwinden. Die Artikel, die sich dem Thema aus einer ganz bemerkenswerten Perspektive naehern, befassen sich mit der aktuellen öffentlichen Debatte, die jegliche Genderforschung und Gendersensitivität zur Ideologie abzustempeln versucht, um ihr so mit dem Zweifel an ihrer Wissenschaftlichkeit jegliche Berechtigung zu entziehen. Im Forum vereinen sich eben jene Stimmen, die Das Wort der Hoffnung in und mit der Welt teilen. Dies oft unter ausserordentlich spannenden Bedingungen.

In the Middle East, women's cries of agony are elevated for the centennial of the Armenian Genocide and the inconceivable Syrian tragedy. In Cyprus, women's lament for their missing loved ones has lasted for half a century, while on the Mediterranean coasts the impoverished voices of the refugees transport the cry of the humanist crisis to Europe, which has already been added to the existing economic and ethical crises. In the European South, angry voices are raised against the unjust distribution of wealth. Corporate Social Responsibility and the Social Economy are pushed as solutions. The ethical crisis is due to the marginalisation of moral values that adjoin communities and ensure the progress of the members and of the whole, but mostly due to self-absorption and the dwindling of religious belief. To remedy it, those who cultivate values must be awakened and create a proper ethos: families, spiritual leaders, educators, the social environment, and all who express a religious belief. In the already multicultural Europe, all religious traditions as well as intellectuals can contribute to the revival of moral values. Particularly important is the awakening of the Christian faith, re-evangelisation, which, according to the common statements of the European Churches, consists their imperative debt. With thoughts, illumined by the resurrectional light that the Myrrh-bearing women encountered, Christian women in today's crisis can convey the experience of the resurrected Christ to numerous recipients: to their children, their students, their relatives, their colleagues, and their interlocutors in the mass media and social media.

Las crisis son momentos de encrucijada. La presente hace que en Europa, aunque no solo en ella, vuelva a sembrarse de nuevo una cuestión que ha atravesado su historia y que con frecuencia reaparece. Se trata de la búsqueda de chivos expiatorios que "expíen" la incapacidad de los seres humanos para encontrar soluciones ante los fracasos de sus modelos sociales. El grito femenino por la igualdad, por la justicia, por la humanización del mundo en tiempos sombríos nos recuerda la herencia universal de la fe. No supone retomar malos sueños, perdidos ya, con los que se pretendía imponer el cristianismo, sino afirmar el diálogo inter-religioso basado en la creencia de que no hay fe que no constituya la afirmación innegociable de la humanidad para todo ser humano.

Sabine Dievenkorn studierte Theologie, Mathematik, Physik und Germanistik. Sie ist Bildungs- und Übersetzungswissenschaftlerin, promovierte Theologin und evangelische Pfarrerin. Als Mitbegründerin der Academía de Teología Femenina „Maria Magdalena" in Santiago de Chile arbeitet sie dort als akademische Direktorin. Sie ist Professorin für Praktische Theologie, Gender und Translation Studies. Zur Zeit ist sie im Sabbatical in Israel.

Dimitra Koukoura Professor of Homiletics, School of Theology, Aristotle University of Thessaloniki (AUTH). Studied Classics, Linguistics and Theology at AUTH, the Sorbonne and the Catholic Institute of Paris. She is involved in the ecumenical movement (WCC, CEC, Global Christian Forum, Elijah Interfaith Institute) and a member of ESWTR and Societas Homiletica. Field of interests: Homiletics, Communication, Women in the Orthodox Church.

Teresa Martinho Toldy es doctora en Teología Sistemática por la Philosophisch-theologische Hochschule Sankt Georgen (Frankfurt), Profesora con agregación en Estudios Sociales de la Universidad Fernando Pessoa (Oporto, Portugal), investigadora del Centro de Estudios Sociales de la Universidad de Coimbra (Portugal) y coordinadora del Observatorio de la Religión en Espacio Público del mismo centro. Publica en las temáticas del feminismo y de la religión. Correo electrónico: toldy@ces.uc.pt

Journal of the European Society of Women in Theological Research 24 (2016) 13-29.
doi: 10.2143/ESWTR.24.0.3170023

Jadranka Rebeka Anić

Anti-Gender Bewegung: Ein Beitrag zur Bewertung des Phänomens

Während der 2012-2013 gab es in verschiedenen Ländern Europas Demonstrationen gegen "Gender-Ideologie" und "Gender-Theorie". Diese Demonstrationen haben nicht nur wegen ihrer massiven und guten Organisation Aufmerksamkeit erregt, sondern auch wegen der Inhalte, die den Ausdrücken "Gender-Ideologie" und "Gender-Theorie" von den Anti-Gender AutorInnen und AktivistInnen zugeschrieben worden sind. Obwohl das ganze Phänomen der Anti-Gender Bewegung[1] noch nicht ausreichend erforscht ist, können auf der Grundlage der bisherigen Forschung einige Merkmale herausgearbeitet werden, die für ein besseres Verständnis des Phänomens und des Umgangs mit ihm dienen können. In diesem Artikel werden skizzenhaft einige Merkmale und Herausforderungen der Bewegung vorgestellt, sowie Empfehlungen für die zukünftigen Umgang mit der Bewegung beschrieben.

Ein Nationales und Transnationales Phänomen

Obwohl man den Eindruck bekommt, dass die Anti-Gender-Bewegungen in mehreren Ländern voneinander unabhängig, und aus im lokalen Kontext relevanten Gründen erschienen, sind immer mehr Autoren einig in der Überzeugung, dass es sich hierbei um ein nationales und transnationales Phänomen handelt. Nach Meinung von Elżbieta Korolczuk, Soziologin und Aktivistin, ist die gegenwärtigen Mobilisierung gegen "Gendernismus", "Gender-Ideologie"

---

[1] Das Phänomen wird häufig von den WissenschaftlerInnen und PublizistInnen als "Bewegung" gekennzeichnet (vgl. zum Beispiel: Heinrich Böll Foundation, *Anti-Gender Movements on the Rise? Strategising for Gender Equality in Central and Eastern Europe*, (Berlin: 2015) Publication Series on Democracy, 38. (https://ua.boell.org/sites/default/files/2015-04-anti-gender-movements-on-the-rise.pdf, 13. November 2015); http://staseve.eu/gegen-gender-und-frueh-sexualisierung-demo-fuer-alle-in-stuttgart-mit-neuem-teilnehmerrekord, 13. November 2015; http://www.wien-konkret.at/soziales/genderwahn, 13. November 2015). Über die Merkmale, die auf die "Bewegung" hindeuten, wird hier nicht diskutiert, weil es den Rahmen dieses Artikels übersteigen würde.

oder der "Gender Loby" nicht nur ein nationales oder lokales Problem, sondern ein transnationales.[2] Eine kurze Definition der Bewegung gibt der Soziologe David Paternotte: Es geht um eine nationale Manifestation der transnationalen Mobilisation gegen die sogenannte Gender-Ideologie und um die internationale Mobilisation der religiös Rechten.[3] Agnieszka Graff, Schriftstellerinn und feministische Aktivistin, schlägt vor, dass die lokalen Bewegungen zwar gründlich erforscht werden sollten, aber man sollte nicht die ganze Breite der Bewegung aus den Augen verlieren. Es gibt gemeinsame Themen und Strategien, die weit über den nationalen Kontext hinausgehen.[4] Nach der Meinung von Andrea Pető, Professorinn an der Abteilung für Gender Studies in Budapest, es geht um ein neues Phänomen in der europäischen Politik, das neue Methoden und Frameworks zu denken erfordert, wenn kohärent man auf sie reagieren will.[5]

Auf den transnationalen Charakter der Bewegung verweist die zeitgleiche Entwicklung der Bewegung in verschiedenen Ländern Europas. Obwohl der Ausdruck "Gender-Ideologie", wenn er nicht im Sinne soziologischer Arbeiten verwandt wurde,[6] schon vor 20 Jahren gängig war,[7] hat er in verschiedenen

---

[2] Vgl. Elżbieta Korolczuk, "'The War on Gender' from a Transnational Perspective – Lessons for Feminist Strategising", 1-9, hier 3. (http://gup.ub.gu.se/publication/210169-the-war-on-gender-from-a-transnational-perspective-lessons-for-feminist-strategising, 3. September 2105).

[3] Vgl. David Paternotte, "Christian Trouble: The Catholic Church and the Subversion of Gender". (http://councilforeuropeanstudies.org/critcom/christian-trouble-the-catholic-church-and-the-subversion-of-gender/, 7. Juli 2015).

[4] Vgl. Agnieszka Graff, "Report from the gender trenches: War against 'genderism' in Poland", in: *European Journal of Women's Studies* 4 (2014), 431-442, hier 434.

[5] Vgl. Andrea Pető, "Epilogue: 'Anti-gender' mobilisational discourse of conservative and far right Parties as a challenge for progressive politics", in: Eszter Kováts / Maari Põim, *Gender als Symbolic glue. The position and role of conservative and far right parties in the anti-gender mobilization in Europe* (Friedrich Ebert Stiftung: Budapest 2015), 126-131, hier 130-131.

[6] In wissenschaftlichen Aufsätzen steht der Begriff "Gender-Ideologie" für ein Set von Glaubenssätzen über Männlichkeit und Weiblichkeit, das die Geschlechterrollen im privaten und öffentlichen Leben definiert und vorgibt (vgl. Amaka C. Ezeife, "Lexical Indices of Authorial Gender Ideology in Sefi Atta's Everything Good Will Come", in: *The Journal of Pan African Studies* 3 (2014), 48-64, hier 50). Es geht um einen Terminus, der darauf hinweist, dass Geschlechterbilder und Geschlechterrollenzuschreibungen kritisiert werden müssen. Vgl. Andrea Günter, "Geschlechtertheorie und Antifeminismus. ‚Gender ideology': Neuer kirchlicher Antifeminismus". (http://www.thkg.de/Dokumente/GunterGender.pdf, 20. August 2015).

[7] Seit der vierten Frauenkonferenz der Vereinten Nationen (1995). Vgl. Barbara L. Marshall, *Configuring Gender. Explorations in Theory and Politics* (Broadview press: Peterborough 2000), 100-123.

Ländern Europas erst im Jahr 2012 - 2013 die öffentliche Debatte erobert. Zum Beispiel ist die katholische Kirche in Spanien schon von 2004 bis 2011 sehr hart gegen die sozialistischen Regimes in Fragen der vereinfachten Scheidungen, der Homosexuellen-Ehe, der Abtreibung und des "betrügerischen Laizismus" aufgetreten. Die so genannte Gender-Ideologie-Debatte entwickelte sich aber erst in den letzten Jahren. David Paternotte fragt, wenn all diese Fragen als ein Teil der Gender-Ideologie verstanden und gegen die sozialistischen Regierungen benutzt wurden, warum wurden sie nicht bereits früher formuliert?[8] An den Universitäten in Polen laufen die Gender Studies-Programme schon seit Jahrzehnten, viele Bücher zur Genderthematik sind veröffentlicht worden. Die Gender-Ideologie-Debatte ist aber erst seit 2013 entfacht worden. Auch Jaroslaw Kuisz und Karolina Wigura fragen, warum thematisierte man dies nicht schon früher?[9] In Kroatien wurden nach den demokratischen Änderungen viele Gesetze zur Geschlechtergerechtigkeit verabschiedet, und es wurden verschiedene Regierungsbehörden zur Förderung der Gleichberechtigung der Geschlechter eingerichtet.[10] Der Begriff Gender ist aber erst nach dem Jahr 2010 problematisiert worden, besonders während der Jahre 2012-2013. Warum erst jetzt?

Dass die Anti-Gender-Bewegung nicht nur ein nationales sondern auch transnationales Phänomen ist, zeigt sich an ihrer internationalen Vernetzung. Die Befürworter der Anti-Gender-Bewegung kritisieren die von ihnen so genannte Gender-Ideologie als ein Diktat der internationalen Organisationen. Das tun sie, obwohl sie selbst zur gleichen Zeit auf internationale Inhalte, Methoden, den Austausch von Erfahrungen usw. zugreifen. Viele Argumente und Anliegen, die heute in verschiedenen Kontexten gefördert werden, sind überraschenderweise dieselben. Zum Beispiel gibt es große Ähnlichkeiten zwischen den Anliegen, Strategien und Argumenten, die in den Vereinigten Staaten von Amerika in den neunziger Jahren vertreten worden sind, und denen, die gegenwärtig in Russland, der Ukraine, in Frankreich oder Deutschland verwendet werden. Es gibt zahlreiche Bücher und Werbematerialien, die unter konservativen Aktivisten in verschiedenen Ländern sehr beliebt sind, wie

---

[8] Vgl. Paternotte, "Christian Trouble".
[9] Vgl. Jaroslaw Kuisz / Karolina Wigura, "Poland's tender dispute. What does it say about Polish society?" (http://www.eurozine.com/articles/2014-03-28-wigura-en.html, 7. Juli 2015).
[10] Vgl. Rebeka Jadranka Anić, "Zwischen Tradition und Postmoderne: Frauen in der Kirche und Gesellschaft Kroatiens", in: Irmtraud Fischer (ed.), *Theologie von Frauen für Frauen?* (Wien: Lit Verlag 2007), 261-293, hier 278-280.

beispielsweise das Buch der deutschen Soziologin Gabriele Kuby, *Die globale sexuelle Revolution: Zerstörung der Freiheit im Namen der Freiheit.* Dieses Buch ist in viele Sprachen übersetzt worden und ist in kirchlichen und konservativen Kreisen sehr populär. Kuby reist durch ganz Europa und hält Vorträge.[11]

Die Bewegung ist nicht nur auf lokaler, sondern auch auf internationaler Ebene gut vernetzt. Elżbieta Korolczuk zum Beispiel führt einige Organisationsformen auf, die auf beiden Ebenen arbeiten, sowohl lokal als auch international. So gibt es internationale nichtstaatliche Organisationen, die sowohl auf Lobbyarbeit spezialisiert sind, als auch auf Gerichtsverfahren vor dem Europäischen Gerichtshof für Menschenrechte in Straßburg, der Europäischen Union oder den Vereinten Nationen, wie zum Beispiel *The European Centre for Law and Justice* in Strasburg. So gibt es neben Parlamentsausschüssen wie beispielsweise *Stop the Gender Ideology* in Polen, oder *Duma's Committee on Family, Women and Children* in Russland,[12] nationale und lokale, nichtstaatliche konservative und katholische Verbände zum Schutz der Familienwerte oder auch lokale Organisationen der betroffenen Eltern, zum Beispiel *La Manif Pour Tous.*[13] Websites, online-Gruppen und offene Plattformen, die Informationen und Bücher austauschen, und Menschen sowohl zum Unterschreiben von Petitionen mobilisieren als auch zur Organisation von Protesten auf der lokalen, regionalen und nationalen sowie internationalen Ebene.[14]

Eine Definition des Begriffs *Gender*, die Manipulationen ermöglicht

Die Befürworter der Anti-Gender-Bewegung behaupten, dass der Begriff *Gender* nicht klar definiert ist. Seit 1995 wiederholen sie diese Behauptung[15] trotz der Literatur inklusive internationaler Dokumente, aus der sie die Bedeutung des Begriffs in verschiedenen wissenschaftlichen Disziplinen überprüfen könnten.[16] Stattdessen, erstellen sie eigene Deutungen der Begriffe *Gender*,

---

[11] Vgl. Korolczuk, "'The War on Gender' from a Transnational Perspective", 5.

[12] Vgl. Korolczuk, "'The War on Gender' from a Transnational Perspective", 4.

[13] Vgl. Brustier, "France", in: Kováts / Põim, *Gender als Symbolic glue*, 19-39, hier 27.

[14] Zum Beispiel offene Plattform www.citizengo.org, registriert in Spanien, ist in 11 Sprachen verfügbar, einschließlich in Kroatisch. Vgl. Korolczuk, "'The War on Gender' from a Transnational Perspective", 4.

[15] Vgl. Jadranka Rebeka Anić, *Kako razumjeti rod? Povijest rasprave i različita razumijevanja u Crkvi* (Split: Institut društvenih znanosti Ivo Pilar 2011), 71-85, 95-96.

[16] Die Europäische Kommission hat ein Glossar veröffentlicht um ein gemeinsames Verständnis des Begriffs Gender auf europäischer Ebene zu ermöglichen. Vgl. European Commission Unit

Gender-Mainstreaming und *Gender-Equality*. Sie ignorieren die Kritik, die zum einen besagt, dass sie den Begriff *Gender* falsch verstehen, und zum anderen einschliesst, dass sie die Debatten im Rahmen der Genderstudies und in gendergerechter Politik nicht differenzieren.[17] Hartnäckiges Beharren auf der falschen Erläuterung der Begriffe *Gender* und *Gender-Mainstreaming* legt nahe, dass es hier nicht um Unwissenheit geht,[18] sondern dass bewusst falsche Deutungen benutzt werden. Warum? Was sind die Ziele?

Die Definition von *Gender*, *Gender-Mainstreaming* und *Gender-Equality* haben die Anti-Gender-Autoren breit angelegt und bewusst für weitere Hinzufügungen von Inhalten offen gelassen. Hier ein Beispiel, das dazu dient, die Kritik am Gender-Konzept in Allgemeinen und in der katholischen Kirche im Besonderen besser zu verstehen. Es geht um die Definition der amerikanischen Journalistin Dale O'Leary aus dem Jahr 1995. Sie hat nämlich auf der 4. *Weltfrauenkonferenz* in Peking ein Essay unter dem Titel "Gender: the Deconstruction of Women" verfasst, in dem sich die konservativ-fundamentalistische Kritik komprimiert findet.[19] Diese Definition übernahm Kardinal Oscar Alzamora Revoredo ohne inhaltliche Abstriche in einem Artikel, der im Lexikon des Päpstlichen Rates für die Familie veröffentlicht ist.[20] Nach der Meinung von Dale O'Leary, sei das Ziel der *gender perspecitve* die Verringerung der Einwohnerzahlen, die Propaganda sexuellen Genusses, die Leugnung der Unterschiede zwischen Mann und Frau. Es wird der geheime Plan unterstellt, durch die Zerstörung der traditionellen Geschlechterrollen einen neuen Menschen zu schaffen. Die Einführung einer 50:50-Quotenregelung und volle Arbeitszeit für Frauen sei lediglich dazu da, die Frauen an der Übernahme der Mutterrolle zu hindern. So erklärt man weiter, dass *gender perspecitve* die frei zugängliche Empfängnisverhütung will, wie die Legalisierung der Abtreibung,

---

in Charge of Equal Opportunities, *100 words for equality. A glossary of terms on equaltiy between women and men.* (http://www.eduhi.at/dl/100_words_for_equality.pdf, 20. Oktober 2010).

[17] Vgl. Anić, *Kako razumjeti rod?* 23-33; Gerhard Marschütz, "Wachstumspotenzial für die eigene Lehre. Zur Kritik an der vermeintlichen Gender-Ideologie", in: *Herder Korrespondenz* 9 (2014), 457-462.

[18] Vgl. Graff, "Report from the gender trenches", 434.

[19] Mehr darüber: Marshall, *Configuring Gender*, 100-117; Sally Baden / Anne Marie Goetz, "Who needs (sex) when you can have (gender)? Conflicting discourses on gender at Beijing", in: *Feminist Review* 56 (1997), 3-25, hier 13.

[20] Oscar Alzamora Revoredo, "Ideologia di genere: pericoli e portata", in: Pontificio consiglio per la famiglia, *Lexicon. Termini ambigui e discussi su famiglia, vita e questioni etiche* (Bologna: Dehoniane 2006, neue erweiterte Ausgabe), 545-560.

dass sie sowohl Propaganda für Homosexualität unternimmt, als auch für den Sexualkundeunterricht für Kinder – der nach Ansicht der Autoren das Elternrecht auf Erziehung ihrer Kinder untergräbt. Man unterstellt weiterhin eine neomarxistische Interpretation der Weltgeschichte und schliesst daher auf die Initiierung einer Geschlechter- und Klassenrevolution der Frauen gegen Männer.[21]

Dale O'Leary und mit ihr Autoren und Autorinnen des Lexikons des Päpstlichen Rates für die Familie verstehen die Begriffe *Gender, Gender-Mainstreaming* und *Gender-Perspektive* nie in dem Sinne, in dem diese Begriffe in den internationalen Dokumenten definiert und benutzt werden und unterscheiden auch nicht zwischen der Genderstudien und gendergerechter Politik.[22] Das Gleiche findet man auch bei anderen die sich gegen das Genderkonzept aussprechen, wie zum Beispiel bei dem deutschem Journalist Volker Zastrow. Seine These ist, dass Gender-Mainstreaming nach dem von ihm so genannten Kaderprinzip funktioniere, wie es "für die Führung der Napoleonischen Wehrpflichtigenarmee ersonnen und von den russischen Bolschewiki weiterentwickelt wurde."[23] Mit einer solchen Interpretation und der These von der politischen Produktion "des neuen Menschen" gerät Zastrows Gender-Konzept assoziativ in die Nähe von Militärregimes und totalitären Staaten. Wie eine solche These in postkommunistischen Ländern verstanden werden kann, bezeugt die Aussage des polnischen Bischof Tadeusz Pieronek. Er sieht in der auch von ihm so genannten Gender-Ideologie eine weitaus größere Gefahr als im Nationalsozialismus und Kommunismus.[24] Die slowakischen Bischöfe verorten hinter "so edlen Begriffen" wie "Geschlechtergleichheit" die "Kultur des Todes" oder das Bestreben "eine sodomitische Ideologie" durchzusetzen.[25] Die polnischen Bischöfe unterstellen der ebenfalls diskreditieren bezeichneten Gender-Ideologie das Bestreben, schrittweise das Recht auf Euthanasie oder Eugenik, das heißt, die Freigabe der Beseitigung kranker, schwacher und

---

[21] Dale O'Leary, *The Gender Agenda* (Louisiana: Vital Issues Press 1997), 156, 207.

[22] Eine Analyse des Begriffes Gender in Lexikon in: Anić, *Kako razumjeti rod?*, 109-116.

[23] Volker Zastrow, "‚Gender Mainstreaming'. Politische Geschlechtsumwandlung", in: *Frankfurter Allgemeine Zeitung*. (http://www.faz.net/aktuell/politik/gender-mainstreaming-politische-geschlechtsumwandlung-1327841.html, 16. August 2015).

[24] Regina Frey / Marc Gärtner / Manfred Köhnen / Sebastian Scheele, *Gender, Wissenschaftlichkeit und Ideologie. Argumente im Streit um Geschlechterverhältnisse* (Berlin: Heinrich-Böll-Stiftung [2]2014), 11-12.

[25] Hirtenbrief der slowakischen Bischofskonferenz zum ersten Adventssonntag 2013. (www.kbs.sk/obsah/sekcia/h/dokumenty-a-vyhlasenia/p/pastierske-listy-konferencie-biskupov-slovenska/c/pastiersky-list-na-prvu-adventnu-nedelu-2013, 20. Oktober 2015).

behinderter Personen zu erkämpfen und durchzusetzen.[26] In den Hirtenbriefen verschiedener bischöflicher Konferenzen findet sich die These, dass es unmöglich sei, den Begriff *Gender* zu benutzen, ohne sich zur Gender-Ideologie zu bekennen.[27]

Zusammenfassend lässt sich sagen: Die Anti-Gender-Autoren haben eine eigene und sehr breite Definition der Begriffe *Gender* und *Gender-Mainstreaming* entwickelt. Der Begriff *Gender* fungiert gewissermaßen als leerer Korb, der nach Belieben mit unterschiedlichen Thesen gefüllt werden kann. Aus so einer Definition kann man das eine oder andere Thema auswählen, das auf nationaler Ebene für politische oder religiöse Zwecke nützlich sein kann. Am Ende geht es so weit, dass es keine Möglichkeit mehr gibt, den Begriff *Gender* zu benutzen, ohne dessen verdächtigt zu werden, selbst Anhängerin dieser so genannten Ideologie zu sein. Agnieszka Graff ist der Meinung, dass es hier explizit nicht um Missverständnisse handelt, sondern um bewusste Nutzung der Sprache, mit der eigene politische Ziele verfolgt werden. Es gibt nichts Irrationales und Unwissendes in der Anti-Gender-Kampagne. Ihrer Meinung nach, sehen wir uns mit einer starken transnationalen Bewegung von religiösen Fundamentalisten und Rechtsradikalen gegen die Gleichstellung der Geschlechter konfrontiert, und darüber hinaus mit einem Versuch, die liberale Demokratie zu untergraben.[28] Nach Korolczuk demonstriert die Anti-Gender Bewegung die Fähigkeit, die Debatte aus dem akadameischen Bereich auf das Gebiet der öffentlichen Meinung zu verlagern und nutzt die Unwissenheit der Bevölkerung aus um so mit Fehlinformationen und bewusst gewählter emotionaler und hyperbolischer Sprache die Atmosphäre der moralischen Panik zu erzeugen.[29]

---

[26] Hirtenwort der Bischöfe über die Gender Ideologie (http://www.civitas-institut.de/index. php?option=com_content&view=article&id=2229:hirtenwort-der-bischoefe-ueber-die-gender-ideologie&catid=1:neuestes&Itemid=33, 20. Oktober 2015). Der Erzbischof Marek Jedraszewski hat die Gender-Ideologie als direkten Weg "zum Tod unserer Zivilisation" gebrandmart. Seiner Meinung nach, könne es sein, dass im Jahr 2050, dass Mann und Frau, wie Indianer in Reservaten gezeigt werden. Vgl. Giuseppe Nardi, "Erzbischof kritisiert Gender-Ideologie: ‚Direkter Weg zur Selbstvernichtung'". (http://www.katholisches.info/2013/11/19/erzbischof-kritisiert-gender-ideologie-direkter-weg-zur-selbstvernichtung, 20. Oktober 2015).

[27] Vgl. Jadranka Rebeka Anić, "Der Begriff ‚Gender' als Anathema. Eine Kampagne der kroatischen Bischöfe als Beispiel", in: *Herder Korrespondenz* 3 (2015), 157-161.

[28] Vgl. Graff, "Report from the gender trenches", 434.

[29] Vgl. Korolczuk, "'The War on Gender' from a Transnational Perspective", 8.

Die Gegenstände der Anti-Gender-Bewegung

Die Debatten in den verschiedenen Ländern zeigen, dass die folgenden Sachverhalte in der Anti-Gender-Kampagne am häufigsten zu finden sind: Erstens die Einführung der "Sexualkunde" bzw. des Erziehung-Programmes gegen Geschlechterstereotypen in das schulische Programm,[30] wie zum Beispiel ABCD of equality[31] und zweitens die homosexuelle Ehe.[32]

Gegenstand der Debatte in den postkommunistichen Ländern ist auch die Einführung einiger gesetzlicher Regelungen gendergerechter Politik. In Polen beispielsweise ist die Einführung der Übereinkommen des Europarats zur Verhütung und Bekämpfung von Gewalt gegen Frauen und häuslicher Gewalt diskutiert worden,[33] in der Ukraine gibt es das Nationale Programm zur Gewährleistung gleicher Rechte und Chancen für Frauen und Männer, in Russland die Einführung der Reform Juvenile Justice.[34]

Die oben genannten Fragen können als Auslöser, nicht aber als der Beginn der Anti-Gender-Kampagne betrachtet werden. Die Debatte wurde bereits durch Artikel und öffentliche Auftritte von Anti-Gender-Autoren und katholischen Aktivisten vorbereitet.[35] Unter ihnen wird in den postkommunistischen Ländern am häufigsten Gabriele Kuby genannt, so in Polen, Slowakei, Kroatien.[36]

Es ist aber beachtenswert, dass es die weite und offene Definition des begriffes *Gender* dies ermöglicht. In Frankreich hatte die Kampagne gegen die

---

[30] Zum Beispiel in Kroatien, Frankreich, Deutschland, Polen, Russland, Armenien, Georgien und der Ukraine. Vgl. Brustier, "France", 30; Korolczuk, "'The War on Gender' from a Transnational Perspective", 2; Weronika Grzebalska, "Poland", in: Kováts / Maari Põim, *Gender als Symbolic glue*, 83-103, hier 91.

[31] Mehr über das Program: Increasing action for equality between girls and boys in schools. (http://www.gouvernement.fr/en/increasing-action-for-equality-between-girls-and-boys-in-schools, 5. September 2015)

[32] Zum Beispiel Frankreich, Kroatien, Slowakei.

[33] Vgl. Grzebalska, "Poland", 90-91.

[34] Vgl. Korolczuk, "'The War on Gender' from a Transnational Perspective", 5.

[35] Die Frage der "Gender-Ideologie" war für die konservative Intellektuelle in Frankreich von Anfang 2000 wichtig, in der öffentlichen Debatte hat sich aber erst im Jahr 2012-2103 entzündet mit dem Ziel der Destabilisierung den französischen Linken. Vgl. Brustier, "France", 20.

[36] Vgl. Korolczuk, "'The War on Gender' from a Transnational Perspective", 5; Jadranka Rebeka Anić, "Gender, Politik und die katholische Kirche. Ein Beitrag zum Abbau der alten Geschlechterstereotypen", in: *Concilium* 4 (2012), 373-382; Anikó Félix, "Hungary", in: Kováts / Põim, *Gender als Symbolic glue*, 62-82, hier 62; Grzebalska, "Poland", 84; Petra Ďurinová, "Slovakia", in: Kováts / Põim, *Gender als Symbolic glue*, 104-125, hier 105. 111.

Gender-Theorie die Öffentlichkeit zunächst nicht mobilisiert. Aber diese hat eine Mobilisierung gegen die Homosexuellen-Ehe entfacht und außerdem geholfen, dass konservative Aktivisten eine Koalition gegen die Homosexuellen-Ehe bildeten.[37]

Ein besonderer Aspekt der Debatte ist die der Gender-Theorie unterstellten und vorgeworfenen Unwissenschaftlichkeit. In Deutschland, zum Beispiel sind besonders Gender Studien als akademische Disziplin angegriffen. Es wird einerseits kritisiert, sie seien zu wissenschaftlich und zu weit weg vom alltäglichen Leben. Andereseits wird behauptet, man betreibe in diesen Studien keine Wissenschaft, sondern nur eine Ideologie. Aufgrund solcher divergierender Vorwürfe, verlangt man ihre Auflösung.[38]

Mit dem Vorwurf, dass die Gender-Theorie nicht wissenschaftlich sei, verschiebt die Anti-Gender-Bewegung die Diskussion vom religiösen Bereich zum säkularen und verbirgt damit ihre religiös-konservativen Inhalte und Strategien. Roman Kuhar nennt als Ziel dieser Strategie "die Säkularisation des Diskurses um die Klerikalisierung der Gesellschaft zu erreichen".[39] Kuhar ist der Meinung, dass der erste Schritt gegen so eine Strategie sei, eigene, unabhängige Strategien zu entwickeln und nicht nur auf den Angriff zu reagieren.

Die Träger der Anti-Gender-Kampagne

In der Anti-Gender Kampagne ist die katholische Kirche aktiv. Die Kampagne hat aber auch ihre politische Dimension.

Die Hierarchie der katholischen Kirche initiiert in einigen Ländern die Anti-Gender-Kampagne und hat direkten Einfluss auf die Polarisierung der Gesellschaft in Gender-Fragen, so zum Beispil in Spanien, Polen, Italien, Slowakei. In den meisten der genannten Länder unterstützt sie Aktivisten und ihre Verbände entweder finanziell[40] oder durch Verlautbarungen oder Dokumente des Heiligen Stuhls.[41] David Paternotte ist der Meinung, dass die Anti-Gender

---

[37] Vgl. Brustier, "France", 20-21.

[38] Vgl. Blum, "Germany", 47. 49; Eine Antwort auf diesen Vorwurf sehe in: Frey / Gärtner / Köhnen / Scheele, *Gender, Wissenschaftlichkeit und Ideologie*.

[39] Vgl. Pető, "Epilogue", 129.

[40] Vgl. Paternotte, "Christian Trouble"; Ďurinová, "Slovakia".

[41] In den vergangenen zwei Jahren haben einige Bischofskonferenzen, unter anderen die Polnische, die Portugiesische, die Slowakische, die Ungarische, Kroatische sowie die Bischöfe Norditaliens, aber etwa auch papst Benedikt XVI. und *Vitus Huonder*, der Bischof von Chur (Schweiz) in öffentlichen Stellungnahmen vor den Gefahren der "Gender-Ideologie" gewarnt (Vgl. Anić, "Der Begriff 'Gender' als Anathema", 157-161).

Kampagne der katholischen Kirche die Möglichkeit gibt, wieder ein öffentlicher und politischer Faktor zu sein.[42]

Auf der politischen Ebene scheint die Rede von Gender-Ideologie ein Ausdruck zu sein, der Folgendem dient:

- der Homogenisierung der rechten politischen Optionen[43]
- der Spaltung der Gesellschaft auf weltanschaulicher Ebene[44]
- dem Schlachtruf der Rechten und der Hierarchie gegen die linken politischen Optionen, wie in Kroatien[45] oder Frankreich[46]
- der Spaltung in einigen rechten politischen Parteien[47]
- zum Bindemittel, das die verschiedenen politischen Optionen eint.[48]

Die rechten Parteien sind in der Regel Anti-Gender-orientiert. Das gilt, obwohl sie sich als die Parteien präsentieren, die die Gleichberechtigung der Frauen und die Verbesserung der Stellung der Mütter befürworten und gegen Gewalt an den Frauen auftreten.[49] Dass die Anti-Gender Kampagne antifeministisch ist, zeigt sich gut am Beispiel Ungarns. Die gegenwärtige Regierungskoalition hat eine so genannte familienfreundliche Politik verabschiedet. De facto wird hier nun statt Gender-Mainstreaming eine Art *Familien-Mainstreaming* durchgeführt. Beide politischen Strategien werden gegeneinander ausgespielt. Das

---

[42] Vgl. Paternotte, "Christian Trouble".

[43] Vgl. Brustier, "France", 34.

[44] Vgl. Ďurinová, "Slovakia", 104.

[45] Vgl. Jadranka Rebeka Anić, "Gender, Gender 'Ideology' and Cultural War: Local Consequences of a Global Idea – Croatian Example", in: *Feminist Theology* 24 (2015) 1, 7–22.

[46] Dabei muss man bedenken, dass in Frankreich die Rechte, die Union für eine Volksbewegung, die seit 2011 in der Regierung sitzt selbst Gender-Mainstreaming und den Kampf gegen die Geschlechter-Stereotypen in das schulische Programm mit eingeführt haben. Als sie Opposition wurden, wandten sie sich gegen das Programm und verurteilen die Position der Linken. Die Mehrheit der konservativen Aktivisten vergisst bis heute diese Tatsache und glaubt, dass das "ABCD of equality"-Programm von Seiten der sozialistischen Regierung eingeführt worden sei. Sie behaupten, das die Homosexuellen-Ehe und die Gender-Theorie Elemente der sozialistischen politischen Agenda seien. Vgl. Brustier, "France", 30.

[47] Zum Beispiel hat sich die Union der Demokraten und Unabhängigen in Frankreich in zwei Richtungen aufgespalten: Eine geht hart gegen die Homosexuellen-Ehe vor, die andere hat eine Strategie der politischen Mäßigung entwickelt. Vgl. Brustier, "France", 26.

[48] Zum Beispiel hat die Kritik der "Gender-Ideologie" in Deutschland zur Einigung verschiedener politischer Optionen beigetragen: sie wird mittlerweile von den christlichen Humanisten über die neoliberalen bis hin zu den radikalen Nationalisten vertreten. Vgl. Blum, "Germany", 47.

[49] Vgl. Blum, "Germany", 42-43; Félix, "Hungary", 63; Grzebalska, "Poland", 90.

Ziel des Familien-Mainstreamings ist es, den Frauen zu ermöglichen, zu Hause zu bleiben.[50]

Rechte Parteien nutzen die sogenannte Gender-Ideologie-Debatte als politisches Instrument, um neue Wähler zu gewinnen und besonders auf lokaler Ebene alte Wähler zu motivieren wie in Frankreich, Deutschland, Ungarn oder Poland. Jüngere Mitglieder positionieren sich in der Regel radikaler als ihre älteren Kollegen in der Partei.[51]

Das Thema Gender wird auch als Druckmittel benutzt. So hat in Frankreich im Februar 2015, *La Manif pour tous* ein Dokument veröffentlicht, das die Kandidierenden, die eine Unterstützung der Konservativen möchten, verpflichtet, sich gegen LGBT zu positionieren und sich gegen den "pro-gender" Verein einzusetzen.[52]

Die Maßnahmen des Gender-Mainstreaming gehören zum Programm linker Parteien. Diese aber reagieren nicht genug auf Anti-Gender-Diskurse und -Praktiken. Sie zögern die konservative Offensive strategisch zu konfrontieren, wie in Frankreich, Ungarn oder Kroatien.[53]

Die Anti-Gender-Kampagne nutzen die politischen Parteien auf unterschiedliche Weise zur Mobilisierung der Wahlberechtigten. Durch die Kritik an der so genannten Gender-Ideologie versuchen zum Beispiel in Frankreich einige rechte Parteien wie die Union für eine Volksbewegung oder die Union der Demokraten und Unabhängigen, Migranten und Migrantinnen zu gewinnen. Sie sind normalerweise konservativ, wählen aber die Linke und werden als solche die Zielgruppe der Wahlwerbung der Rechten. Die rechte Partei Marine Le Pens, die Front National, akzeptiert allerdings die Unterstützung von Frauen und den Schutz der homosexuellen Bevölkerung und enthält sich eines offenen Engagements in der Anti-Gender-Kampagne. Diese Partei sieht die größte Gefahr in islamischen Migranten.[54]

In Ungarn wird die Anti-Gender-Kampagne gegen Migranten benutzt. Die Europäische Union wird als ein Teil der "globalen Verschwörung" betrachtet, die als Hauptziel die Zerstörung der Nation hat. Ungarn muss vor einer "Kolonisierung" des Landes geschützt werden. Man soll sich am "Kulturkampf"

---

[50] Vgl. Félix, "Hungary", 64.

[51] Vgl. Brustier, "France", 34; Blum, "Germany", 51; Félix, "Hungary", 76; Grzebalska, "Poland", 83. 96-97.

[52] Vgl. Brustier, "France", 29.

[53] Vgl. Brustier, "France", 35; Blum, "Germany", 57; Félix, "Hungary", 78.

[54] Vgl. Brustier, "France", 34.

beteiligen und die eigene Tradition bewahren. Indem sie die Politik der Gleichstellung der Geschlechter mit Staatssozialismus verbinden, nutzen die rechten Parteien eine antikommunistische Stimmung für die Mobilisierung gegen die Gender-Ideologie, die der marxistischen Ideologie zugeschrieben wird.[55] In diesem Sinne erscheint *Gender* als ein symbolisches Bindemittel, das antieuropäische, antikommunistische und homophobe Einstellungen verbindet. Gender-Mainstreaming wird als trojanisches Pferd vorgestellt, das auf die Zerstörung der vermeintlichen natürlichen Ordnung gerichtet sei, auf die Beseitigung von Mutterschaft und Vaterschaft, Familie und Ehe. Die Schöpfer der Gender-Debatte seien die zionistischen Oligarchien, die Homosexualität legitimieren wollen, und Homosexualität bewirke einen Rückgang der Geburtenrate. Das nun aber sei das eigentliche Ziel der Oligarchie, weil sie damit die Akzeptanz der Einwanderung rechtfertigt. Damit sei die nun als "Gender-Ideologie" bezeichnete Auffassung eine Gefahr für die traditionellen Werte und für die ungarische Gesellschaft. Sie führe zu einem Zusammenbruch der Nation.[56]

Anti-Gender-Bewegung als *backlash*?

Wie kann die Anti-Gender-Bewegung gedeutet werden?

Obwohl diese Bewegung von Anfang an eine zutiefst antifeministische Bewegung ist,[57] ist Korolczuk der Meinung, sie kann als *backlash* auf die Frauenemantipation verstanden werden, wenn es um die USA gehe. Das geht aber nicht im Hinblick auf Länder wie Polen, die Ukraine oder Russland. *Backlash* bedeutet eine Reaktion auf etwas, was Popularität, Ansehen oder Einfluss gewonnen hat. Die Proteste in Polen, in der Urkaine oder in Russland ziehlen oft auf die Gesetze, die noch nicht beschlossen oder umgesetzt worden sind. Die Mobilisierung gegen Gender-Theorien und -Auffassungen erinnert vielmehr an die Tatsache, dass der Prozess der Gleichstellung noch weit von einer Umsetzung entfernt ist. Die Anti-Gender-Kampagne sollte in diesen Ländern mehr als unvollendete feministische Revolution gedeutet werden, nicht aber als *backlash* in Bezug auf etwas, was schon erreicht worden ist.[58] Das Hauptproblem der Anti-Gender-Bewegung ist nach der Meinung von

---

[55] Vgl. Félix, "Hungary", 76-77.
[56] Vgl. Félix, "Hungary", 70, 76-77. In den Diskussionen in Polen, die Europäische Union wurde als kultureller Kolonisator angesehen, der, die unschuldige polnische Kinder korrumpiert und die polnische Nationalkultur unterdrückt. Vgl. Grzebalska, "Poland", 92.
[57] Vgl. Marshall, *Configuring Gender*, 100.
[58] Vgl. Korolczuk, "'The War on Gender' from a Transnational Perspective", 8.

Korolczuk das Ausmaß der staatlichen Eingriffe in das Privatleben durch Institutionen wie Schulen, Krankenhäuser, Justizwesen usw. Hier geht es um das Verhältnis zwischen dem Staat und den Bürgern. Die Anti-Gender-Bewegung wendet sich aber gegen jede Idee, dass der Staat, um die Rechte von einzelnen zu verteidigen, in den privaten Bereich eingreifen darf.[59]

Gegen-Strategien

Die Reaktionen gegen die Anti-Gender Kampagne sind in einigen Ländern kaum oder nur sehr schwach vorhanden. Zum Beispiel kann in Kroatien der Widerstand auf wenige Akteurinnen reduziert werden.[60] In der Regel aber schweigt und ignoriert die wissenschaftliche Gemeinde die Anti-Gender-Wissenschaftler oder Wissenschaftlerinnen und Aktivisten.Diese Situation ist anders in Polen. In der Antwort auf den Anti-Gender-Diskurs haben sich viele engagiert: Männer und Frauen in der Wissenschaft, in der Politik, den Medien und in NGOs.[61] Es gibt auch verschiedene Strategien, wie auf die Anti-Gender-Kampagne reagiert wird. Eine besonders populäre Gegenstrategie geht davon aus, dass die Anti-Gender-Kampagne unzureichende Kenntnis habe.

---

[59] Vgl. Korolczuk, "'The War on Gender' from a Transnational Perspective", 7.

[60] Ein Buch (Anić, *Kako razumjeti rod?*) und die Artikel von Anić und Brnčić (Anić, "Gender, Politik und die katholische Kirche"; Anić, "Der Begriff ‚Gender' als Anathema"; Jadranka Rebeka Anić / Jadranka Brnčić, "Missverständnisse um den Begriff ‚Gender'. Überlegungen anlässlich einer Botschaft der kroatischen Bischofskonferenz", *Concilium* 1 (2015), 121-126), zwei öffentlichen Stellungnahmen der Soziologische Gesellschaft Kroatien zum Missbrauchs der wissenschaftlichen Forschung in der Anti-Gender-Kampagne (Hrvatsko sociološko društvo, IV. elektronička sjednica predsjedništva Hrvatskog sociološkog društva. http://www.hsd.hr/web/images/Zapisnik_IV%20Elektronicka%20Sjednica%20Predsjednistva%20HSD-a_28_11_01_12_2013.pdf , 27. Juli 2015), eine Reaktion des Frauennetzwerkes an die falschen Deutung von Gender-Mainstreaming durch den Erzbischof von Zadar (Izjava Ženske mreže Hrvatske u povodu sve češćih istupa protiv politike rodne ravnopravnost. http://www.zenska-mreza.hr/izjave/napad_na_teoriju_roda_napad_je_na_zenska_prava.html, 20. Juli 2015); die kroatische Sektion der ESWTR hat die Übersetzung von Artikeln von Gerhard Marschütz initiiert, in denen er das Buch von Gabriele Kuby wissenschaftlich kritisiert (Gerhard Marschütz, "Rod – trojanski konj? Teološke napomene uz nedavnu raspravu o rodu na katoličkom području", *Nova prisutnost* 2 (2014), 181-203; Gerhard Marschütz, Dokidanje biološkog spola? Teološke napomene o raspravi o rodu na katoličkom području, *Riječki teološki časopis* 2 (2015), 359-378), eine Gruppe von Autoren hat in einem Brief die Botschaft der Katholischen Bischöpfen über die Gefahren der Gender-Ideologie kritisiert (Križ života, "Osvrt na poruku HBK o rodnoj ideologiji 'Muško i žensko stvori ih!'". http://www.kriz-zivota.com/osvrt-na-poruku-hbk-o-rodnoj-ideologiji-musko-i-zensko-stvori-ih/, 3. September 2015).

[61] Darüber auch: Ulrike Kind, "Drang zur Mitte. Wie sich Gesellschaft und Kirche in Polen verändern", *Herder Korrespondenz* 3 (2015), 149-154, hier: 151.

Diese Strategie hat das Ziel, der Öffentlichkeit konkrete Informationen über Gendertudien zu geben und die Politik des Gender-Mainstreamings durch wissenschaftliche Konferenzen, Artikel und Aussagen von Gender-Experten und Expertinnen zu erklären.[62]

Die zweite Strategie übt Druck auf staatliche Institutionen aus, um sie zu zwingen, Position gegenüber der Anti-Gender-Kampagne zu beziehen. In diesem Sinne werden verschiedene Bürgerinitiativen, öffentliche Proteste und förmliche Beschwerden organisiert, wie zum Beispiel "Supreme Audit Office",[63] in dem verlangt wird, die katholischen Einrichtungen, die von den EU-Strukturfonds finanziert werden, daraufhin zu kontrollieren, ob sie die Anforderungen der Gleichstellung der Geschlechter respektieren. Es wurde auch ein Brief an Papst Franziskus von dem Frauenkongreß gesendet.[64]

Eine dritte Strategie war der Versuch, einen Dialog zwischen denen, die die Anti-Gender Kampagne unterstützen, und jenen, die sie kritisieren, zu initiieren. So gab es zum Beispiel eine Diskussion zwischen Feministinnen und katholischen AktivistInnen.

Auf der anderen Seite des Spektrums stand die Strategie, die Anti-Gender-Debatte lächerlich zu machen. Nach Meinung von Weronika Grzebalska haben sich diese Gegenstrategien wirksam erwiesen. Zum Beispiel hat die Regierung die Istanbul-Konvention der Europaratskonvention zur Verhütung von Gewalt gegen Frauen ratifiziert und 89 % der Polen(??) haben diese Ratifizierung unterstützt.[65]

Empfehlungen

Als Abschluss werden noch einige Empfehlungen zusammengefasst, wie an die Anti-Gender-Bewegung reagiert werden kann. Die Autoren und Autorinnen, die die Bewegung erforscht haben, schlagen Folgendes vor:

---

[62] Diese Strategie folgt auch der Katholischer Deutscher Frauenbund, der eine die Broschüre veröffentlicht hat mit der Intention, eine Orientierung über "Gender, Gender Mainstreaming und Frauenverbandsarbeit" zu biten (Vgl. Katholischer Deutscher Frauenbund (ed.), *Gender, Gender Mainstreaming und Frauenverbandsarbeit*. http://www.frauenbund.de/themen-und-projekte/gender/, 22. Oktober 2015). In der Slowakei haben WissenschaftlerInnen des Instituts für soziale Kommunikation Manipulationen über die Meinung zu Gender-Mainstreaming aufgedeckt; es wurden Informationen und ein E-Kurs über Gender-Mainstreaming Politik angeboten (vgl. Ďurinová, "Slovakia", 117-118.).

[63] Vgl. Grzebalska, "Poland", 98.

[64] Vgl. N. N., Papież Franciszek rozumie problemy kobiet. (https://www.kongreskobiet.pl/plPL/news/show/papiez_franciszek_rozumie_problemy_kobiet, 4 März 2014)

[65] Vgl. Grzebalska, "Poland", 98.

- Die Anti-Gender-Bewegung sollte eher als ein langlebiges, transnationales Phänomen analysiert werden, denn als eine lokale, nationale Bewegung. Um sie zu verstehen, braucht man eine komparative Analyse des Phänomens, die zeigt, wie es sich entwickelt hat in verschiedenen nationalen und transnationalen Räumen.

- Auf die Anti-Gender-Mobilisierung sollte auf der wissenschaftlichen, politischen und aktivistischen Ebene reagieret werden, weil das Fehlen einer umfassenden Reaktion sowohl Anti-Gender-Aktivisten als auch reaktionären Gruppen hilft, das Vertrauen der Allgemeinheit zu gewinnen. Es sollte eine gute Ausbildung für Lehrende, Sozialarbeiter und Sozialarbeiterinnen geben, sowie Informationen für Medien und andere MultiplikatorInnen gewährleistet werden.

- Weitere Empfehlungen: Man sollte weiter

- die Öffentlichkeit über die Bedeutung und die Durchführung von Gender-Mainstreaming-Politik und deren Bedeutung informieren, die in diesem Prozess eine geschlechtersensible Erziehung hat; es sollte erklärt werden, dass es nicht um die Aufhebung des Geschlechteridentität geht, sondern um die Aufhebung der der Geschlechtersterotipe;

- darlegen, dass die Gender-Mainstreaming-Politik nicht nur ein so genanntes Frauenthema ist und dass die geschlechtsspezifischen Probleme in weitere soziale Probleme eingebettet sind;

- die Befürchtungen der Eltern verstehen, die an der Anti-Gender-Bewegung partizipieren, und ihnen fundierte Antworten auf den Anti-Gender-Diskurs bieten;

- eine geeignete Sprache finden, um angemessen auf die Sprache der Angst und die moralische Panikmache antworten zu können. Es sollten die Aspekte von Gerechtigkeit, Verteilung von Macht und Solidarität betont werden;

- an statt der menschlichen Natur oder der so genannten "traditionellen Werte", sollen die Gerechtigkeit und das Teilen von Macht und Reichtum betont werden;

- einen breit angelegten sozialen Dialog über die Gleichstellung der Geschlechter initiieren;

- die Bedeutung der christlichen, konservativen Frauenbewegung in der Diskussion und der weiteren Entwicklung evaluieren: Werden sie mit der Rechten kooperieren oder nicht?

- größere Aufmerksamkeit auf die Art und Weise legen, wie die Kampagne auf lokaler Ebene durchgeführt und verwendet wird, um ein Netzwerk zwischen konservativen Politikern, religiösen Aktivisten und Kirchenbeamten zu etablieren.

– den Kontext des so genannten Kulturkampfs überwinden, den der Anti-Gender Diskurs vorschlägt.

– Strategien, die dem Spott oder der Verteufelung des Anti-Gender Diskurses dienen, als kontraproduktiv ablehnen. Vielversprechender sind die Strategien, die aufzeigen, dass es sich im Streit über Gender mehr um einen Interessenkonflikt, als um einen Identitätskonflikt handelt.

– auf nationaler und EU-Ebene ein Netz von NGOs für Menschenrechte und die Gleichstellung der Geschlechter schaffen. Es ist notwendig, Erfahrungen über bewährte Praktiken auszutauschen und sich gegenseitig zu beraten.

– eine Schritt-für-Schritt-Strategie entwickeln.[66]

– Diesen Vorschlägen kann noch hinzugefügt werden, verschiedene Fragen, die unter dem Konzept der "Gender-Ideologie" gesammelt sind, zu separieren und so eine klar formulierte Position zu denen von den Anti-Gender-Aktivisten suchen.

Während der Jahre 2012 und 2013 gab es in verschiedenen Ländern Europas Demonstrationen gegen eine so genannte Gender-Ideologie und gegen die Gender-Theorie. Diese haben nicht nur wegen ihrer massiven und guten Organisation, breite Aufmerksamkeit geweckt, sondern auch wegen der Inhalte, die den Ausdrücken *Gender-Ideologie* und *Gender-Theorie* von den Anti-Gender-AutorInnen und -AktivistInnen zugeschrieben worden sind. Obwohl das Phänomen der Anti-Gender-Bewegung noch nicht ausreichend erforscht ist, werden auf der Grundlage der bisherigen Forschung in diesem Artikel einige Merkmale und Herausforderungen herausgearbeitet. Es wird diskutiert, in wie weit es sich um ein nationales oder transnationales Problem handelt; wie die Definition des Begriffes Gender in der Anti-Gender-Bewegung manipuliert wird; was die Gegenstände und wer die Träger dieser Bewegung sind; welche Organisationsformen die Anti-Gender-Bewegung hat; ob die Bewegung als *backlash* verstanden werden kann und welche Gegen-Strategien gibt es, und was die Empfehlungen für die zukünftigen Umgang mit der Bewegung sein können.

During 2012-2013, demonstrations against "gender ideology" and "gender theory" were held in various European countries. These demonstrations attracted attention not only because of their mass and organisation, but also because of the ways in

---

[66] Vgl. Korolczuk, "'The War on Gender' from a Transnational Perspective", 7; Blum, "Germany", 58; Ďurinová, "Slovakia", 119-120; Félix, "Hungary", 79-80; Brustier, "France", 36; Grzebalska, "Poland", 99.

which their anti-gender thinkers and activists considered "gender ideology" and "gender theory". Although the whole phenomenon of the anti-gender movement has not been adequately researched, some characteristics and challenges based on previous research are presented in this article. The current discussion addresses the following questions: Is the anti-gender movement a national or international issue? How are definitions of gender in the anti-gender movement manipulated? What are the issues and who are the bearers of this movement? What are the organisational forms of the anti-gender movement? Can this movement be understood as a "backlash"? What counter-strategies exist and what is recommended for dealing with this movement in the future?

Jadranka Rebeka Anić ist Mitglied der Kongregation Franziskanischer Schulschwestern Christi des Königs – Provinz Split. Sie promovierte zum Dr. theol. an der Kath.-theol. Fakultät der Universität Wien. Seit 2007 arbeitet sie als Wissenschaftlerin im Institut für Sozialwissenschaften Ivo Pilar – Regionalzentrum Split, Kroatien. Bibliographie: http://bib.irb.hr/lista-radova?autor=277285.

Journal of the European Society of Women in Theological Research 24 (2016) 31-45.
doi: 10.2143/ESWTR.24.0.3170024

Nuria Calduch-Benages

Miriam, May Your Hope Give Us Hope! (Exod 2:1-10)

Introduction

Popular wisdom is interested in numerous aspects and themes of human life. One of these is hope. Curiously, in Italian, for instance, there are many proverbs on hope which express negativity, scepticism or even sarcasm. Here are some of their translations into English: "Too much hope kills a man", "Hope is a deceiver", "In the land of hope, there is neither lunch nor dinner" and its variant "In the land of hope, one does not put on weight". Fortunately, there are other proverbs which are more positive and very encouraging, such as: "While there's life, there's hope", "Hope is the first to be born and the last to die", "The one who hopes does not despair", "More miles are covered with good hope than with a good horse", "No sowing without hope".

Hope is a property of being human. The ancients said so in various ways: "Hope is the only good common to all; those who have nothing else possess hope still" (Thales of Miletus) and the moderns repeat it: "To live without hope is to cease living" (Theodor Dostoyevsky), "Today is always forever" (Antonio Machado), "If I help a single person to have hope, I shall not have lived in vain" (Martin Luther King), "Without hope, who would dare to begin any activity, to perform any task? Who would have the courage to face a future that is murky, uncertain and unpredictable?" (Francesco Alberoni).[1]

Hope in the Bible

In the Bible, hope is never something general: it consists in hoping for something good that comes from God. Closely linked with faith, biblical hope is an expectation, which is eager, fervent, and active and which has nothing to do with kidding oneself with regard to the troubles of the present moment. To the extent in which faith in God is faith in His promise, faith is also hope. To hope, then, means to trust: to trust in His rewards, in eternal happiness and in His mercy (cf. Sir 2:7-9).

---

[1]   These are all my free translations from Italian.

The journey of hope begun with Abraham (cf. Gen 12:1-3) reaches its goal in Christ; however, it will have its full realisation only in the Parousia. In the course of this journey, the Bible presents numerous examples of hope: the patriarchs and the matriarchs hoped in the promise of descendants and land; the prophets hoped in the conversion of Israel; the psalmists and worshippers hoped for the salvation of God; righteous Job hoped against all hope in the manifestation of his Lord and closest friend; the sage, Daniel, announced a message of hope in a situation of political oppression and religious persecution, and so many other biblical characters whose stories encourage us to hope in a better future for our people and for the whole of humanity.

Miriam in the Bible

With the object of illustrating the theme of hope in the Bible, I have decided to concentrate on the most important female character in the books of Exodus and Numbers, namely, Miriam. Known mainly as the sister of Moses and Aaron, she is described as daughter, leader of the people, and prophetess. Miriam does not stand out for her deeds, wars, and victories, not even for her beauty like other biblical heroines (Judith, Esther, and so on).[2] As Phyllis Silverman Kramer rightly observes, "The Bible contains no physical description of Miriam; her personality emerges only through her actions."[3] In the account of Moses being saved from the water (Exod 2:1-10), Miriam appears as a young girl and in the account of the passage through the sea (Exod 15:20-21), she appears as a young woman. In the latter, we see her singing and dancing together with the other women to celebrate the saving intervention of the Lord. In the book of Numbers, she is punished, together with Aaron, for having criticised her brother Moses (Num 12:1-16), an episode which is recalled in Deut 24:9: "Remember what the Lord your God did to Miriam during the journey when you came out of Egypt."[4] Again in the book of Numbers, specifically in the census of the Levites, the name of Miriam appears together with her two brothers: Aaron, Moses, and Miriam (Num 26:59). In 1 Chr 5:29 they are cited in the same order. A text of Micah is worthy of

---

[2]   Cf., by contrast *Soṭah* 11b.12a; *Exod. Rab.* 1:21 and *Pirqe R. Eliezer* 45.
[3]   Phyllis Silverman Kramer, "Miriam," in: Athalya Brenner (ed.), *Exodus to Deuteronomy* (Academic Press: Sheffield 2000), FCB. Second Series, 104-133, here 105.
[4]   Here and throughout the paper, all quotes are my translations from the Hebrew of *Biblia Hebraica Stuttgartensia. Editio Minor. Editio secunda emendata opera W. Rudolph et H.P. Rüger*, Stuttgart: Deutsche Bibelgesellschaft, 1984.

mention. There the prophet considers Miriam as a leader of the people who was commanded by God, along with her brothers, to carry out this task: "Was it because I brought you out of the land of Egypt, I redeemed you from the house of bondage and I sent before you Moses, Aaron and Miriam?" (Mic 6:4). One notes that, in these last three texts, the order in which the three siblings are mentioned is not the order of their birth: Miriam, the firstborn, is always mentioned last. All three of these texts have been extensively studied by Rita J. Burns (1987) and Ursula Rapp (2002).[5]

In recent years, the academic discussion about Miriam has been concerned mainly with her prophetic and cultic function. The most studied texts have been Exodus 15 (the Song of the Sea) and Numbers 12 (the murmuring of Miriam and Aaron). By contrast, we intend to focus on the figure of Miriam as a woman of hope and for this reason we have chosen Exod 2:1-10 as our point of reference. In this connection, it is not to be forgotten that Philo of Alexandria, in his treatise *De Somnis*, attributes to Miriam the symbolic name of ἐλπίς (hope):

> For this reason they say, that the sister of Moses also (and she is called Hope by us, when speaking in a figurative manner) was contemplated at a distance by the sacred scriptures, inasmuch as she kept her eyes fixed on the end of life, hoping that some good fortune might befall her, sent by the Giver of all good from above, from heaven.[6]

The Prologue of Exodus and the Women

The book of Exodus begins with a brief genealogy of the family of Jacob (Exod 1:1-7), its function being to demonstrate continuity with the story narrated in the book of Genesis (see Gen 50:24). Even if this genealogy contains only the names of the twelve sons of Jacob, taken as a whole, the first three chapters of Exodus (considered as a prologue for the entire work) are characterised by a

---

[5] Rita J. Burns, *Has the Lord Indeed Spoken Only Through Moses? A Study of the Biblical Portrait of Miriam* (Society of Biblical Literature: Atlanta, GA 1987), SBLDS 84; Ursula Rapp, *Mirjam. Eine feministisch-rhetorische Lektüre der Mirjamtexte in der hebräischen Bibel* (Walter de Gruyter: Berlin / New York 2002), BZAW 317; cf. also, Mercedes García Bachmann, "Miriam, Primordial Political Figure in the Exodus," in: Irmtraud Fischer / Mercedes Navarro Puerto with Andrea Taschl-Erber (eds.), *Torah* (Society of Biblical Literature: Atlanta, GA 2011), The Bible and Women. Hebrew Bible/Old Testament 1.1, 329-374.

[6] Philo, *De Somnis*, II, 142. (http://www.earlyjewishwritings.com/text/philo/book21.html, 7 June 2016)

female presence: the midwives Shiphrah and Puah, Moses' mother, his sister, the daughter of the Pharaoh of Egypt, Zipporah, Moses' wife and her six sisters, daughters of the priest of Midian. Twelve women in total. According to Joppie Siebert-Hommes, these twelve daughters are the counterpart of the twelve sons of Jacob who are presented as the origin of the people.[7]

If it is the two midwives who determine the pace of events in Exod 1:8-22, in Exod 2:1-10, the protagonists proper are a mother, a sister and a daughter. Their role is to save the life of the newborn Moses. Little importance, however, is to be attached to the seven daughters of Reuel,[8] Zipporah included. Of the latter, we know only that she was given in marriage to Moses and bore him two sons named Gershom (Exod 2:21-22)[9] and Eliezer (Exod 18:3-4). Despite this difference in importance, the fact remains that it is women who dominate the stage. "It is a women's story, men are strikingly absent", comments J. Cheryl Exum. A little later, she adds, ironically: "Without Moses there would be no story, but without the initiative of these women [she is referring to the twelve daughters mentioned before NCB], there would be no Moses!"[10] Since, for reasons of space, we cannot take into consideration all these texts, we confine ourselves to Exod 2:1-10, the passage known as "the birth of Moses".

Miriam in Exod 2:1-10[11]

[1]A man of the family of Levi went and took as his wife a daughter of Levi. [2]The woman conceived and bore a son; she saw that he was beautiful/good and kept him hidden for three months. [3]Not being able to keep him hidden any

---

[7]   Jopie Siebert-Hommes, *Let the Daughters Live! The Literary Architecture of Exodus 1–2 as a Key for Interpretation* (Brill: Leiden 1998), BIS 37; idem, "The Female Saviors of Israel's Liberator: Twelve "Daughters in Exodus 1 and 2," in: Fischer / Navarro Puerto (eds.), *Torah*, 295-312; cf. also Irmtraud Fischer, *Women Who Wrestled with God. Biblical Stories of Israel's Beginnings*. Translated from the second German edition into English by Linda M. Maloney (Liturgical Press: Collegeville, MN 2005), 114-115.

[8]   In other traditions, he is called Jethro (Exod 3:1; 4:18; 18:1-27) or else Obab (Jdg 4:11; Num 10:29).

[9]   On the figure of Zipporah, cf. Ursula Rapp, "The Vanishing of a Wife," in: Fischer / Navarro Puerto (eds.), *Torah*, 313-328.

[10] J. Cheryl Exum, "You Shall Let Every Daughter Live: A Study of Exodus 1.8–2.10," in: Athalya Brenner (ed.), *A Feminist Companion to Exodus to Deuteronomy* (Academic Press: Sheffield 1994), FCB 6, 37-61, here 52.

[11] For a predominantly synchronic study of the text, cf. Gordon F. Davies, *Israel in Egypt. Reading Exodus 1–2* (Academic Press: Sheffield 1992), JSOTSup 135, especially 86-117.

longer, however, she took a basket of papyrus, daubed it with bitumen and pitch, put the baby in it and set it among the reeds on the bank of the river Nile. [4]His sister stood afar off to know what would happen to him. [5]Now, Pharaoh's daughter went down to the Nile to bathe while her maids walked along the edge of the Nile. She saw the basket among the reeds and ordered her slave-woman to fetch it. [6]She opened it and saw the baby: it was a little boy and he was crying. She took pity on him and said: "He is one of the Hebrews' babies". [7]Then his sister said to Pharaoh's daughter: "Can I go and call a nurse for you from among the Hebrew women so that she can breastfeed the child for you?" [8]"Go," Pharaoh's daughter said to her. The girl went to call the baby's mother. [9]Pharaoh's daughter said to her: "Take this baby away with you and wet-nurse it for me; I shall pay you for it". The woman took the child and wet-nursed it. [10]When the baby had grown, she brought him to Pharaoh's daughter. He became her son and she called him Moses, saying: "I saved him from the waters!"

Two Daughters, Two Mothers

The second chapter begins with a touch of irony. The Pharaoh of Egypt (whose name has been deliberately suppressed) has just given the order not to kill the daughters of Israel: "Every male who is born to the Hebrews you shall throw into the Nile, but you shall let every daughter live" (Exod 1:22). Now the story begins precisely with one of these daughters. Not only that; further on, the story will continue with another daughter, in this case not an Israelite, and that is the daughter of Pharaoh. Hence, two daughters disobey the order given by Pharaoh in such a way as to ruin the plan conceived by the highest authority in the empire. Let us look more closely at these two daughters.

The first daughter mentioned in the story is a daughter of Israel. She is the daughter of a Levite woman married to a man of the tribe of Levi, a tribe particularly involved in the teaching of the Torah (cf. Deut 33:9-10). The text reads: "A man of the family of Levi [Amram NCB][12] went and took as his wife a daughter of Levi" (Exod 2:1). The author refers to Moses' mother as a daughter of Levi, a somewhat unusual epithet: we would have expected rather an expression such as "a woman/wife of the house of Levi". She always appears anonymous in the account, whether as a daughter of Levi or as a

---

[12] Cf. Num 26:59.

mother of Moses. We do know her name, however, because it is mentioned in Exod 6:20 and Num 26:59. She is called Iochebed (in Hebrew, "Yahweh is glory, might"). Let us listen to a rabbinic exegesis about her name:

> As his life-companion Amram had chosen his father's sister Iochebed, born on the same day as he. She was a daughter of Levi and her name, which means 'divine splendour' referred to the heavenly light which radiated from her face.[13]

We should note – and here, the art of the narrator shines through – that both the daughter of Levi and the daughter of Pharaoh will become the mother of Moses. The story tells of two mothers who help each other because they are pursuing the same goal: saving the life of a baby in danger. According to Athalya Brenner, these two mothers cause us to recall the different paradigms with which the biblical authors tell of the birth of a hero. Just as in the book of Ruth, where there are two mothers (Ruth and Naomi) for one child (Obed), in our passage, both Iochebed and Pharaoh's daughter are presented as the mothers of Moses, two mothers who complement each other.[14] Our passage, "a concise legend" has several similarities with the accounts of the birth of Sargon the Great or King Oedipus, Romulus and Remus, and Cyrus the Great. Catherine Vialle has recently characterised Moses as "the biblical Sargon".[15]

The Baby's Mother

We now concentrate on the first example and mother number one. Moses' mother does not speak; she only acts. Let us thus examine her actions (Exod 2:2) and pay attention to the verbs (all active) employed by the narrator: "conceive", "bear", "see", and "hide". The object of these actions is always her son. What we have here, in fact, is an account that is technically considered as a "birth announcement", that is, an account which announces the birth of a hero (compare, for example. 1 Sam 1–3). In accounts of this type, there is

---

[13] Louis Ginsberg, *Le leggende degli ebrei. IV. Mosè in Egitto, Mosè nel deserto* (Adelphi: Milani 2003), Biblioteca Adelfi 440, 30 (translation ours).

[14] Athalya Brenner, "Female Social Behavior: Two Descriptive Patterns within the 'Birth of the Hero' Paradigm," in: *Vetus Testamentum* 36 (1986), 257-273, here 260.

[15] Catherine Vialle, «Échec au roi d'Égypte: le récit de la naissance de Moïse», in: Christian Cannuyer / Catherine Vialle (eds.), *Les naissances merveilleuses en Orient. Jacques Vermeylen (1942-2014) in memorian* (Société Belge d'Études Orientales: Bruxelles 2015), Acta Orientalia Belgica 23, 189-200, here 191. See in the same volume the articles by Alexandre Tourovets and Stéphanie Anthonioz on the same topic.

always a moment in which the father (or mother) gives the baby a name. In our text, however, this element is highly irregular, because the baby receives his name later than usual, where it is given not by his father or mother, but by the daughter of Pharaoh, that is, his adoptive mother.

The text does not speak of the name here, but adds a valuable piece of information: having conceived and borne him, the baby's mother "saw that he was beautiful/good" (in Hebrew, *ṭôb*). According to the rabbinic writings, this phrase refers to the priestly account of the creation in Gen 1:1–2:4a, specifically to the creation of light performed by God on the first day of Creation. "God saw the light and it was good/beautiful, *ṭôb*" (Gen 1:4). This is the rabbinic comment: "At the birth of the child, the whole house is filled with a light like that of the sun and moon together".[16]

Moses' mother is aware that hiding the baby could turn out to be dangerous, and so she reacts feverishly with great energy and haste: she takes a basket of papyrus, daubs it with bitumen and pitch, places the baby inside, and sets it among the reeds at the bank of the Nile (Exod 2:3). All these actions are related with great care, in all their details, revealing the mother's great concern. She is extremely decisive. She will do everything possible to save the baby and she will do it on her own, without the help of her husband of whom we know nothing.

Once again, we are faced with the narrator's irony. The Pharaoh had ordered the male babies to be thrown into the Nile, and Moses' mother obeyed the order by "placing" (not throwing) her baby in the river. She does it, however, in such a way, that instead a place of death, the river becomes a place of life and salvation. Let us add one more detail. In Hebrew, a "basket" is called *tebah*, the same word employed in Genesis 6 to designate Noah's ark. Moreover, this is not the only coincidence between the two accounts. Noah and Moses, the two protagonists, were both saved from the waters. Furthermore, Noah builds a huge ark and the mother of Moses prepares the basket which is, in fact, a kind of little ark.

The Baby's Sister

We thus arrive at Exod 2:4, a verse located in a strategic position in the text, that is, at the centre of what is technically called the "complication" of the account: "His sister stood at a distance to know what would happen to

---

[16] Ginsberg, *Le leggende degli ebrei*, 33 (translation ours). Cf., also, the midrash *Exod. Rab.* 2:2.

him."[17] Our protagonist emerges unexpectedly, "when the action is well under way."[18] Until this point, no one could guess that the new-born baby had a sister. Her existence has not even been mentioned. But her presence is as surprising as it is essential, because it links the two principal themes of this story: that of the mother and her son and that of the princess and her baby. With great literary skill, the narrator describes the opposition between the daughter of Levi (biological mother of Moses) and the daughter of Pharaoh (adoptive mother of Moses).[19] One a Hebrew, the other an Egyptian; one a slave, the other free; one of common stock, the other of royal blood; one poor, the other rich; one hides her son, the other finds him; one remains silent, the other speaks.[20] Two separate women who are brought together thanks to a third woman acting as an intermediary: she, too, is a daughter, but is presented by the narrator as "his sister" (Exod 2:4 and 7) or "the girl" (Exod 2:8). All three female protagonists are anonymous. Moses alone has a name.

Miriam is a figure highly admired in rabbinic literature:[21] there are many legends about her prophecy (she prophesied that one day her brother would save Israel), her fountain and her death. For the rabbis, Miriam could have been a perfect model, but she was not, for two reasons: she never married and did not have any children,[22] and, furthermore, she murmured against Moses her brother. If this had not been the case, Miriam would have been one of the few women about whom the rabbis would possibly have had nothing bad to say (*b Ber.* 19a).

However, let us return to our text. From the narrative point of view, there is no connection between the actions of the mother and her daughter. Moreover, as we have just mentioned, the young woman is described not as a daughter

---

[17] The book of *Jubilees* adds a very poetic detail to the biblical text: "Your mother came by night to suckle you, and, during the day, your sister, Miriam, protected you from the birds" (47:5).

[18] Davies, *Israel in Egypt*, 91.

[19] Tradition has identified her with a number of figures: Thermuthis (Josephus, *Ant.Jud.* II, 9,5 and *Jubilees*, 47), Merris (Eusebius, *Praep. ev.* 9,15, quoting Artapanus), Bithiah (*Exod. Rab.* 18:3; *Lev. Rab.* 1:3; 1 Chr 4:18).

[20] Phyllis Trible, "Bringing Miriam out of the Shadows," in: Brenner (ed.) *A Feminist Companion to Exodus to Deuteronomy*, 166-186, here 167.

[21] Deborah Steinmetz, "A Portrait of Miriam in the Rabbinic Midrash," in: *Prooftexts* 8 (1988), 35-65 and Kramer, "Miriam," esp. 106-115.

[22] According to some traditions, she married Caleb with Bezalel as issue of the union (*Soṭah* 11b). Cf. Ginsberg, *Le leggende degli ebrei*, 25.

but as "his (Moses') sister". Thus, Irmtraud Fischer comments, "her act of rescue is to be seen independently of her mother and whatever orders she may have given. She does not act as a dependent of the family, but in family solidarity."[23] By contrast, for Mercedes Navarro, "the mother and sister of Moses hatch a plan to save the baby."[24] Even if the narrator is silent in this regard, this common strategy between mother and daughter seems completely logical and understandable if we take the context into account.

Let us now analyse the behaviour of Moses' sister in this episode. The text says that she stands "afar off". We should note that the verb used here for "stand" is not, as one would expect, *'amad*, but the imperfect Hithpa'el of *yaṣab*, the primary meaning of which is defined by the vertical position of the body: to get to one's feet (the dynamic-inchoative aspect), or to be on foot (the static-continuative aspect). This verb, observes Siebert-Hommes, "often indicates assuming a particular stance: the subject takes a certain position in tense expectation of what is to take place."[25] A good example is Exod 14:13, where Israel is in a desperate situation, threatened both by the sea and by Pharaoh's army. It is then that Moses encourages the terrified Israelites with these words: "Do not fear! Stand firm and you will see the salvation of the Lord". A similar situation in our passage. Faced with the risk of losing her little brother among the reeds on the bank of the Nile, Miriam stations herself to share in God's action on behalf of Moses. Even if God is never mentioned in the text, His explicit absence indicates the implicit way in which He is taken to be present.[26]

The second word which deserves our attention is *meraḥoq*, "afar off", although many prefer the translation "at a distance" which puts more emphasis on the spatial dimension. However, the Hebrew term may have an extra level of meaning, namely inaccessible, so far off that it comes to mean unreachable, elusive, impenetrable. In other words, rather than being a matter of quantitative distance, it is a question of qualitative distance. Completely defenceless, the baby is fated to die and no one can do anything to prevent it. According to Siebert-Homes, "It seems legitimate to infer that the author intends to suggest that Moses' sister stood there in order to see how God

---

[23] Fischer, *Women Who Wrestled with God*, 118.
[24] Mercedes Navarro / Carmen Bernabé, *Distintas y distinguidas. Mujeres en la Biblia y en la historia* (Publicaciones Claretianas: Madrid 1995), Débora 3, 35 (translation ours).
[25] Siebert-Hommes, *Let the Daughters Live!*, 118.
[26] Navarro / Bernabé, *Distintas y distinguidas*, 35.

would deal with the matter".[27] This inference is confirmed by the use of the Hithpa'el of the verb *yaṣab* of which we have just spoken.

To continue, the first appearance of Miriam in Exodus 2 is closely bound up with both the waters of the Nile and her brother. This is also the case with her second appearance, in Exodus 15, after the passage through the Sea of Reeds. Both form a fine feminine inclusion. If, in Exodus 2, Miriam lingers in order to know what will happen (the saving of Moses), in Exodus 15 she already knows what has happened (the saving of the people). Together with Moses, Aaron and all the people, she is witness of the liberation performed by the Lord. It is precisely from this life-giving experience that there arises her song of thanksgiving, with which the first part of the book of Exodus concludes: "Sing to the Lord, for he has triumphed gloriously" (Exod 15:20).

The Daughter of Pharaoh

In the two following verses (Exod 2:5-6), exactly in the middle of the story,[28] Pharaoh's daughter goes down to the Nile to bathe while her maids walk on the edge of the river. However, the only one who discovers the basket is the princess (Exod 2:5).[29] Let us look closely at her actions: she goes down to the river, she sees the basket, she sends a slave to get it, she opens the basket and sees the baby who is crying (Exod 2:6). Then, in the twinkling of an eye, we pass from actions to emotions: "she took pity on it" and then to the words: "He is one of the Hebrews' babies". The careful description of the actions of the princess recalls the preparation of the basket on the part of Moses' mother in Exod 2:2-3. Where the princess is concerned, we know of her actions, her emotions, and even the words which she speaks. Thus we know that she was aware of the decree of her father, the Pharaoh, a decree which she is prepared to disobey without any regret. From the narrative point of view, "She is the one who pulls the strings. The other personages, the mother and the sister are immobilised as though arrested in an image of a movie."[30]

---

[27] Siebert-Hommes, "But if She Be a Daughter... She May Live! 'Daughters' and 'Sons' in Exodus 1–2," in: Brenner (ed.) *A Feminist Companion to Exodus to Deuteronomy*, 62-74, here 69.

[28] According to Gordon F. Davies, the "turning point" of the account comes in 6c: "and, behold, a boy crying! (*Israel in Egypt*, 99). Jopie Siebert-Hommes, on the other hand, places it in 6b: "and she saw the baby" (*Let the Daughters Live!*, 119).

[29] In the Islamic Kora,n it is Pharaoh's wife rather than his daughter who rescues the child from the river (*Surah* 28).

[30] Siebert-Hommes, *Let the Daughters Live!*, 119.

The attitude of the princess towards the baby anticipates that of God's towards the people.[31] She saw the baby in the basket, felt compassion towards him, and decided to save him.[32] We should note that she felt compassion not only towards a baby who was crying, but towards a Hebrew baby. So too God, upon seeing the suffering of His people in Egypt and listening to their cry, has compassion for them and goes down to save them from their oppressor (Exod 3:7-9). In saving Moses from the waters of death, the princess allows him to be born again. God does the same with his people: He saves them from the deathly waters of the Sea of Reeds and leads them to the freedom which awaits them on the other bank.

It should be noticed that in Exod 2:7, there is the encounter between the baby's sister and Pharaoh's daughter, an encounter that is unexpected from the narrative point of view (it is surprising to hear the voice of Miriam), but already prepared for in advance. At first sight, it appears that the initiative for saving the baby originates from the princess. But this is not so. Miriam approaches the princess and makes a request which in reality, is not quite a request but rather a suggestion as to how to resolve the situation: "Can I go and call a nurse for you from among the Hebrew women so that she can breastfeed the child for you?" With this solution, the sister prepares covertly for the reunion of the mother with her son. The repetition in the Hebrew of the expression "for you" after the verbs "to call" and "to breastfeed" make us think of a person who stands at the service of another (the sister at the service of the princess). However, the twofold "for you" is "for us" (for me and my mother). In other words, the solution proposed by the sister is appropriate for all. Thanks to his sister, therefore, Moses will be saved from death.

The princess accepts the suggestion without hesitation, even if she replies with a brusque "Go", an order appropriate to her social standing (Exod 2:8a). "The princess's one-word command – comments Davies – is set against the blustering and irrational orders of her father in Exod 1,8-14. In a single breath, she undoes her father's authority and contributes indispensably to a movement of rebellion that will eventually bring the destruction of the whole Egyptian army (cf. Exod 12,31-32)".[33] Miriam's reaction is immediate. Obediently, she

---

[31] In this context, cf. Navarro / Bernabé, *Distintas y distinguidas*, 36-37.

[32] Exum, "You Shall Let Every Daughter Live," 58: "Just as the midwives' fear of God provides the explanation of their conduct, so the princess's compassion furnishes the motivation of hers."

[33] Davies, *Israel in Egypt*, 114.

goes to call the baby's mother, that is, her own mother (Exod 2:8b). The dialogue between the girl and the princess is filled with irony. The Pharaoh has been deceived not only by a daughter of Israel (in Exod 1:22 he allowed the Hebrew daughters to live because he regarded them as harmless), but even by his own daughter, who does not hesitate to disobey his orders. Apparently, she does not know that the Hebrew nurse is actually the baby's biological mother.

A Happy Ending

After this shrewd intervention, Miriam disappears completely from the scene, and from that moment on, events develop quickly. The narrator's irony lurks behind every word. Firstly, Pharaoh's daughter decides to pay a certain sum of money to the baby's mother in return for her work in feeding him. Without uttering a word, the mother complies with the o princess' order (presumably with great pleasure!) and suckles the child. Moses is adopted by the Egyptian princess.[34] It is she, as his mother, as if she had been the one giving birth to him, who assigns him the name of Moses. Thus, the child destined to free Israel from the yoke of Egypt grew up in the oppressor's own house, that is, in Pharaoh's own palace and under the protection of the princess.

Miriam, a Woman of Hope

The story has a "happy ending" thanks to a woman who appears on the biblical stage from the shadows, without a genealogy to identify her, without any notice of her birth or name-giving ritual: she is, in fact, nameless in our story. She appears all of a sudden, when no one would have expected it, and, standing upright, observes the scene from afar. With her shrewd action and her wise and opportune words, she succeeds in bringing together two very different women for a single purpose: saving the life of a baby. Having completed her mission, our protagonist disappears in silence. In point of fact, the story of the Exodus owes its beginning not to Moses but to Miriam and the other women who helped her. Miriam's patience is transformed into hope, hope of life for the child, for her family, for the people of Israel, and, finally, for all of us who still today are struck by this story and this extraordinary character.

---

[34] Scholars discuss the legality of such an adoption and also the baby's name. Moses' name is Egyptian, but its explanation ("saved from the waters") is an association based on the sound of the name Moses. Cf. Werner H. Schmidt, *Exodus (1,1–6,30)* (Neukirchener: Neukirchen-Vluyn 1988), Biblischer Kommentar Altes Testament II/1, 73-75.

Figure 1. Rescuing Moses, Dura Europos Synagogue (245 C.E.),
National Museum, Damascus, Syria.

Figure 2. Rescuing Moses (detail), Dura Europos Synagogue (245 C.E.)

Miriam is among the women of Exodus 1–2: the midwives and the women
giving birth, a mother and a daughter, a Hebrew slave and an Egyptian princess. Leaping over the barriers imposed by nationality, culture, society, and
even age, all of them act in solidarity to attain their aim: "to maintain life

43

against a death-dealing command!"[35] Each in her own way strives against the power of the Pharaoh who, in fear, wishes to guarantee his power with the death of the innocents. Without wasting time in useless requests, without compromised solutions, all these women opt for "civil disobedience."[36] Apparently harmless women, who in reality are shrewdly subversive.

In this world of ours, gripped by fear and violence, by tyrants blinded by power and greedy for innocent blood, the story of the anonymous sister is, above all, an injection of hope. Miriam encourages us not to cease striving for life, not to fear losing our security, to act in solidarity and to use our intelligence to defend justice; to know how to hope for the right moment, to stand and observe from afar before acting, not to live off vain illusions but to be anchored in hope. Miriam, may your hope give us hope!

With the object of illustrating the theme of hope in the Bible through an example, this paper concentrates on the most important female character in the books of Exodus and Numbers, namely, Miriam. Known mainly as the sister of Moses and Aaron, she is described as daughter, leader of the people, and prophetess. Miriam does not stand out for her deeds, wars, and victories, not even for her beauty like the other biblical heroines (Judith, Esther…). In recent years the academic discussion about Miriam has been concerned mainly with her prophetic and cultic function. The most studied texts in this context have been Exodus 15 (the Song of the Sea/ the Song of Miriam) and Numbers 12 (the murmuring of Miriam and Aaron). By contrast, we intend to focus on the figure of Miriam as a woman of hope and for this reason have chosen Exod 2:1-10 as our point of reference. In this regard, it should not be forgotten that Philo of Alexandria, in his treatise *De Somnis* (II,142), attributes to Miriam the symbolic name ἐλπίς, meaning hope. In point of fact, the story of the Exodus owes its beginning not to Moses but to Miriam and the other women who helped her. Miriam's patience is transformed into hope, hope of life for the child, for her family, for the people of Israel, and, finally, for all of us who today are still struck by this story and by Miriam's extraordinary character.

Con el objetivo de ilustrar el tema de la esperanza en la Biblia con un ejemplo, este artículo se concentra en el personaje femenino más importante en los libros del Éxodo y Números, s decir, Miriam. Conocida principalmente como la hermana de Moisés y Aarón, es presentada como hija, jefe del pueblo y profetisa. Miriam no destaca por sus hazañas, batallas o victorias, ni siquiera por su belleza como otras heroínas bíblicas (Judit, Ester). En los últimos años las discusiones académicas se

---

[35] Fischer, *Women Who Wrestled with God*, 122.
[36] *Ibid.*

44

han ceñido, en su mayor parte, a su función profética y cultual. Los textos más estudiados han sido Éxodo 15 (el canto del Mar/el canto de Miriam) y Números 12 (las murmuraciones de Miriam y Aarón). Nosotros, en cambio, vamos a focalizar nuestra atención en la figura de Miriam en cuanto mujer de esperanza, y por esta razón hemos escogido Ex 2,1-10 como texto de referencia. A este respecto, no hay que olvidar que Filón de Alejandría, en su tratado *De Somnis* (II,142), atribuye a Miriam el nombre simbólico de ἔλπις (esperanza). Humanamente hablando, la historia del Éxodo debe su inicio, no a Moisés, sino a Mirian y a las otras mujeres que le ayudaron. La paciencia de Miriam se transformó en esperanza, esperanza de vida para el recién nacido, para su familia, para el pueblo de Israel y, finalmente, para todos nosotros que todavía nos dejamos impresionar por esta historia y por este extraordinario personaje.

Nuria Calduch-Benages is currently Professor of Old Testament Exegesis at the Pontifical Gregorian University in Rome. She is Book Review Editor of *Biblica* and member of the editorial board of *Vetus Testamentum* and *Estudios Bíblicos*. Consultant at the Cardinal-Bea-Center for Jewish Studies and Vice-President of the ISDCL (International Society for the Study od Deuterocanonical and Cognate Literature). Since 2014 is member of the Pontifical Biblical Commission.

Journal of the European Society of Women in Theological Research 24 (2016) 47-62.
doi: 10.2143/ESWTR.24.0.3170025

Rita Perintfalvi

The True Face of the "Gender Ideology" Discourse: Religious Fundamentalism, or Questioning the Principle of Democracy?

Introduction

The aim of my study is to analyse a recent phenomenon, which is rooted in political and/or religious fundamentalism. Fundamentalist thinking sees a threat in changing male and female social roles and also in changes to the traditional family model. Rather than understand this diversity, it tries to reduce it, and does so through irrational argumentation. One model, deemed good and morally appropriate, is selected and absolutised of the many existing ones, while everything else is seen as wrong and morally inappropriate.

My study looks at a phenomenon that sees a threat in changing feminine and masculine gender roles as well as in gender studies, the branch of science describing these changes. It also sees a threat in gender mainstreaming, the policy and strategic principle fighting for social equality. The analysis reveals that, in fact, anti-gender attacks are much deeper than they seem: it is not only the concept of gender and the related policy strategy that is under attack, but indeed the entire political consensus based on the language of human rights after World War II [WWII]. These attacks question, in essence, not only the existence of the European Union [EU], but the fundamental European principle of democracy.

The first section of my paper analyses anti-gender attacks on the Central-East-European front. The second section looks at the same phenomenon at the level of Church texts. The concluding section examines the role played by Gabriele Kuby in aggressive anti-gender attacks in Central-East-Europe.

Anti-Gender Attacks in European Political Wars

As Eszter Kováts and Eszter Petronella Soós put it in their study, "after the earlier sporadic interest in the theme, *gender* has recently become an issue, what's more, a transnational issue."[1] As Andrea Pető states in her article, "The 'gender

---

[1] Eszter Kováts / Eszter Petronella Soós, "Félelem a dominó-elvtől? A gender-ellenes európai mobilizáció jelensége: Francia esettanulmány és magyar kilátások" [Fear of the Domino

Rita Perintfalvi
The True face of the "Gender Ideology" Discourse: Religious Fundamentalism,
or Questioning the Principle of Democracy?

ideology' debate opens up a new chapter in the political, cultural and social landscape of Europe that questions previous political chasms."[2] The analysis in this study focuses on Central-East-Europe, in particular Hungary, Poland, and Slovakia, as I had the opportunity to personally study anti-gender movements in these countries. Of course, the picture is only full if we admit that this phenomenon is not specific to the Central-East-European region, but also appears in other countries in the wider region, including Germany, Switzerland, Austria, Italy, and France, as well as countries in the nearer region, such as Croatia or Slovenia.

The term gender became the image of an enemy suitable for mobilisation. Initially, only a small professional community knew the term gender, but then – through expressions like "gender ideology", "gender theory", "gender totalitarianism", and "genderism" – a language and definition-based fight began within associated wide-ranging social movements. These arbitrarily distorted reinterpretations lead to a false – and very often ridiculed and demonised – interpretation of the term gender, "in which neither gender policy experts, nor scholars involved in Gender Studies recognise themselves."[3] In this distorted and falsified sense, gender becomes a synonym for the promotion of homosexuality, free choice of sex and sexual orientation, the elimination of the sexes, paedophilia, sexualising children, and "the culture of death."

According to some scholars, this phenomenon is not merely a classical conservative backlash movement against gender and Lesbian, gay, bisexual, transgendered, and queer [LGBTQ] equality, but a sign that a new kind of fundamentalism has reared its head. What seems at first sight as an attack on the gender perspective, is in fact much more in that, since "gender is a symbolic glue."[4] The issue runs deeper, as these movements question the post-WWII consensus over a political language centred on human rights and disenchantment as well as a neoliberal, policy-based approach to foster political change.

Principle? The Phenomenon of the Anti-Gender Mobilisation in Europe: French Case Study and Hungarian Prospects.], in: *Társadalmi Nemek Tudománya e-Folyóirat*, (2/2014), 106-124, here 109. (tntefjournal.hu/vol4/iss2/kovats_soos.pdf, 1 May 2015). My translation from Hungarian; emphasis in the original.

[2] Andrea Pető, "'Anti-Gender' Mobilisational Discourse of Conservative and Far Right Parties as a Challenge for Progressive Politics," in: Eszter Kováts / Maari Põim (eds.), *Gender as Symbolic Glue: The Position and Role of Conservative and Far Right Parties in the Anti-Gender Mobilizations in Europe* (Friedrich Ebert Stiftung: Budapest 2015), 126-134, here 126. (http://library.fes.de/pdf-files/bueros/budapest/11382.pdf, 10 November 2015)

[3] Kováts / Soós, „Félelem a dominó-elvtől?," 109. My translation from Hungarian.

[4] Pető, "'Anti-Gender' Mobilisational Discourse," 127.

Rita Perintfalvi
The True face of the "Gender Ideology" Discourse: Religious Fundamentalism,
or Questioning the Principle of Democracy?

The buzzword "gender" integrates, in a peculiar way, a series of concerns and criticism – not only against gender or LGBTQ equality, but also against gender as a symbolic glue, which thus integrates anti-EU, anti-liberal, anti-communist, and homophobic attitudes.

Pető writes about the deeper objective of the anti-gender debate: "This is a fight to redefine neoliberal representative democracy and this process is creating new political chasms."[5] This political objective may lead to an unprecedented strengthening of the extreme right, which entails immense dangers: "The real and new challenge is that after 1945 anti-modernist alternatives have never received so many votes in democratic elections as viable alternatives. The rise of the far right is a fact and in their electoral success anti-genderism works as a symbolic glue."[6]

The Emergence of the Anti-Gender Debate in Poland[7]

The anti-gender outbreak began in the years 2012-2013. There were three important reasons that had brought this discourse to the surface: the Istanbul Convention, a Paedophilia Scandal in the Polish Catholic Church, and the World Health Organisation [WHO]'s recommendations for sex education in schools. Weronika Grzebalska gives the following summary of the role of political parties in the outburst of the debate:

> In 2014, 'gender ideology' was directly addressed in the programs of three parties – Law and Justice, United Poland and the National Movement – and pictured as a foreign-imposed threat to traditional family and national identity. In their statements, right-wing politicians often used fear-arousing language conflating gender equality with deviations and pathologies.[8]

---

5 Ibid., 130.
6 Pető, "'Anti-Gender' Mobilisational Discourse," 130-131.
7 In order to understand the events in Poland, see the following texts: Agnieszka Graff, "Report from the Gender Trenches: War against 'Genderism' in Poland," in: *European Journal of Women's Studies* 21 (2014), 431-442; Magdalena Grabowska, *Cultural War or "Business as Usual"? Recent Instances, and the Historical Origins of a "Backlash" against Women's and Sexual Rights in Poland* (Heinrich-Böll-Stiftung: 2014). (http://pl.boell.org/sites/default/files/uploads/2014/10/cultural_war_or_grabowska.pdf, 10 November 2015); Agnieszka Graff, *Gender és politika, de az az igazi* (Friedrich Ebert Stiftung: Budapest 2014). (http://www.fesbp.hu/common/pdf/Graff_gender_es_politika_de_az_az_igazi.pdf, 5 May 2015).
8 Weronika Grzebalska, "Poland," in: Eszter Kováts / Maari Põim (eds.), *Gender as Symbolic Glue: The Position and Role of Conservative and Far Right Parties in the Anti-Gender Mobilizations in Europe* (Friedrich Ebert Stiftung: Budapest 2015), 83-103, here 83.

Rita Perintfalvi
The True face of the "Gender Ideology" Discourse: Religious Fundamentalism,
or Questioning the Principle of Democracy?

The anti-neo-colonial, Eurosceptic rhetoric is also present as a mobilisation factor: "The discursive figure of the EU as a cultural coloniser, corrupting innocent Polish children and suppressing the Polish national culture, was used ubiquitously,"[9] says Grzebalska. According to her, the main stakeholders in the anti-gender debate in Poland are

> the Catholic Church, right-wing politicians both on the local and national level, parliamentary committees (e.g. 'Stop gender ideology'), conservative academics (e.g. Marta Cywińska, Warsaw University of Life Sciences), Catholic and pro-life NGOs (e.g. Healthy Family Association) and Internet platforms (e.g. *stop-seksualizacji.pl*).[10]

However, the role of foreign Catholic anti-gender authors who have played a major role in the coarsening of the debate cannot be neglected either. These include Lucetta Scaraffia, Dale O'Leary, Christine de Marcellus de Vollmer, and Gabriele Kuby.

As demonstrated above, the Catholic Church has been one of the key stakeholders in the unfolding of the gender debate in Poland. A pastoral letter was read out to the episcopal conference on Angelus Sunday, 29 December 2013. The faithful and representatives of various Church movements and associations were called upon to act courageously against this ideology. Many rallies, demonstrations, Internet campaigns etc. ensued with thousands of people cussing out "genderism" and "gender ideology" as "anthropological heresy". "Gender ideology is worse a threat that National Socialism and communism combined."[11] It destroys family and nation.

Hungary and the gender discourse

In Hungary, anti-gender discourse and the mobilisation against the so-called "gender ideology" has not intensified at the same level as in Poland or Slovakia. Still, there are several triggers, actors, and documents relating to this issue that would make a more intensive mobilisation possible in the near future: the debate may explode at any moment.[12]

---

[9] Grzebalska, "Poland," 92.

[10] Ibid., 90, emphasis in the original.

[11] Cf. Tadeusz Pieronek, Polish bishop on the "gender problem". (http://www.nytimes.com/2014/01/27/opinion/sierakowski-the-polish-churchs-gender-problem.html?_r=0, 27 May 2015)

[12] The examination of anti-gender attacks has just begun in Hungarian social research, with, for example, Nikolett Kormos' introduction to the special issue of the Replika journal on Hungarian

Rita Perintfalvi
The True face of the "Gender Ideology" Discourse: Religious Fundamentalism,
or Questioning the Principle of Democracy?

The debate first appeared in 2010, when the then governing left-liberal coalition was ousted by the new, conservative government of *Fidesz-KDNP* (Christian Democratic Party). Already in 2010, the Gender Equality Department was disbanded and merged into the Division of Equal Opportunity under the Ministry of Human Resources. The new Family Protection Act which came into force in 2012 reiterates foetus protection from conception, and redefines family as composed of the marriage of a heterosexual couple and their children, or relatives in direct line.

Currently, the gender debate infiltrates the discourse held around the issue of migration. Talking at the Budapest Demographic Forum on 5 November 2015, prime minister Viktor Orbán pointed out as important that communities can sustain themselves even without the involvement of external resources. "Who will inhabit Europe?" is a key question for Orbán, and the anti-gender rhetoric appears in this context again:

> It would be worth the while to talk about this seriously, but somehow there is much more time, attention, energy, and money for other things and debates that are alienated from life. Gender debate, homosexual marriage, and we could certainly mention a few more. These things are cute and important, but are secondary after all; they will not move Europe from the economic and societal pitfall.[13]

Gender Studies, "Előszó: A genderideológiáról," in: *Replika* (1-2/2014), 7-11. The above-mentioned study by Eszter Kováts and Eszter Petronella Soós, as well as Lídia Balogh's paper of February 2015 entitled "A nemek közötti egyenlőség normái a 'gender-ideológia' diskurzusának tükrében" [Norms of Gender Equality in Light of the Discourse of '[Norms Ideology']], in: *Állam és Jogtudomány* (4/2014), 3-25. Eszter Kováts / Maari Põim (eds.), *Gender as Symbolic Glue* looks at the role of right and extreme right parties in the mobilisation around the "gender ideology" discourse, with two Hungarian studies included: Anikó Félix, 62-82 and Andrea Pető, 126-132. One of the defining studies in gender debate in Hungary is the article of Gerhard Marschütz, "A biológiai nem megszüntetése? Teológiai megfontolások a katolikus területen folyó gender-vitához" [Dissolving Biological Sex? Theological Considerations of the Debate on Gender within Catholicism], in: Szécsi József (ed.), *Keresztény - Zsidó Teológiai Évkönyv 2014* (Keresztény–Zsidó Társaság: Budapest 2014), 160-177. (http://teologusnok.hu/files/temak/gender/201504_Gender-ideologia_Prof.Marschutz.pdf, 30 May 2015). Marschütz looks at the phenomenon of the gender debate from a theological perspective, and points out that the concepts of Gabriele Kuby, who has been of definitive importance in this debate, are strongly questionable from a theological perspective.

[13] The prime minister's speech is published on his website: http://www.miniszterelnok.hu/cikk/az_eu_nem_epitheti_a_jovojet_csaladok_helyett_bevandorlasra, 10 November 2015. My translation from Hungarian.

Rita Perintfalvi
The True face of the "Gender Ideology" Discourse: Religious Fundamentalism,
or Questioning the Principle of Democracy?

In the domains of theology and the Church, the first books that attempted to explain why "gender ideology" was dangerous appeared in 2008. Prime examples are the volumes *Die Gender Revolution – Relativismus in Aktion*[14] and *Die globale sexuelle Revolution. Zerstörung der Freiheit im Namen der Freiheit*[15] by Gabriele Kuby, and the essay *A szexuális forradalomtól a gender-forradalomig* [From Sexual Revolution to Gender Revolution] by pater Ferenc Tomka.[16] Tomka assumes Kuby's entire gender conspiracy theory without any critique whatsoever.

Another definitive piece of work for the theological discourse is the volume of the Austrian auxiliary bishop Andreas Laun, *Keresztény ember a modern világban* [Christian Man in the Modern World], also published in Hungarian in 2014.[17] Laun introduced his book personally at a book presentation held at the Pázmány Péter University in October 2014. According to the extreme right-wing associated website "eredetimiep.hu", Andreas Laun highlighted that

> National Socialism and Communism tried to disable the Church's work; and we hoped that we would not face any attacks anymore. Alas, we were wrong because the gender movement appeared, which represents the absurd concept that there are no essential differences between being a man or a woman, and it is only a matter of socialisation if someone becomes a man or a woman.[18]

The Possible Emergence of a Movement; Preventive and Halting Strategies

If we look at the countries where a significant societal anti-gender movement has emerged, it is easy to map the first steps of a movement, the necessary structural requirements and focal point around which the discourse intensified. The first steps of such emerging movements exhibit, milder mobilisations as

---

14 Gabriele Kuby, *Die Gender Revolution – Relativismus in Aktion* (fe-medienverlag: Kißlegg 2006). The book was also published in Hungarian: *A nemek forradalma. A gender forradalma – A nevelés államosítása* (Kairosz: Budapest 2008).

15 Gabriele Kuby, *Die globale sexuelle Revolution. Zerstörung der Freiheit im Namen der Freiheit* (fe-medienverlag: Kißlegg 2012). The book was also published in Hungarian: *Globális szexuális forradalom – A szabadság elpusztítása a szabadság nevében* (Kairosz: Budapest 2013).

16 Ferenc Tomka (in collaboration with László Bíró, Ilona Ékes, and Péter Roska), "A szexuális forradalomtól a gender-forradalomig", in: *Magyar Bioetikai Szemle* (1-2/2010), 63-74. (http://makab.sk/Hu/anyagok/gender.pdf, 10 November 2015)

17 Andreas Laun, *Keresztény ember a modern világban*, (Kairosz: Budapest 2014).

18 A summary of Andreas Laun's speech can be read at the following link, under the title "Gender Ideology is Demonic and Also Destroys Families: http://www.eredetimiep.hu/fuggetlenseg/2014/november/14/13.htm, 10 November 2015. My translation from Hungarian.

Rita Perintfalvi
The True face of the "Gender Ideology" Discourse: Religious Fundamentalism,
or Questioning the Principle of Democracy?

an initial step, followed, in the right moment, by a burst up of a much stronger societal movement. The theoretical background work, the arguments and materials had usually been at hand for several years already.

The lack of two of these structural conditions slows down the intense emergence of anti-gender attacks in Hungary. One is that the integration, organisation, and civic relations of the Catholic Church in Hungary are all very weak due to its historical background; and it is not very likely that it would be able to build up and operate enduring civil organisational structures that are independent of party politics.[19] A second, very important, structural factor lacking in Hungary, is that contrary to Slovakia, Poland, or Croatia, for instance, Hungarian legislation pushed gender mainstreaming completely to the background since 2010 in, making any fundamentalist backlash quite senseless. The Hungarian government implements a non-liberal (illiberal) cultural agenda, so that anti-gender attacks are meaningless. However, there is already a risk of gender attacks: there are political actors, journalists, Church personalities, and conservative non-governmental organisations that stimulate and may lead on gender attacks. The theoretical background material is already available.

The reasons immediately preceding an outburst are different in different countries. For example, in Slovakia, it was the discussion around government strategy with regard to human rights that set attacks in motion, while in Poland, the financial and paedophiliac scandals of the Church led to similar results.

It seems very feasible that the government itself can also kick-start an anti-gender movement should a new enemy be sought when the immigrant agenda is depleted. An attack against the benchmark human rights and equal opportunity norms of the European Union would very comfortably fit the freedom-fighting, anti-EU rhetoric of the government and its strategy of mobilising its own civil organisations. Possible points of explosion could be abortion, or the topic of LGBTQ rights, or even the current, highly intense issue of immigration.

The main question for preventive and halting strategies, is whether progressive social stakeholders are able to develop a competitive frame, a political narrative that renders comprehensible and politically attractive the critical contents of gender concepts frequented by the actors of gender studies. Seeking dialogue between conservative and progressive thinkers, political scientists and gender studies experts, sociologists, theologians, journalists, opinion leaders, etc., is pivotal. Such a search for dialogue has been going on with increasing intensity since early

---

[19] Kováts / Soós, „Félelem a dominó-elvtől?," 120.

Rita Perintfalvi
The True face of the "Gender Ideology" Discourse: Religious Fundamentalism,
or Questioning the Principle of Democracy?

2014, with the forums of Friedrich-Ebert-Stiftung, the public political activity of the Hungarian chapter of ESWTR, and the production and translation of theological works trying to remedy the almost completely lacking gender perspective in theological approach in Hungary, playing an essential role. The purpose of the dialogue is to prevent, on all levels, the development of an enemy stereotype, and the escalation helix built upon fear and hatred.

Misunderstanding and Misreading Gender-Conscious Thinking in Church Texts in Slovakia

I have selected texts to which an adequate theological response can be given. One, such text is the pastoral letter of the Conference of Slovak Bishops, published on 1 December 2013, available on the Internet in Hungarian, and read out aloud in various Hungarian churches.[20] I would like to point out the rhetorical topoi of the anti-gender campaign that emerged and became widespread not only in Slovakia, but also in Poland, among others.[21]

After the pastoral letter, the politics in Slovakia were polarised in relation to the idea of gender equality and "gender ideology". There were, of course, some debates on this issue previously connected with the German sociologist, Gabriele Kuby, and her lectures on state sex education for children, homosexuality, and pornography. The strategies of human rights and of gender equality are closely linked with the emergence of the anti-gender discourse. There had been a strong resistance on the part of several NGOs and the Slovak Bishops Conference against the gender equality strategy for the years 2014–2019. Representatives of catholic schools issued a declaration warning of the gender ideology and early sexualisation of children at schools. Oľga Pietruchová, Head of the Gender Equality Department in the Ministry of Labour, Social Affairs, and Family, who has actively participated in the preparation of the human rights and gender equality strategy, has had to deal personally with very aggressive attacks and threats.

---

[20] Cf. Conference of Slovak Bishops, "Pastoral letter on the first Sunday of Advent in 2013". (http://www.kbs.sk/obsah/sekcia/h/dokumenty-a-vyhlasenia/p/pastierske-listy-konferencie-biskupov-slovenska/c/pastiersky-list-na-prvu-adventnu-nedelu-2013, 27 May 2015). Available in Hungarian: (http://www.magyarkurir.hu/hirek/szlovak-katolikus-puspoki-konferencia-adventi-korlevele, 27 May 2015)

[21] Cf. The pastoral letter of the Conference of Polish Bishops appeared on Sunday of the Holy Family, 2013. (http://episkopat.pl/dokumenty/listy_pasterskie/5584.1,Pastoral_letter_of_the_Bishops_Conference_of_Poland_to_be_used_on_the_Sunday_of_the_Holy_Family_2013.html, 15 May 2015)

Rita Perintfalvi
The True face of the "Gender Ideology" Discourse: Religious Fundamentalism,
or Questioning the Principle of Democracy?

"Followers of 'the culture of death' proclaim the sameness of the sexes"
Let us look at the pastoral letter of the Conference of Slovak Bishops.

Advocates of "the culture of death" came up with the new concept of "gender ideology", and in its name they proclaim the sameness of the sexes. When hearing the concept for the first time, one may think that the main objective is to ensure equal rights and dignity to both males and females. However, when referring to "gender equality", the promoters of gender equality mean something totally different. Promoters of gender equality want to convince the public that none of us has been created as a man or a woman; and therefore, they aim at taking away the man's identity as a man, and the woman's identity as a woman, and the family's identity as a family.[22]

The greatest problem with the term "gender ideology" is that it does not refer to any clear reality. This is, in fact, an empty term which can be filled with any preferable content. The term "gender ideology" is used in the debate to assault anything that has to do with gender or feminism, rendering many the following concepts suspicious: gender perspective, gender studies or gender theories, gender mainstreaming, feminism, feminist philosophy, feminist social theory, feminist theology, feminist ethics, etc.

What then is the point and purpose of using this term? During the heated debate in Poland, one could hear utterances such as "'gender ideology' is more dangerous than communism and fascism combined."[23] After the fall of the iron curtain, the Church had to face the burden of the pluralism of the modern age within a short time. This confrontation also concerns religious people, who do not side with the Church nowadays as unanimously as they did during communism in the form of shared resistance. Thus, the question today is whether resistance to "gender ideology" will be able to mobilise and unify Catholics.[24]

What else is the problem with the quotation above? "Advocates of 'the culture of death' came up with the new idea of 'culture ideology', and in its name they proclaim the sameness of the sexes".[25] By stating so, the pastoral

---

[22] Conference of Slovak Bishops, "Pastoral letter." My translation from the Hungarian version.

[23] See note 11.

[24] Gerhard Marschütz, „Trojanisches Pferd Gender? Theologische Anmerkungen zur jüngeren Genderdebatte im katholischen Bereich," in: Kerstin Schlögel-Flierl / Gunter M. Prüller-Jagenteufel (eds.), *Aus Liebe zu Gott – im Dienst an den Menschen: Spirituelle, pastorale und ökumenische Dimensionen der Moraltheologie* (Aschendorff: Münster 2014), 433-456, here 438.

[25] See note 20.

Rita Perintfalvi
The True face of the "Gender Ideology" Discourse: Religious Fundamentalism,
or Questioning the Principle of Democracy?

letter assumes that the term "gender" entails an "equality of man and woman" that is dissociated from biology and understood as "gender sameness", as a material lack of differentiation. This quotation from the pastoral letter suggests that the so-called "gender ideology" is about the elimination and disappearance of biological sex. However, gender studies' concern with gender equality – the formal equality of genders –, is in the context of human dignity. This means that it is also concerned with examining, from the perspective of their non-reflective biological fixations, the gender differences between man and woman assumed to be self-evident in both everyday discourse and science, and which often hinder such equality, and with demonstrating that these are predominantly socially constructed.

Biological sex is a given and does not change. Gender, on the other hand, can change: it is dependent on the cultural context and on other factors. And the term "gender equality" means that "the different behaviour, aspirations and needs of women and men are equally valued and favoured and do not give rise to different consequences that reinforce inequalities."[26] Thus, the possibility of gender-based discrimination and the unequal treatment (of either women or men) is precluded.

"Introducing 'Sodomite Ideology' into Schools"
Let us examine another thought, the topoi of which are repeated many times and in many different contexts in anti-gender alarmism in Slovakia:

> Advocates of the "sameness of the sexes" never give up, but they are waiting for the suitable moment to grab, with the help of legislation, the process of education, and introduce this "Sodomite ideology" into schools and kindergartens. They promote an educational process, which would not only deprive children of their dignity, but also would make them into moral and psychological cripples. Children would not be given the chance to develop into mature men and women.[27]

This quotation refers to the introduction of "sexual education" into schools, which, in the view of the supporters of anti-gender attacks, leads to the early sexualisation of children and the spreading of "gender ideology".

---

[26] EUROPEAN COMMISSION: EMPLOYMENT & EUROPEAN SOCIAL FUND, *EQUAL Guide on Gender Mainstreaming*, (Luxembourg, 2005), 3.
(http://ec.europa.eu/employment_social/equal_consolidated/data/document/gendermain_en.pdf, 10 November 2015).

[27] Conference of Slovak Bishops, "Pastoral letter." My translation from the Hungarian version.

Rita Perintfalvi
The True face of the "Gender Ideology" Discourse: Religious Fundamentalism,
or Questioning the Principle of Democracy?

An Immediate Political Call with a Combative Tone

Before finishing this chapter, let us look at a final quotation:

> The culture of death really threatens the existence of the nation. In such a situation previous generations did not hesitate to sacrifice their lives in the interest of their motherland. From our part, for the time being, no such great sacrifice is demanded, but let's remain vigilant! We warn leaders on every level, parents, local authorities at schools, and every well-meaning citizen to take precautions. Let's reject the culture of death at the very beginning! At any elections, vote for those candidates who exclusively reject the culture of death. Otherwise, we would belittle our ancestors who sacrificed their lives.[28]

The expression "sacrifice of lives" reminds one of a manifesto for war, which would definitely not promote dialogue or peace in society. Referring back to war suggests, that just as a certain ideology – fascism – had to be fought against in the past, we must now fight with the same resolution against the equally dangerous notion of "gender ideology".

The reason for writing this text, and for gender suddenly becoming the focus of attention, is clearly shown by the following sentence: "At any elections, vote for those candidates..." This clearly shows the intention behind the pastoral letter, namely to exert influence in the context of the presidential elections that took place in March 2014.

The Impact of Gabriele Kuby in the Gender Debate in Eastern and Central Europe

Die Gender Revolution 2006,[29] *Die globale sexuelle Revolution 2012*[30]

If we seek to identify the texts which may have influenced the anti-gender campaign in Slovakia, Poland, and Croatia, it does not take long to come up with Gabriele Kuby. Kuby is a German publicist, translator, and sociologist, a Christian fundamentalist who is very popular in politically (ultra)conservative circles in her homeland ,and equally in Hungary, too.

The popularity of Kuby's book can be easily understood: it can be downloaded free of charge from the websites of the Christian Democratic People's

---

[28] Ibid. My translation from the Hungarian version.

[29] Kuby, *Die Gender Revolution*. The book was published in Hungarian (2008), Polish, Croatian, and Italian translations as well.

[30] Kuby, *Die globale sexuelle Revolution*. The book was published in Hungarian (2013), Slovakian, Czech, and Croatian translations as well.

Rita Perintfalvi
The True face of the "Gender Ideology" Discourse: Religious Fundamentalism,
or Questioning the Principle of Democracy?

Party *[KDNP]* and the Piarist Order. This finally led to the situation that the book became the ultimate standard for understanding gender in certain circles of the Church in Hungary as well as in the political field. It has been recommended and popularised with great enthusiasm, and without any criticism.

According to Marschütz, "Kuby's books function in European postcommunist countries as 'the' Catholic answer to challenges of the modern age concerning, especially, the morality of marriage, family and sexuality, with special regard to 'gender ideology.'"[31] We must note, that Kuby has no academic qualifications in theology, and is therefore not acquainted with the specific modern literature of moral theology, which discusses these questions with academic precision and an openness to the challenges of the modern age. While gender-aware approaches appear in all disciplines in theology in Western Europe, and there is a great number of research projects held and many publications written, the concept of gender is unfortunately completely alien to theology in Central and East-Europe. Therefore, Kuby's concepts are met with (almost) no critique. It is only recently, that the first articles in German-speaking countries which seriously criticise the book on a theological basis have been published.[32]

Quotations from Kuby's "Die Gender Revolution"[33]

> In our age we are experiencing the most extreme manifestations of relativism: they [advocates of "gender ideology" R.P.] deny what is obvious and conceivable for every human being, and what is, since the dawn of humanity, as self-evident as the alternation of day and night: *humans exist in two sexes – male and female.* Anyone who hasn't met this way of thinking may see it as morbid hubris, which is unnecessary to deal with. However, this perspective has, since the last decade, (silently)

---

[31] Marschütz, „A biológiai nem megszüntetése?" [Dissolving Biological Sex?], 166. My translation from Hungarian.

[32] Marschütz, „Trojanisches Pferd Gender?" 433-456; Marschütz, „Wachstumspotenzial für die eigene Lehre. Zur Kritik an der vermeintlichen Gender-Ideologie," in: *Herder Korrespondenz* 68 (9/2014), 457-462. (http://www.hk-on.de/HKOnlineDocuments/HTML%20Einzelbeitraege/ 2014/Heft%209/HK_68_2014_09_Ss_457ff.htm and http://st-theoethik-ktf.univie.ac.at/fileadmin/ user_upload/p_theologische_ethik/Klarstellung_zu_Kuby_HK11-2014.pdf, 10 November 2015). Rebeke J. Anić, „Der Begriff 'Gender' als Anathema: Eine Kampagne der kroatischen Bischöfe als Beispiel," in: *Herder Korrespondenz* 69 (3/2015), 157-161; Rebeka J. Anić / Jadranka Brncic, „Missverständnisse um den Begriff 'Gender': Überlegungen anlässlich einer Botschaft der kroatischen Bischofskonferenz," in: *Concilium* 51 (1/2015), 121-126; Rebeka J. Anić, „Gender, Politik und die katholische Kirche: Ein Beitrag zum Abbau der alten Geschlechterstereotypen," in: *Concilium* 48 (4/2012), 373-382.

[33] Kuby, "Die Gender Revolution." Henceforth, my translations from Hungarian.

Rita Perintfalvi
The True face of the "Gender Ideology" Discourse: Religious Fundamentalism,
or Questioning the Principle of Democracy?

become the guiding principle of the UN, the EU and national governments, leading to a social revolution, shaking the very foundations of human existence.[34]

We can see that Kuby portrays so-called "gender ideologists" as people who want to relativise male and female sex. This misinterpretation was the focus of anti-gender attacks in Slovakia and Poland. The anti-UN and anti-EU political orientation of the idea is obvious.

Gender as Synonym for the Dissolution of Biological Sex in Kuby's Writing

They argue that the sexual difference between men and women is a social construction, invented by "heterosexual patriarchy".[35]

The "compulsory heterosexuality" must be exceeded, as long as people are free to define – independent of their biological sex – their gender.[36]

The struggle is fought with the artificial term "gender". In 1995, on the Fourth World Conference of Women in Beijing, feminists, in a manipulative way, exchanged the term "sex" with "gender", in order to deliver the sexual difference between man and woman to the arbitrariness of subjective decision.[37]

The purpose of gender activists is the "dissolution of the obvious sexes" and creating a malleable identity.[38]

From these quotations, it turns out that Kuby interprets and condemns the term "gender" as the dissolution of "biological sex". "By doing this, doesn't she intentionally misinterpret the concept of 'gender', turning it into a threatening target which must inevitably be rejected?" – asks Marschütz.[39]

"Sex" is nothing else but biological and anatomical differences between men and women. In opposition to this, "gender" refers to socially constructed differences. In this sense, "gender" is a social construction, because it is constantly changing with the social context. However, the fact that different cultures define the socially desirable behaviour, roles, and personality traits of men and women (that is, gender) differently does *not* mean that with a constantly changing and socially constructed gender, biological sex also changes. This claim of Kuby's is an absurdity.

---

[34] Kuby, *Die Gender Revolution*, 62. Emphasis in the original.
[35] Kuby, *Die Gender Revolution*, 63.
[36] Ibid.
[37] Ibid.
[38] Ibid., 65.
[39] Marschütz, „A biológiai nem megszüntetése?" [Dissolving Biological Sex?], 167. My translation from Hungarian.

Rita Perintfalvi
The True face of the "Gender Ideology" Discourse: Religious Fundamentalism,
or Questioning the Principle of Democracy?

Manifestations of Homophobia in Kuby's Writing

> The minority of homo-, bi- and trans-sexuals, which is not discriminated against anymore at all, but, on the contrary, is discriminating others, is making an effort to force its values, during the process of a social revolution unprecedented in history, on the majority.[40]
>
> So far [advocates of "gender ideology" R.P.] were talking about gays, lesbians, bi- and trans-sexuals, but now even the fight for paedophilia and polygamy is going on as well.[41]

These claims are equally absurd and dangerous. They portray the endeavours towards gender equality as a homo-, bi- and trans-sexual conspiracy, who no longer fight against hate and discrimination, but want to transform society, and want the majority to become like them. What is more, Kuby "informs" us that these movements are fighting for the legalisation of paedophilia and polygamy as well.

In this claim, Kuby consciously confounds the categories of "minority" and "majority", depicting the "minority" as the enemy by ignoring the discrimination it is facing from the "majority", and, by a twisted logic, shifts the emphasis onto the "minority", which is supposedly threatening the normality and existence of the "majority". But how would any "minority" be capable of doing this?

Summary

The most dangerous scenario would probably be, if the culture war attacking gender studies and gender mainstreaming would lead to a situation where one would no longer be permitted to talk about gender equality, or where certain groups of people have to suffer even more discrimination and hatred than they have so far due to their sexual orientation. And who knows what else is concealed under the mask of this *Kulturkampf*? What does the face of new political and religious fundamentalism look like in the 21st century?

N. Docekal recognises that the fight for gender equality can only be successful if it transcends national frameworks:

> Any attempt to implement the objective of equitableness within the constraints of individual states is deemed to fail. Therefore, the claims for a participatory parity

---

[40] Kuby, *Die Gender Revolution*, 64.
[41] Kuby, *Die Gender Revolution*, 66.

Rita Perintfalvi
The True face of the "Gender Ideology" Discourse: Religious Fundamentalism,
or Questioning the Principle of Democracy?

of genders are being devised now also in the context of contemporary blueprints for a "global democracy" [...] This means, with relevance for the feminist cause, that a joint engagement for gender equality that reaches beyond national borders, can be justified from the moral theological perspective.[42]

All of this is particularly true in the context of anti-gender attacks.

Theology has to carry a societal responsibility: if certain processes are set into motion in society that threaten social equality and human dignity, then theology must not remain silent. Responsibly lived faith is what can liberate us from social injustice, oppression, poverty and exclusion. A just society can only come about if we are able to discover the face of the suffering God in the face of fellow humans who suffer discrimination and despite. We must not pass them by without doing anything.

This study aims to analyse a recent phenomenon, which is rooted in political and/ or religious fundamentalism. Fundamentalist thinking sees a threat in changing male and female social roles and also in changes to the traditional family model. Rather than understand this diversity, it tries to reduce it and does so through irrational argumentation. It selects one of the existing models and absolutizes, it declaring it proper and morally right, while everything else is seen as improper, morally wrong, and even dangerous. As a consequence, both politics and the Church give rise to transnational movements which aggressively attack gender studies as the descriptive science of changes, and gender mainstreaming as the political strategic principle that fights for the social equality of men and women. The "gender ideology" debate opens up a new chapter in the political, cultural, and social landscape of Europe, questioning previous political chasms. The current analysis shows that anti-gender attacks are about more than they seem to be at first sight. The issue runs deeper, as these movements question the post-WWII consensus over a political language centred on human rights and disenchantment as well as a neoliberal, policy-based approach to foster political change. Gender here serves as "only a symbolic glue". Finally, these are movements that question not only the existence of the EU, but also the fundamental European principle of democratic functioning.

In meinem Aufsatz analysiere ich ein höchst aktuelles transnationales Phänomen, was im politischen bzw. religiösen Fundamentalismus tief verwurzelt ist. Denn die

---

[42] Herta Nagl-Docekal, „Philosophische Reflexionen über Liebe und die Gefahr ihrer Unterbestimmung im zeitgenössischen Diskurs," in: Herta Nagl-Docekal / Friedrich Wolfram (eds.), *Jenseits der Säkularisierung. Religionsphilosophische Studien* (Parerga: Berlin 2008), 111-142, here 141. My translation from German.

Rita Perintfalvi
The True face of the "Gender Ideology" Discourse: Religious Fundamentalism,
or Questioning the Principle of Democracy?

neue fundamentalistische Denkweise sieht in den wandelnden männlichen und weiblichen Geschlechterrollen und der damit enhergehenden Veränderungen der traditionellen Familienmodelle eine große Gefahr. Anstatt dass Gründe dieser Änderungen verstehen zu wollen, wird versucht, die so eben entstehende Vielfalt sofort wieder zu reduzieren. Dies geschieht mit zum Teil irrationalen Argumenten. Aus den vielfäligen Familien- und Beziehungsmodellen wird ein verabsolutiert und somit einzig als moralisch richtig deklariert. Alle anderen Modelle fallen in die Kategorie „moralisch schlecht" und „verwerflich", oder gar „gefährlich", wobei die wissenschaftliche Geschlechterforschung aggressiv attackiert und als wird. „Gender-Ideologie" deklariert wird. Aus meiner Analyse wird klar werden, dass es bei der sog. Anti-Gender-Bewegung um viel mehr geht als um eine bewusste Miss-interpretation des Begriffs „Gender". Es werden nicht nur Gender als analytische Kategorie und die sich daran anschließenden politischen Strategien in Frage gestellt, sondern auch das damit verbundene Grundprinzip der europäischen Demokratie.

Rita Perintfalvi is a theologian of the Roman Catholic faith with a PhD in Old Testament Studies. She is a teacher of religion, Manager of Culture and Social Affairs specialising in psychosocial prevention. She currently works as the scientific and pedagogical advisor to Österrechisches Katholisches Bibelwerk, and as lecturer at the University of Vienna (Theological Research of Men, Women and Gender). She is working on her habilitation under the tutorship of Prof. Dr. Gerhard Marschütz, on the topic of "Transformation possibilities of various forms of religious and social exclusion from a theological perspective." The examination of the "gender ideology" discourse is an integral part of this research.

Journal of the European Society of Women in Theological Research 24 (2016) 63-80.
doi: 10.2143/ESWTR.24.0.3170026

Elina Vuola

Finnish Orthodox Women and the Virgin Mary

Questions related to gender and religion have suffered from a double blindness in scholarship: blindness to religion in gender studies, on the one hand, and blindness to gender in religious studies, including theology, on the other. The situation is changing, but it is still very much on the level of acknowledging the importance of gender in religious studies and theology, and of religion in gender studies, respectively. Scholars of religion and gender, including feminist theologians, share the concern for this double blindness. However, from the perspective of theology, I wish to add yet another possible blindness at the core of the study of religion and gender, namely some kind of blindness to theology – or avoidance of it, to put it more mildly. I will also argue that another blind spot is that of lived religion in theology, including feminist theology: ordinary women's theological thinking and interpretation have not occupied a central place in feminist theology, which has centred on academic theological critique of religious traditions.

Continuity and change

The history of Judaism, Islam, and Christianity testifies how pressures for change do not necessarily come from the "secular". It is thus important that we understand how changes happen through new interpretations of sacred texts and theological doctrines. This is a two-way dynamic: different cultural contexts and changes in society influence religious communities such as churches; new interpretations and self-understanding of religious communities, including their relationship to society, influence not only the communities themselves but also the surrounding society. Different liberation theologies, including feminist theology, are examples of this dynamic of continuity and change, which stem from both (internal) theological developments and (external) changes in society.

Feminist theology – and other liberation theologies – are examples of how theological reinterpretations, "from within" and not from outside a given religious community, can become sources of change, not just in the religious sphere but also a more general context. Latin American liberation theology, for example, played such an important role in repressive political situations. Because of its location at the intersection of theology and gender studies, feminist theology has relevance beyond the academy that no other form of gender theorizing has.

The role of theology

Methodologically, it is important to pay attention to the ways in which ethnographic and textual methods may enrich each other in theology, religious studies, and anthropology of religion. On the one hand, it is rare to see a theologian, even a feminist or liberation theologian, using ethnographic methods. On the other hand, questions related to doctrine and scriptures are too easily bypassed in much of religious studies, especially in the study of vernacular religion, and even when such questions would be crucial in understanding a specific religious phenomenon.

Feminist theologians have not made extensive use of ethnographic methods. Neither have they drawn on insights gained by anthropologists of religion in developing a feminist theology, that would also be attentive to women's lived religious practices and ways of understanding their religious identity. The emphasis has been on the interpretation of texts, doctrines and traditions. The more practical dimension of feminist theological work is most often related to issues of ethics, particularly sexual and reproductive ethics. There is, thus, a vacuum at the heart of feminist theology: it does not stem from ordinary women's ways of being and acting as religious persons, does not include their own interpretations of their religious traditions, even when the mainstream self-understanding of feminist theology has been rooted in orthopraxis. By and large, this is a methodological issue: how do we know what this orthopraxis consists of if we do not use non-textual methods? As important as it is to critically analyse and interpret sacred texts and the history of theology, feminist theologians in different contexts should pay more attention to the variety of women's lived experiences. In other words, if there is some sort of blindness to theology in religious studies and anthropology, there is also a blindness towards different forms of lived religion and popular religiosity in feminist theology.

For its own part, ethnographic study of religion is of course valid without theological knowledge and analysis. If textual analyses do not suffice for understanding the interplay between gender and religion, much the same can be said of mere ethnographic analysis. The relevance of different methods obviously depends on the object of research. For example, it is a different thing to analyse and deeply understand new religious movements or spiritu-alities that lack – often even reject – systematic theology or dogma, than it is to study Muslim, Jewish or Christian women, whose struggles and self-under-standing are more directly tied to sacred texts, their interpretations, authoritative teachings, the development of dogma, and so on. At least in the three mono-theistic religions, women's ways of thinking theologically, and of interpreting the teachings at the core of their tradition, form a central part of their religious identity and should not be ignored by scholars.

How do the adherents of these communities – especially women – negotiate between the obvious patriarchal elements of their tradition and the ideals of equality both within that tradition and in the secular society? What is the relationship between the core religious elements (the sacred, spirituality, tran-scendence, God) and people's everyday lives (community, family, ritual, meaning of life, values)? What is the relationship between one's sense of belonging and the institutionalised structures of the given tradition? And what does all this mean in relation to the secular society?

Especially in the context of the three so called Abrahamic religions, theo-logical ideas and doctrinal interpretations make up an essential part of people's religious identity and agency. Attention to how people create their theological worldview as part of their religious identity is important when scholars aim to understand how people negotiate with their religious inheritance. This nego-tiation is often a complicated, layered, and conflicted process, especially with regard to gender, women's position, and sexuality. "Religious agency" thus always includes theology and theological agency. In order to understand it, scholars need to understand the core theological doctrines and their develop-ment over time.

Anne M. Blackburn makes a similar point when analysing the relationship between textual and empirical analysis of religion:

> There is a danger, however, that the turn to studies of ritual and everyday life, especially in the context of an apologetic retreat from the study of texts, leaves scholars of religion in an intellectually untenable position. We may fail to recognise the often profoundly influential connections between texts and devotional practice, for example, and to neglect the very high value accorded to textual composition, transmission, and interpretation within the communities we seek to understand.[1]

---

[1] Anne M. Blackburn, "The Text and the World," in: Robert Orsi (ed.), *The Cambridge Companion to Religious Studies* (Cambridge University Press: Cambridge 2012), 151-167, here 155.

Blackburn does not speak of theology as such, since her case study is Thai Buddhism, but in my view, her point is just as accurate in the case of Christianity and the other monotheistic religions – perhaps even more so since the authority of ancient texts is considered sacred and normative: they are textual religions, their theology drawn and interpreted on the basis of these texts. Blackburn thus pays attention not only to the importance of texts but also to their interpretation as an essential part of religious renewal.

An ethnographic study of the Virgin Mary – an interesting and common subject for scholars of religion and gender – can be substantially enriched by a theological analysis of Mary's central place in Christian theology. I would even argue that such an analysis is necessary in order to understand how Catholic or Orthodox women, for example, interpret the Mariological tradition of their church.

Case study: The Orthodox Church in Finland

The Orthodox Church of Finland features as a case study in a larger research project, "Embodied Religion. Changing Meanings of Body and Gender in Contemporary Forms of Religious Identity in Finland."[2] The project focuses on the study of certain religious minorities in Finland, especially from the perspective of gender and minority status. Part of the following is based on interviews conducted with over sixty Orthodox women in my home country in 2013-14.

The project questions approaches to religion and religious women that are either culturally obtuse (see secularisation as inevitable and natural) or openly negative (see people, particularly women, as victims). Such constructions of women's absence or victimhood are discursive forms of otherness, in which the issue of religious difference has remained relatively unexplored.[3] Taking religious people's – especially women's – agency as a starting point, the project aims to highlight the dynamics between the above mentioned continuity and change within the tradition.

Because of its geographical location, Finland has been an area of encounter and conflict between two great religious currents. The south-eastern part of the country, Karelia, is still today the main home base of the Eastern Orthodox faith, whereas the western part has been Protestant since the sixteenth century. The Catholic Church prevailed approximately 400 years before the Reformation.

---

[2]   http://blogs.helsinki.fi/embodied-religion/vuola, 19 February 2016

[3]   Saba Mahmood, *Politics of Piety: The Islamic Revival and the Feminist Subject* (Princeton University Press: Princeton 2005), 1.

Until 1808, current day Finland belonged to Sweden. It was then formally a part of Russia until 1917, when it gained its independence in the aftermath of the Russian revolution.

Figure 1: Map of Finland[4]

Parts of Karelia were lost to the Soviet Union in World War II [WWII], and a minor part belongs to Finland to this day. As in many other areas in which competing superpowers have interests, the borders of Finland have constantly shifted over the centuries. While the region has formally belonged both to the West (Sweden) and to the East (Russia) along the years, it has been able to maintain its distinct culture and language, which is neither Indo-European nor Slavic. The Orthodoxy under discussion is thus a culture-specific Orthodoxy, influenced by both East and West, as well as by pre-Christian traditions.

Just before WWII, poetry, incantations, and ritual laments were still being recorded by folklorists in the area. The Karelians belonged to the Orthodox

---

4   https://commons.wikimedia.org/wiki/Atlas_of_Finland, 24 February 2016

Church, although in many ways their Orthodoxy was intertwined with elements of pre-Christian religion.[5] The culture of this area, including its religion, has been shaped by influences from both East and West, and its diverse origins have resulted in a rich and hybrid heritage.[6] As a consequence of WWII, Finland ceded to the Soviet Union large parts of Karelia in the south-east, and Petsamo (Pechenga) in the north-east. From both regions, a large number of evacuees was relocated to different parts of Finland; many of the evacuees, including the entire population of the Skolt Sámi indigenous people in the north-east, were Orthodox by religion.

Figure 2: Areas ceded in 1944[7]

Most of the ancient Finnish Karelian folk poetry, including materials built into the Finnish national epic "Kalevala", has been collected in Karelia and

---

5 Kaija Heikkinen, "The Role of Own and 'Other's' Everyday in the Construction of Identity. The Case of Finnish-Karelian Families," in: Satu Apo, Aili Nenola, and Laura Stark-Arola (eds.), *Gender and Folklore: Perspectives on Finnish and Karelian Culture* (Finnish Literature Society: Helsinki 1998), 278-291.

6 Henni Ilomäki, "The Image of Women in Ingrian Wedding Poetry," in: Satu Apo, Aili Nenola, and Laura Stark-Arola (eds.), *Gender and Folklore: Perspectives on Finnish and Karelian Culture* (Finnish Literature Society: Helsinki 1998), 143-174.

7 https://commons.wikimedia.org/wiki/Atlas_of_Finland, 24 February 2016

Ingria, largely in the 19th century. This oral material, only partly published and translated, is housed in the Finnish Literature Society Folklore Archives in Helsinki, one of the largest folklore archives in the world. Parts of this poetry are pre-Christian and reflect the ancient Finnish religion, while other parts show Christian (primarily Orthodox) influence, though often in syncretised form. Karelia preserved elements of an indigenous non-Christian belief-system for much longer than neighbouring regions in Finland.[8] Interestingly the figure of the Virgin Mary plays a central role in this material – in poetry, incantations, laments, and songs.[9] Some of the contemporary informants in Northern Karelia (on the Finnish side of the border) interviewed for this study were knowledgeable of the ancient oral poetic tradition, including the role of the Virgin Mary in it. One of them, a living embodiment and dictionary of Karelian culture, performs regularly in public events – song and public lamentation, and teaches both to other women. This Karelian tradition of female ritual singers is alive in Finland to this day.

Contemporary Finnish Orthodox Women and the Virgin Mary

The Finnish Orthodox Church is today an autonomous Orthodox archdiocese of the Patriarchate of Constantinople. With its roots in the medieval Novgorodian missionary work in Karelia, the Finnish Orthodox Church was part of the Russian Orthodox Church until 1923. Today, the Church has about 60,000 members, accounting for 1.1 percent of the population of Finland. At least until the 1960s, the public image of the Orthodox Church in predominantly Lutheran Finland was stereotypically and openly negative: "the Church of the Russians" (*ryssänkirkko*) points to both Russophobia and the view of Orthodox Christians as "icon worshippers". This is why many Orthodox Karelian evacuees in fact converted to the Lutheran Church.[10] Nowadays, the tide has been almost reversed: there are more and more Lutheran converts to the Orthodox Church, often considered more sensual and embodied than the word-centred Lutheranism. Thus, in a short span of time, the Orthodox Church

---

8   Senni Timonen, "The Mary of Women's Epic," in: Anna-Leena Siikala and Sinikka Vakimo (eds.), *Songs Beyond the Kalevala: Transformations of Oral Poetry* (Finnish Literature Society: Helsinki 1994), 301-329.

9   See Elina Vuola, "*La Morenita* on Skis. Women's Popular Marian Piety and Feminist Research of Religion," in: Sheila Briggs and Mary McClintock Fulkerson (eds.), *The Oxford Handbook of Feminist Theology* (Oxford University Press: Oxford 2011), 494-524.

10   Helena Kupari, *Sense of Religion: The Lifelong Religious Practice of the Evacuee Karelian Orthodox Women in Finland* (University of Helsinki: Helsinki 2015).

has changed from the despised Other to the favorite Other in the Finnish cultural and religious landscape.

In 2013 and 2014, I conducted 62 interviews in different parts of Finland. The ages of the women interviewed varied from just under 30 to almost a hundred years old. Of these, 26 were born and raised Orthodox, 17 were converts to the Orthodox Church, and 19 were Skolt Sami, all cradle Orthodox. My main question was "What does the Mother of God mean to you?" Based on my earlier research among Costa Rican Catholic women,[11] I assumed that instead of asking women how they see their role and position in the Orthodox Church, asking about Mary would be an easier, less tendentious task, that would provide a richer window or lens into women's lives. Indeed, this is exactly what happened. Almost without exception, at some point in the interview, the women started talking about issues of gender hierarchy, sexism, and women's position in the church, exhibiting a variety of opinions and positions towards these issues. However, talking about Mary rather than about women's roles, opens up the entire spectrum of issues in women's lives – relationships, marriage, motherhood, sexuality, and spirituality – often by reflection through the meaning of Mary for women and the broader theological framework in which Orthodox Mariology is presented. Thus, the Mother of God – or the God-Bearer or Birth-Giver of God (*Theotokos*), the more common terms used in the Orthodox tradition – is not only an icon (understood as the divine presence in material, visual form) to be venerated and used as a window to transcendence, but also a window to immanence: talking about Mary with believing Orthodox women was to open a window to the entirety of their lives.

Responses from converts were greater than expected. In the process of doing the interviews, I started asking converted women somewhat different questions from those I asked women who were born and raised Orthodox. For some of the former, the presence of Mary in the Orthodox tradition, unlike in the Lutheran Church, had been a pulling factor. For others, the rich Marian devotion in liturgy, prayer, iconography, and Orthodox theology, had come as a "surprise" which they slowly embraced. A few of them recounted how the

---

[11] See Elina Vuola, "Seriously Harmful for Your Health? Religion, Feminism and Sexuality in Latin America," in: Marcella Althaus-Reid (ed.), *Liberation Theology and Sexuality: New Radicalism from Latin America* (Ashgate: London 2006), 137-162; Elina Vuola, "Patriarchal Ecumenism, Feminism and Women's Religious Experiences in Latin America," in: Hanna Herzog and Ann Braude (eds.), *Gendering Religion and Politics: Untangling Modernities* (Palgrave MacMillan: New York 2009), 217-23; and Vuola, "*La Morenita* on Skis".

centrality of Mary in the Orthodox Church had been a source of suspicion even as they felt drawn to convert for other reasons; this was accentuated in the stories of women who had been active participants and believers in the Lutheran Church, in which the absence of Mary is notorious.

The Orthodox tradition and gender

The Orthodox tradition is less studied from a gender perspective than other Christian traditions. This includes both ethnographic and theological research. There is a considerable and recognised meagreness, or even lack of, feminist theology in the Eastern Orthodox tradition.

Mary and Marian theology in the Orthodox tradition is both different from and similar to the Catholic tradition. From the perspective of gender, a major difference (possibly a variation) is the emphasis on Mary as the model for humanity, independently of gender: the most divine and holy (*panagia*) person, a model of *theosis*, deification, for both men and women to follow. The Church does not present Mary as the ideal model for women only. Also, especially in liturgy and stories of miracles attached to certain icons, the role of Mary is that of the leader in battle, a powerful woman who protects. And finally, there is an emphasis on incarnation, which also makes human deification possible: incarnation is not possible without Mary, thus she is and should be at the centre of the Church, liturgy, prayer and spirituality.

All these notions were reflected in the interviews. In what follows, I focus on two themes that came up practically in all interviews, in one way or another: a) motherhood and womanhood, and b) women in the Church. Let me start by introducing the meaning of icons in the Orthodox tradition.

Iconic piety

One of the interviewed women, aged 28, from Helsinki, began the interview by producing an icon of the Mother of God of Valaam from her bag and placing it on the small table, where it stayed for the entire interview. She told how she and her husband had been suffering from infertility. They had gone to the New Monastery of Valaam in Heinävesi, where the original icon is placed, and prayed together in front of it, having heard of miracles especially in cases of infertility. They now have two children. When the first one was born, the woman's brother-in-law had brought the small icon to the hospital, and ever since it has been on their bedroom wall.

> Me and my husband wanted to have a child, but when nothing happened, we visited Valaam monastery and prayed in front of this icon [...] we experienced a kind of

response to our prayers. We just recently visited Valaam with our family and we told our children about this. My brother-in-law brought this icon to the hospital when our daughter Maria was born, and now it is on our bedroom wall.[12]

Figure 3: Mother of God of Valaam[13]

This icon is considered as one of the greatest treasures of the Finnish Orthodox Church, said to work miracles. It was originally placed in the Old Valaam Monastery's Church of the Dormition, in the region ceded to the Soviet Union after WWII, and later transported to safety in Finland. It now occupies a prominent position in the main Church of the New Valaam Monastery.

A.'s way of speaking of the icon and her story related to it was not uncommon among the women interviewed. Most of them had an icon of the Mother

---

[12] Unpublished interview with A., born 1976, on 8 July 2013; my translation from Finnish.

[13] http://www.ortodoksi.net/tietopankki/esineet/ikonit/jumalansynnyttajan_ikonit/valamolainen_jumalanaiti.htm, 19 February 2016

of God, which was particularly dear to them, even though not all had experienced a miracle related to the icon. It is important to note that Eastern Orthodox spirituality is impossible to understand without understanding the central role of the icons and their veneration. This may be called visual piety,[14] or, more specifically, iconic piety.[15] This piety is not merely visual, since the relationship with the icons includes prayer, body movements like bowing, touching, kissing, lighting of candles, smelling (the wax, the incense), decorating the icon, and so on.

Iconic piety is about a true relationship with a holy person. It is a face-to-face interaction in the context of prayer and silence. The gaze goes both ways. In the words of David Morgan, "…a face receives one's attention and returns it. Like a face, an icon is both a surface and a depth, which combine to create a sense of presence."[16] At the same time, the icons are thought of as bringing the divine into presence, as being the locus of divine presence, mediating the divine to the person in front of the icon. Icon veneration is thus about relationship and presence. In front of the icon, a space is created in which worshipers believe that human and divine relate to each other and communicate in a shared presence, which is always both individual and communal.

In the words of Vera Shevzov,

> […] icons are not merely depictions of persons or events in sacred history; they are also thought to convey the presence of that which they depict. In this sense, icons can be considered a means by which the faithful can know God and participate in the sacred reality that the images manifest. The stories surrounding icons are intimately connected to this theology of presence, telling of an individual's or community's perceived encounter with "the holy" by means of a particular icon.[17]

Iconic piety implies also the possibility of wordlessness and the inability or unwillingness to put issues in words. This notion came up in several interviews, when women were asked about their devotional practices: that one can

---

[14] David Morgan, *Visual Piety: A History and Theory of Popular Religious Images* (University of California Press: Berkeley 1999).

[15] Vera Shevzov, "Iconic Piety in Modern Russia," in: Amanda Porterfield (ed.), *Modern Christianity to 1900*, vol. 6 of *People's History of Christianity* (Fortress Press: Minneapolis 2007), 178-208.

[16] David Morgan, *The Embodied Eye: Religious Visual Culture and the Social Life of Feeling* (University of California Press: Berkeley 2012), 89.

[17] Vera Shevzov, "Icons, Miracles, and the Ecclesial Identity of Laity in Late Imperial Russian Orthodoxy," in: *Church History* 69:3 (2000), 610-631, here 616.

just go in front of an icon, whether at home or at church, light a candle, kiss the icon, stand there in its presence, and not say or think anything, just be. Many of them called it "to rest".

Much more can be said about the meaning of icons in Eastern Orthodox tradition. For the purpose of the following discussion on motherhood and womanhood, it suffices to say that in addition to the devotional aspects discussed above, icons play an important role in mediating theological truths. Thus, in the case of Marian icons, the different types – conventional and repetitive – all convey theological ideas.

Motherhood and womanhood

The single most frequent point of reference for the interviewed women with relation to the Mother of God or The Birth-Giver of God, was, perhaps obviously, motherhood. Most of the women were mothers themselves, but even those who were not talked about motherhood, about having a mother. The younger ones, still without children, brought up thoughts about future motherhood. As in other contexts, talk of motherhood included talk of not being able to become a mother (infertility and miscarriages), the difficulties of being a mother (including being a single or divorced mother), not wanting to become a mother (including abortion), and the importance of motherhood to one's identity as a woman.

Like the Catholic women interviewed in Costa Rica,[18] the Finnish Orthodox women also stressed the role of the Mother of God as an example and intercessor for them, especially in issues more relevant and urgent in women's lives, with motherhood being the most important. Women's closeness to Mary was often expressed in terms such as: "she understands especially us women and mothers"; "she is a woman and a mother herself"; "she is closer to me than God or Jesus"; and "she is the mother of all mothers". Thus, the idea of being able to talk to the Virgin Mary about everything, without shame or self-control, seems to be central in women's devotion of her in both Catholic and Eastern Orthodox traditions. It is the Protestant tradition which seems to be the great exception here.

Let us turn to two examples of how Mary is experienced, first as another woman (identification), and second, as someone who has the power and willingness to protect women in particular. Both quotations were made by single

---

[18] Vuola, "Seriously Harmful for Your Health?"; Vuola, "*La Morenita* on Skis"; and, Vuola, "Patriarchal Ecumenism, Feminism and Women's Religious Experiences".

mothers, which is not accidental: it was due to their situation that these two roles of Mary were felt with special intensity, as is also reflected in the fact that both women cried while talking.

The identification with Mary's earthly lot was expressed with special intensity by S.:

> I have this thought [about Mary E.V.], it is maybe awful to say it, but I am a single mother, I gave birth to my son alone, and somehow... when Mary learned that she is pregnant, she too had to suffer the anguish of being a single mother, the shame and things like that... So it is also because of this experience that Mary is so human, so very close to me... that I have experienced all these things in my own life [...] I prayed [to Mary E.V.] for strength: *"you who have gone through the same."*[19]

S.'s identification with Mary was a source of great comfort for her. This understanding and lived experience of Mary as someone who not only shares the lot of other women, but also understands and protects them, was expressed by another single mother:

> If you live as a single mother or have a child outside marriage or that you are a manless woman [...] you have to be really strong. You feel rejected even by people you would never believe that they would. [When I was pregnant with x E.V.] the story of Mary comforted me [...] But then on the other hand it was difficult for me to approach the church from this position of the sinful woman. X [son E.V.] was baptised in the church, but I could not even think that I would have invited all my family there. Because of the shame [...] But Mary protects women, she is good to women. She is a compassionate mother. She is like a shield between me and the patriarchal world, the church too. That's how I experience her. She is women's shield.[20]

Women in the Church

Because of the gendered teachings of the Orthodox Church, the women interviewed had different ways of negotiating them as women, and Mary was an important part of this negotiation. Due to of the lack or meagreness of feminist theology in the Orthodox tradition, ordinary women do not have a similar theological basis for their critique of certain practices and teachings as do women in the Catholic Church and in most Protestant churches. This does not mean that no theologians reinterpret the Orthodox tradition from women's

---

[19] Unpublished interview with S., born 1949, on 14 May 2014; my translation from Finnish.
[20] Unpublished interview with H., born 1960, on 21 July 2013; my translation from Finnish.

perspectives, but a systematic de- and re-construction of the gendered nature of Orthodox theology is still quite lacking.

In a country like Finland, the surrounding society and the majority-serving Lutheran Church serve the Orthodox Church as mirrors in issues of gender equality. Most of the interviewed women were educated, working women, who sometimes saw the interviewer as a representative "outsider" who would often hold a stereotypical view of the Orthodox tradition as especially patriarchal. This added a certain defensive tone to the way some of them spoke about gender issues in their Church. One of the most frequent comments in this respect, was the comparison of the Lutheran Church and the Orthodox Church in a way that emphasised the more masculine and anti-feminine character of the Lutheran Church, in spite of it having female pastors and even one female bishop. The centrality of the Mother of God, the importance of a variety of female saints, and the over-all more sensuous, embodied liturgy of the Orthodox Church were contrasted with the wordiness, the meagreness of emotion, warmth and the senses, and the lack of Mary in Lutheran liturgy and spirituality. Thus, women's ordination did not serve as a yardstick for gender equality for these women, who claimed that the all-male priesthood does not pose any problem for them.

This contrasting and comparing was especially accentuated among converted women, who thus justified their decision to convert from the more gender equal Lutheran Church to the more traditional Orthodox Church. Some said this was among the most frequent questions they were asked by others following their conversion: how could they convert to such a patriarchal church after the Lutheran Church had finally opened up ordination for women.

Those who were born and raised Orthodox did not have a similar point of comparison of traditions, and thus, the issue of women's roles and gender issues in the Church were framed somewhat differently. Here are two examples. First, about all-male priesthood:

> We don't have female priests... I have been thinking about it sometimes, but on the other hand I think that this is how it must be – that we have men as priests, as fathers in the Church, as we say. The fathers of the Church and then this mother, Mother of God, as the female side. That this is why I think we don't have female priests. And it is not a problem for me.[21]

---

[21] Unpublished interview with Sh., born 1948, on 14 May 2014; my translation from Finnish.

and second, about the practice of gendered division of space in the church:

> I think the practice of having men's side and women's side in the Church is in fact
> quite fine. Maybe a long time ago it meant putting women in the corner or aside
> [...] but for me it is also a kind of protection that you are among other women.
> I don't have to think if there is some guy behind me when I am bowing, or if my
> hair is fine.[22]

The most critical voices questioning sexism and patriarchal practices came
from cradle Orthodox. Some of the women interviewed were daughters, sisters
or wives of priests, and had thus a very down-to-earth view of priesthood:

> Well, we have this institution, this Church, and it has certain rules and norms.
> I think all members should be equal, as they are in front of God. Men can talk to
> male priests, we women also have to talk to male priests, and I think we should
> have the opportunity [...] People are just so used to it and do not question [...] OK,
> I will comply, but don't give those stupidities as reasons to me. I have a right as a
> person to my opinion.[23]

and once again H., the single mother quoted above:

> They always say this [that Mary gives women worth] and that women have their
> important role and duties in the Church, which are valuable. But I don't believe it,
> because you always see that women do not have the same position as men. There
> are women who would like to be priests, like a friend of mine, who then became a
> flight attendant [...] Well, at least she got to the heavens [laughs E.V.]. And I think
> *I* would make a good priest.[24]

A different kind of comparison between churches concerning Mary came
from a woman who in her youth was active in the ecumenical student movement:

> When I went to ecumenical meetings, I did not understand what Protestant women
> were talking about when they said Mary is a model of submission [...] It was an
> 'aha experience' for me – that my image of her in the Orthodox Church as the

---

[22] Unpublished interview with B., born 1955, on 12 May 2014; my translation from Finnish.
[23] Unpublished interview with C., born 1969, on 17 July 2013; my translation from Finnish.
[24] Unpublished interview with H., born 1960, on 21 July 2013; my translation from Finnish;
emphasis in the original.

God-Bearer was something totally different [...] I was thinking about her images, the icons. I see a strong and independent woman, not a mellow young girl. I don't recognise the submissive image of Mary.[25]

And finally, one example of the answers given to the question, if the devotion to the Virgin Mary is somehow related to women's position in the Church – and if yes, how:

The Mother of God is important for women's position in the Church. It is difficult to say how, but it is something empowering, also for us as women. If you want like a comment on why women can't be priests because we have Mary... it is a quite distant thought for me, like we could get some compensation. But the Virgin Mary is the holiest of all [*Panagia* E.V.], she is a woman and she is the most holy person.[26]

Conclusion

The Mother of God is extremely important in the Orthodox tradition and in theology in general, but it seems that she is especially and differently important for women: Mary is easy to approach in issues such as maternity, family, sexuality, and everyday life. This is based on women's strong identification with her as another woman, sister, and mother. She is believed to understand women by being a woman and mother herself. However, she is also believed to be stronger and holier than any other human being. She thus functions both as a mirror of human identification and a source of divine protection. The experience of it being often easier to approach Mary than God or Christ is theologically based on her role as the intercessor. She is seen as close to humans, being human herself, but also closer to God and Christ, bringing the petitions of her believers to them, praying for humans in front of God.

In the lived experience of Orthodox women, Mary gives worth to women in the Church in spite of exclusive male leadership and priesthood. Because of her and other female saints, the Orthodox Church is considered "more feminine" than the Lutheran Church. There is a female presence at the heart of its liturgy and spirituality. However, this does not exclude a critique of male dominance in the Church, even though this is not necessarily or only related to all-male priesthood.

---

[25] Unpublished interview with L., born 1961, on 4 October 2013; my translation from Finnish.
[26] Unpublished interview with B., born 1955, on 12 May 2014; my translation from Finnish.

Finnish Orthodox women negotiate with the gendered teachings and practices of their Church in multiple ways. Many of the women interviewed for this project expressed critical views which could be seen as feminist, but not explicitly theological in nature. They expressed their critique on the basis of their lived experience as women. Their critique was aimed at the Church as an institution, which holds and exercises all kinds of power – not just within itself but in the broader society and culture.

However, the Orthodox Church is a minority church in Finland, which is why the majority-serving Lutheran Church often served as a mirror and point of comparison. The societal influence of the Lutheran Church is obviously much greater. The secular society with its ideals of gender equality was another point of comparison: for example, all-male priesthood was not seen as a problem even though gender equality outside of Church was taken for granted. Those women who were most critical of sexism in the Church, tended to think that the Church should not be an exception in society, and that the broadly shared gender equality should be extended to it as well.

Theology, including feminist theology, is not only academic, but an individual and communal way of reflecting intellectually on one's faith and beliefs. This always takes place within a continuum of tradition – and continuum includes both continuity and change. Though I have not emphasised the interviewed women's theological views in this article, this kind of scholarly attentiveness means locating the theology in their speech when it occurs. Mariology is a case in point: even less educated laypeople are usually aware of the theology concerning Mary in different Christian churches. The women interviewed in the course of these research projects, first Catholic and then Orthodox, both maintained a distance from these teachings and at times affirmed them, always reflecting upon them and negotiating with them.

The first part of this paper analyses some methodological issues concerning the use of ethnographic methods in theology. It is important to pay attention to how ethnographic and textual methods may enrich each other in theology, religious studies, and anthropology of religion. Feminist theologians have not widely used ethnographic methods or included the insights of anthropologists of religion in the development of such a feminist theology, that is also attentive to women's lived religious practices and ways of understanding their religious identity. In the course of research, over 60 Finnish Orthodox women had been interviewed in 2013-14 regarding their perceived relationship with the Virgin Mary. Preliminary results show, that in the lived experience of Orthodox women, Mary gives worth to women in the church in spite of exclusive male leadership and priesthood. However, this does not exclude a critique of male dominance in the Church, even though this is not necessarily or only related to all-male priesthood. Finnish Orthodox women negotiate with the gendered teachings and practices of their church in multiple ways. Many of the informants expressed critical views which could be seen as feminist, on the basis of their lived experience as women. Their critique was aimed at the Church as an institution which holds and exercises all kinds of power – not just within itself but in the society and culture at large.

En la primera parte del presente artículo, son analizadas algunas cuestiones metodológicas sobre la utilización de métodos etnográficos en teología. Es importante tener en atención que, en áreas como la teología, estudios sobre la religion o antropología, los métodos etnográficos y textuales se podrían enriquecer mutuamente. Las teólogas feministas no han recurrido mucho al uso de métodos etnográficos, ni han incluído las ideas de los antropólogos de religion para el desarrollo de una teología feminista centradas en las prácticas religiosas vividas por las mujeres y sus formas de entender su identidad religiosa. Durante los años 2013 y 2014, entrevisté más de 60 mujeres ortodoxas finlandesas sobre su relación con la Virgen María. Algunos resultados preliminares de este estudio muestran que, para estas mujeres ortodoxas, la Virgen María valoriza a las mujeres, a pesar de que el liderazgo en la Iglesia y sacerdocio sea ejercido exclusivamente por hombres. Sin embargo, esto no excluye críticas a la dominación masculina en la Iglesia, aunque este aspecto no está ni necesariamente ni únicamente relacionado con el sacerdocio exclusivamente masculino. Las mujeres ortodoxas finlandesas negocian con aquellas enseñanzas y prácticas que se relacionan con cuestiones de género diferentemente. Muchas de las mujeres entrevistadas espresaron ciertas críticas, que pueden ser interpretadas como feministas, a partir de su experiencia vivida como mujeres. Las críticas fueron dirigidas hacia la iglesia como institución, que mantiene y ejerce varias formas de poder – no únicamente dentro de la iglesia sino también, de una forma más amplia, en la sociedad y cultura.

Elina Vuola is Academy Professor of the Academy of Finland, the Faculty of Theology, University of Helsinki, Finland. She directs the research project *Embodied Religion. Changing Meanings of Body and Gender in Contemporary Forms of Religious Identity in Finland* (http://blogs.helsinki.fi/embodied-religion/vuola). She has been a visiting scholar at Northwestern University (2014-15), at the Women's Studies in Religion Program, Harvard Divinity School (2002-03), and at the *Departamento Ecuménico de Investigaciones* in San José, Costa Rica (1991-93 and 1999-2000).

Journal of the European Society of Women in Theological Research 24 (2016) 81-105.
doi: 10.2143/ESWTR.24.0.3170027

Heleen Zorgdrager

Does Hope Need Heroes? Towards a Feminist Political Theology in the Context of the Russian-Ukrainian Conflict

Introduction

The following is a quotation from my 22-year-old student Nina from Lviv, describing her Maidan experience: "There were people from all regions in Ukraine. The cooperation was great. It didn't matter which language you spoke. People did not think about themselves but about the other. They were prepared to sacrifice their lives, so strong was the feeling of community." Her friend Ulyana adds, "Maidan was like a big church in the open air. We could breathe in that open air. That was the Holy Spirit."[1]

Half a year later, after the annexation of Crimea and the Russian-backed separatist war in Eastern Ukraine, the students are tired and disappointed, and express their feelings of helplessness.[2] They now wonder what they can do and believe that only prayer can unite them. They simply hope for something better. They try to reduce their feelings of powerlessness by volunteering: collecting goods and money for the army, visiting wounded soldiers in the hospitals, helping refugees, and attending prayer services at church for peace and the wellbeing of the nation.

The non-declared but very real war in the east of the country has changed the lives of all Ukrainians. Many families are anxious about husbands, fathers, and sons serving in the Anti-Terrorist Operation [ATO] zone. Many families are mourning the death of loved ones, be it civilians killed by shelling or soldiers on the battlefield. Relatives have become separated from one another by new physical borders and by mental borders of diverging pro-Ukrainian or

---

[1] Unpublished interviews conducted with students of the Ukrainian Catholic University and Ivano Franko State University, Lviv, 26 and 28 March 2014. The interviews were conducted in English or Ukrainian; the quotations here and henceforth are all taken from interviews conducted in the English language.

[2] Unpublished interviews conducted with students of the Ukrainian Catholic University and Ivano Franko State University, Lviv, 7 November 2014.

pro-Russian loyalties. Friends have decided to reduce their conversations to an indispensable minimum or to freeze relationships completely till better times come. Ukrainians face a situation that is usually ignored in descriptions of wars: the shelling and shooting is destroying friendships and relationships more often than lives. Russian friends tell me that this collateral damage (or is it the core damage?) of war is also splitting their circle of friends, relatives, and colleagues.

In this article I want to reflect on the following questions:

1. What is the post-Maidan situation and what roles do Ukrainian women play in it, and how do they respond creatively and critically to that reality?
2. Regarding the political theology of the churches, which road maps to the future, which narratives of salvation do the churches offer to the faithful?
3. Why is it that right in the midst of wartime the churches continue their "war on gender"?
4. How can women build a peace-promoting, de-escalating theology in the context of this war today? How might our narrative of salvation look?

In the end, I suggest building blocks for a feminist political theology in the context of the Russian-Ukrainian conflict.[3] My position is that of a committed outsider. I am only partially entitled to give voice to Ukrainian women's concerns and hopes. But I can give voice to my own hopes. The method can only be that of dialogue, or polylogue. Therefore, I am grateful for the responses and comments of my colleagues and friends both from Ukraine and Russia which have enriched the contents of this article.[4]

---

[3] As for the part of a theology of reconciliation in the context of this conflict, I am inspired by reflections of Fr Cyril Hovorun, Alfons Brüning, Cinta Depondt, Lydia Lozova, and Frans Hoppenbrouwer, shared at the conference "The Churches and the War in Ukraine," 4 April 2015, Tilburg (Netherlands), organised by Foundation Communicantes and the "Endowed Chair of Orthodoxy and Peacebuilding" of Protestant the Theological University and VU University.

[4] This article is based on a keynote lecture presented at the ESWTR conference, Orthodox Academy of Crete, 17-21 August 2015. Halyna Teslyuk of the Ukrainian Catholic University in Lviv was the first invited to respond to the paper, followed by Marina Shishova of the Orthodox Christian Academy in St Petersburg, and Elena Volkova, former professor at the Moscow State University and currently active at the Sacharov Centre. Their responses were followed by a panel discussion.

Ukrainian Women in the Post-Maidan Situation

Women's Agency in Wartime

Participation in the EuroMaidan protest increased civic and political awareness and agency among women. Men and women participated in the Maidan movement in near equal numbers: 41 to 47 percent of the participants were women. Their roles were manifold.[5] They were engaged in traditional, supportive tasks such as kitchen work and distributing food for protesters; sorting donated clothes, food, and medication; cleaning up the protest spaces; coordinating logistics; administering services; and writing press reports. Women were also active in roles that placed them in riskier situations, as on-site doctors and nurses, on-the-scene journalists and photographers, and lawyers for arrested protesters. When the protests turned more violent, women were excluded from the barricades. The narrative on Maidan became man-centred. Men were celebrated as the new Cossacks. Heightened patriotic discourse and expansion of violent protest strategies strengthened patriarchal attitudes towards women. (Neo)traditionalist gender-scripts assigned them the roles of "mothers of the nation" and "inspiration for male protesters." It sparked heated discussions among women about the relation between the feminist and nationalist-patriotic agenda. Loyalty to the nation's struggle for independence is deeply entrenched in the history of the Ukrainian women's movement and needs our particular attention below.

Despite the rule excluding them from the barricades, some female protesters still joined the clashes and prepared Molotov cocktails or threw them themselves.

---

[5] Olga Onuch, "EuroMaidan Protest Participant Survey. Ukrainian Protest Project". (http://ukrainianprotestproject.com/, 6 November 2015) [The Ukrainian Protest Participant Survey was conducted from November 26, 2013 – January 10, 2014. It is the only on-site continuous multi-day survey of the EuroMaidan Protest Participants]; Olga Onuch, *Mapping Mass Mobilizations: Understanding Revolutionary Moments in Ukraine and Argentina* (Palgrave Macmillan: London 2014); Olga Onuch and Tamara Martsenyuk, "Mothers and Daughters of the Maidan: Gender, Repertoires Of Violence & The Division of Labour in Ukrainian Protests," in: *Social, Health, and Communication Studies Journal* 1 (2014) 1, 105-126; Sarah Phillips, "The Women's Squad in Ukraine's Protests: Feminism, Nationalism and Militarism on Maidan," in: *American Ethnologist*, 41 (2014) 3, 414-426, here 415; Olesya Khromeychuk, "Gender and Nationalism on the Maidan," in: David R. Marples and Frederick V. Mills (eds.), *Ukraine's Euromaidan: Analyses of a Civil Revolution* (Columbia University Press: New York 2015), 123-146; Olena Petrenko, "Women and Men of the Euromaidan: Revitalizations of the Heroic National Narrative," paper presented at Danyliw Seminar 2014. (http://www.danyliwseminar.com/#!olena-petrenko/c4sv, 6 November 2015); Heleen Zorgdrager, "Women's Bonding in a Spiritual Revolution: The Maidan and Post-Maidan Experience," to be published in the conference proceedings of the ESWTR conference Gniezno, Poland, 2014.

There were also three all-female self-defence brigades formed, called the *Zhinocha Sotnias* (Women's Squads or Women's Hundreds).

After Maidan, many young women continued their activist roles in the volunteer movement, which is a rather new phenomenon in Ukrainian society. They have become involved in NGOs, in grassroots initiatives for social and political reform, in critical art projects, in university initiatives promoting exchanges between East and West Ukraine, and in numerous initiatives to support the army with food, clothes, bulletproof vests, and medical supplies. While men continue to dominate the traditional political sphere (the new government of Ukraine has only one woman, the Minister of Finance, Natalie Jaresko), women are expressing their political engagement in new civil and local networks, as leaders of NGOs and as undertakers of volunteer initiatives.

An interesting shift in public opinion has occurred. According to a poll on public trust conducted in May 2016 by the Razumkov Centre,[6] Ukrainians mostly trust volunteer organisations (trusted by 63.7% of respondents) and the Armed Forces of Ukraine (61.8%). They have taken over the lead from churches, which were until March 2015 still the most trusted institution (66.2%),[7] and now follow as third with a trust level of 60.5%.

Volunteer organisations	63.7%
Armed forces	61.8%
Churches	60.5%
Volunteer battalions	58.5%
National Guard of Ukraine	57.3%
New patrol police	43.9%
NGO's	46.8%
President of Ukraine	24.3%
Government	15.8%
Parliament	14.6%
National Bank	11.2%
Courts	10.5%
Prosecutor's office	9%

Figure 1. Public trust poll, Razumkov Centre, May 2016

---

6 http://www.ukrinform.net/rubric-society_and_culture/2015941-poll-ukrainians-trust-volunteers-army-and-church.html, 26 May 2016.

7 Poll conducted by the Razumkov Centre, March 2015. (http://www.razumkov.org.ua/eng/poll.php?poll_id=1030, 20 May 2016)

The traditional political sphere, dominated by men and notorious for its corruption, is highly mistrusted. The voluntary organisations, with their high degree of female participation, and the churches, traditional citadels of male power, are competing for the first position.

Gendering the Front

A process of militarisation, which had already begun during Maidan, sped up after the annexation of Crimea and the war in Donbas.

Militarism sharpens gender dichotomies. The social reality gets divided into the categories of fighting front and home front, a gendered division of reality. Politics of masculinity and femininity are produced to support the war effort.[8] The ideology of "man-making" serves the, in theory, absolute separation of military and civilian worlds of the battlefield and the home front.[9] The symbol for the home front is the mother. There is a firewall between the battle zone and the home front, namely the security policy of maintaining strict control over communication and information, suggestively 'for the good of the mothers'.[10] In Russia, this information ban is complete: mothers know nothing and are deceived about the fate of their sons, at times carrying empty coffins because the bodies of their sons killed in the "war that does not exist" are not given back to them.[11]

Expert Cynthia Enloe shows that the military system, in reality, is not separate from, but profoundly dependent on manipulations of motherhood, family and kinship.[12] The maternal sacrifice is the fertile soil from which the military draws its lifeblood. While men are fighting, women are mourning – or praying, as they are every Saturday morning in Lviv at the special Mothers of Soldiers prayer service.

The tight intertwinement between patriarchy and militarism is also evident in a policy that promotes births and motherhood, a pro-natalist policy.

---

[8] Cynthia Enloe, *Maneuvers: The International Politics of Militarizing Women's Lives* (University of California Press: Berkeley/Los Angeles/London 2000); Joshua S. Goldstein, *War and Gender: How Gender Shapes the War System and Vice Versa* (Cambridge University Press: Cambridge 2001).

[9] Steven L. Gardiner and Angie Reed Garner, "Relationships of War: Mothers, Soldiers, Knowledge," in: Robin M. Chandler, Linda K. Fuller, Lihua Wang (eds.), *Women, War, and Violence: Personal Perspectives and Global Activism* (Palgrave Macmillan: London 2010).

[10] See Gardiner and Reed, "Relationships of War"; Nira Yuval-Davis, *Gender and Nation* (Sage Publications: London 1997).

[11] See Elena Volkova, "Every Son's Mother: Human Rights Mariology," in this volume.

[12] Enloe, *Maneuvers*, 244-260.

"Militarizing motherhood often starts with conceptualizing the womb as a recruiting station," as Enloe puts it.[13] Militarised regimes tend to see mothers as breeders of the nation and of future soldiers. The ideological intertwining is succinctly captured in a phrase that is attributed to Benito Mussolini: "War is to man what motherhood is to woman."[14] Military war and demographic war tend to ally. This can be observed in the Ukrainian situation as well.

The empirical reality of the demarcation between the fronts, however, has always been more complicated. In Ukraine there are women present at the front, as soldiers, as liaison officers, as doctors and nurses, as engineers, and as prostitutes.[15]

A special case is Nadiya Savchenko, a 34-year-old first lieutenant in the Ukrainian Ground Forces and Air Force pilot. Nadiya, whose name means "hope," joined as a volunteer the Aidar battalion in the ATO in Donbass. She was captured by pro-Russian rebels and handed over to Russia. While in captivity, Savchenko was elected as deputy to the Verkhovna Rada (Parliament) in November 2014. Savchenko has become a symbol of the struggle for Ukraine. President Poroshenko awarded her with the title "Hero of Ukraine", the highest national honor.[16] He said, "Nadiya is a symbol of unbroken Ukrainian spirit and heroism, a symbol of the way one should defend and love Ukraine, a symbol of our victory."[17] Patriarch Filaret awarded her with the Holy Order of St George for her brave fight against the evil dragon of Putin's Russia.[18]

Savchenko is Christ-like, Mary-like, and Pussy Riot-like. Like Pussy Riot, she writes letters from prison, is supported by a famous French philosopher (Bernard-Henry Lévi in her case),[19] and the pictures of her behind bars and on hunger strike for 83 days have become iconic.

Ukraine has in Savchenko its *"Berehynia* of the war". The *Berehynia* was a female spirit in Slavic mythology that transformed in 19th-century discourse

---

[13] Enloe, *Maneuvers*, 248.

[14] Source unknown.

[15] According to statistics from 2009, in peacetimes, women made up almost 13% of the Armed Forces of Ukraine; 7% of these women were officers. (https://en.wikipedia.org/wiki/Women_in_the_military_by_country#Ukraine, 6 November 2015)

[16] "Poroshenko Awards Savchenko Highest National Honor," 2 March 2015. (http://www.rferl.org/content/savchenko-award-highest-national-honor/26878078.html, 1 November 2015)

[17] https://en.wikipedia.org/wiki/List_of_heroes_of_Ukraine, accessed 1 November 2015

[18] Ibid.

[19] "Nadiya Savchenko's Letters From Prison," Part 2, 12 May 2015. (http://www.huffingtonpost.com/bernardhenri-levy/nadiya-savchenkos-letters_b_7264172.html, 1 November 2015)

into the mother and protector of the nation.[20] As a young, slender yet tough woman with big eyes, she symbolises in the popular representation the human face of the Ukrainian armed forces that will gain the world's sympathy for Ukraine's unequal struggle.[21]

As the following examples will show, women are breaking down the barrier between home front and battlefield in alternative ways as well. In the powerful movement of volunteers supporting the Ukrainian army with food, goods, technical equipment, and medical supplies, women often carry out the transport themselves and deliver the goods right behind the frontlines. Mothers of soldiers sometimes take to the streets and demand that Russia stop the war. Female journalists and photographers cross the front lines, and subvert the information ban by reporting about the ambiguous, ugly, and not so heroic realities of the war (such as violence against women in the war-zone and the increase of domestic violence committed by servicemen on leave). And finally, there have been explicit dialogue initiatives by women who seek communication with those on the other side of the frontline.[22]

Dialogue Initiatives by Women

We should be cautious to call these "dialogue initiatives" rather than "anti-war" or "peace-building" initiatives, since Russian internet trolls have seized the name of a so-called Ukrainian Peace Movement.[23]

---

[20] Oksana Kis, "'Beauty Will Save the World': Feminine Strategies in Ukrainian Politics and the Case of Yulia Tymoshenko," in: *spacesofidentity.net*, 7 (2007) 2. (http://soi.journals.yorku.ca/index.php/soi/article/view/7970/7101 , 6 November 2015). In a more profound feminist analysis, following Enloe, the case of Savchenko would perfectly demonstrate the efforts military officials and political leaders make to divide groups of militarised women (women soldiers, wives, mothers, prostitutes, nurses, raped women) to ensure that each of these groups feels special and separate, and will not join in alliance. See Enloe, *Maneuvers*, xiii.

[21] See for example "Бог нам послав НАДІЮ!" July 11, 2014, by Yuriy Havrylyuk (http://www.halynaklymuk.com/nadiya-means-hope-in-ukrainian/) This Facebook post honours her in ecstatic wordings: "For Ukrainian woman, she is the sun and the air around us. She is mother – one that gives birth; and wife – one that makes a man a human being. Nadiya Savchenko – she is even *Berehinya* the Protectoress who is not afraid to stand up against those who are tearing Ukraine apart and spill its blood! She is like the Mother of God. And the picture of Nadiya with the helmet – it is like an icon. [...] God has given us Nadiya – HOPE."

[22] International Centre for Policy Studies [ICPS], *Mapping of Dialogue Initiatives to Resolve the Conflict in Ukraine*, January 2015.

[23] See for instance "Victoria Shilova – Leader of the Ukrainian Anti-War Movement Has Been Abducted and Imprisoned by the Kiev Regime". (http://www.liveleak.com/view?i=a46_1428 573966#MQCPUCAi81D3RoeA.99, 6 November 2015)

In late August 2014, the popular singer Ruslana (Stepanivna Lyzjytsjko), who acted as a courageous moderator on the Maidan stage, made a trip to Donbas. After the trip, she gave a press conference in Kiev. Her main message was "Stop firing at countrymen." Ruslana is convinced that Ukrainians from both sides should stop shooting countrymen and unite against the real enemy, the foreign aggressor.[24]

In December 2014, the journalist, lawyer, and politician Tetiana Montian went to the rebel-controlled territories of Luhansk and Donetsk. The trip resulted from agreements reached during a teleconference on Channel 17 between Tetiana Montian and Oleksii Mozgovyi, field commander in the so-called LPR (Luhansk People's Republic). During Montian's visit to Donbas, Mozgovyi released a soldier who had been held captive since August 2014. Moreover, Montian held public meetings in Luhansk and Donetsk and answered journalists' questions. After coming back to Kiev, Tetiana Montian together with Channel 17 journalist Dmytro Filatov gave a press conference titled "Humanitarian disaster in Donbas."[25]

The initiatives of these women are characterised by the readiness to have a face-to-face encounter with the enemy, and a deliberate kind of *naiveté*. The expectation is that perhaps the other side can teach one something that one does not yet know. Perhaps reality is different from the propaganda both sides want people to believe. By challenging the dichotomy of home front and battlefield, and listening and talking to real people, civilians, and combatants, these women at least trouble the mythologies of war.[26]

The women's movement as a collective is not really visible in the initiatives for dialogue. In June-July 2014, there was an initiative of the "Union of Ukrainian Women" to appoint the organisation's leader Valentyna Semeniuk-Samsonenko and her deputy Hanna Osova as heads of Donetsk and Luhansk Regional State Administrations. The initiative was meant to promote de-escalation of violence and conflict resolution. After the death of Semeniuk-Samsonenko under unclarified circumstances on 27 August 2014, there were no further reports on dialogue initiatives by the Union of Ukrainian Women.[27]

---

[24] ICPS Report, *Mapping of Dialogue Initiatives*, 25f.

[25] Ibid.

[26] Debra White-Stanley, "Cultural Perceptions of Gender in War Films," in: Karen A. Ritzenhoff and Jakub Kazecki (eds.), *Heroism and Gender in War Films* (Palgrave Macmillan: London 2014), 135.

[27] ICPS Report, *Mapping of Dialogue Initiatives*, 25. Valentyna Semeniuk-Samsonenko was the former Head of the State Property Fund of Ukraine.

Feminism and Patriotism

Why are women's initiatives for dialogue so exceptional? To answer this question, we have to discuss the relation between feminism and patriotism. Can patriotic goals serve the interests of women? For Westerners, feminism and patriotism appear to be incompatible. As far as I can see, Western feminists have become deeply suspicious of any kind of nationalism. Their moral compass has been shaped by the historic experiences of national-socialism and fascism. They associate nationalism with war-making, imperialistic aspirations, and compulsory motherhood policies that assign to women the function of biological and symbolical reproduction of the nation. Mainstream Western feminists feel comfortable with the trajectory of cosmopolitanism and anti-militarism. They fail to understand the specific Central- and Eastern-European situation. In these regions, women's emancipation in the nineteenth and twentieth century went hand in hand with the formation of nation states and the fight against imperialistic powers. Though not without problems and ambiguities, the interests of women and nation, both victims of totalitarian statehood, could converge in numerous ways.[28]

Feminism is not imported from the West. Historian Oksana Kis dryly comments:

> In analyzing the process of feminism's flourishment in independent Ukraine, both in the sphere of public activism and in the academic milieu, it should be remembered above all that feminism can hardly be seen as alien. It had taken root and borne fruit in Ukrainian scholarship and public life a century ago. Feminism in its essence and consequences (though perhaps not in its declared goals and form) was the powerful women's movement in Galicia and in eastern Ukraine in the early twentieth century.[29]

Ukrainian women significantly expanded their range of social and political roles by joining the nationalist organisations that from the 1920s till the 1950s fought for the ideal of an independent Ukrainian state.[30] Significant numbers

---

[28] Tatiana Zhurzenko, "Feminist (De)Constructions of Nationalism in the Post-Soviet Space," in: Marian J. Rubchak, *Mapping Difference: The Many Faces of Women in Contemporary Ukraine* (Berghahn Books: New York/Oxford 2011), 173-192.

[29] Oksana Kis, "Feminism in Contemporary Ukraine: From 'Allergy' to Last Hope," 2013. (https://www.academia.edu/4890934/Feminism_in_Contemporary_Ukraine_From_Allergy_to_Last_Hope, 1 November 2015)

[30] Olena Petrenko, "Makellose Heldinnens des Terrors. Die Organisation der Ukrainischen Nationalisten im Spannungsfeld zwischen Heroisierung und Diffamierung," in: Christine Hikel

of women participated in the Organisation of Ukrainian Nationalists [OUN] and its military wing, the Ukrainian Resistance Army [UPA].

Departments of gender studies in Ukraine (in Lviv, Kiev, Odessa) embrace the concept of "national or patriotic feminism."[31] It is a concept of pragmatic feminism. The scholars in these departments have set out to participate critically as feminists in the process of nation building, and in the process of constructing collective memory and national identity.

For example, feminist historian Oksana Kis works on the ethnological discourse that has been developed since the 1990s in the field of "Ukrainian Studies." She deconstructs the essentialist concept of Ukrainian culture that dominates the scene, focuses on family, kinship, customs, tradition, and promotes maternalistic discourses.

Not all gender scholars share the "national (or patriotic) feminism" approach. The defining narrative in western Ukraine is the nation-centred narrative, whereas in parts of eastern Ukraine, the transnational narrative of the Soviet past still shapes minds and hearts.[32] The Charkiv feminist scholar Irina Zherebkina, who elaborates on the gender theories of Judith Butler, criticises her Ukrainian colleagues for their narrow ethnocentrism, whereas the latter defame the Russo-centric, anti-Ukrainian, imperialistic attitude of the Charkiv school.

It is important to note that Ukrainian "national feminism" is not as provincialist as it may seem. Women scholars from the Ukrainian diaspora in the U.S. and Canada actively take part in research and discussions, and there is a steady exchange of scholars, students, programs, methods, and ideas between the continents.

The Role of Churches and their Narratives of Salvation
Salvation and the Nation
Which road maps to the future, which visions of hope do the churches offer to the faithful? What kind of political theology do they present? It is important

---

and Sylvia Schraut (eds.), *Terrorismus und Geschlecht: Politische Gewalt in Europa seit dem 19. Jahrhundert* (Campus Verlag: Frankfurt am Main 2012), 191-208.

[31] Zhurzenko, "Feminist (De)Constructions of Nationalism."

[32] Oksana Kis has analysed women's biographical narratives in eastern and western Ukraine, and shows on the basis of oral history research the fundamental differences in their patriotic sentiments, as determined by their differing political loyalties – whether to the Soviet regime or to the independent Ukrainian nation-state. Kis, "Biography as Political Geography: Patriotism in Ukrainian Women's Life Stories," in: Marian Rubchak (ed.), *Mapping Difference: The Many Faces of Women in Contemporary Ukraine* (Berghahn Books: New York/Oxford 2011), 89-108.

to note, that there is no clearly dominant (majority) church in Ukraine, and the confessional landscape is very pluralistic (see figure 1). In order to trace the political theology of the churches, I shall look at both the Russian Orthodox Church and two important Ukrainian churches and analyse the latest Easter messages issued by their leaders (April 2015). These messages have a major public impact. They are read aloud after the Easter liturgy and widely spread through the media.

Ukrainian Orthodox Church of Moscow Patriarchate	26%
Ukrainian Orthodox Church of Kyiv Patriarchate	31%
Ukrainian Autocephalous Orthodox Church	2%
Ukrainian Greek-Catholic Church	8%
Roman-Catholic Church	0.6%
Protestant Churches:	
Baptist, Pentecostal, Evangelical, Lutheran,	
Reformed (Hungarian & Ukrainian), Charismatic,	
Seventh-Day Adventist, Methodist...	2-3%
Muslims (Crimean Tatars)	500,000
Jews	100,000
(Source: U.S. State Department's International Religious Freedom Report 2011)	

Figure 2. Plural confessional landscape of Ukraine

Patriarch Kirill (Gundyayev) of the Russian Orthodox Church calls the Resurrection of Christ a gift of hope. He calls Christ "the First Warrior in the battle for our salvation."[33] The military metaphor inspires him to dwell on "spiritual heroism" as the way to imitate Christ. This heroism consists of active love and the willingness to sacrifice oneself in service. First it is service to the suffering, the sick, the lonely, and the downcast, but, in a rhetoric shift, the Patriarch expands this service to the "entire people," and it becomes a forthright patriotic speech. He pictures spiritual heroism as "the hearts of millions of people [...] ready to defend their Fatherland." By great spiritual achievements, "the nation acquires enormous strength which no disasters or enemies are capable of overcoming." The "enemies" are not clearly identified,

---

[33] Paschal Message by Patriarch Kirill of Moscow and All Russia, 1 April 2015. (https://mospat.ru/en/2015/04/11/news117689, 1 November 2015)

and could basically be anyone from inside or outside who attacks the homeland.[34]

The image of hope is the glorious resurrection of the Russian people and nation, surely affirmed by the Resurrection of Christ, but even so, "evidently attested by the Victory in the Great Patriotic War." It is difficult to determine which event is most decisive. The suffering nation will stand up in eternal glory. Patriarch Kirill speaks here of the resurrection of Holy Russia, in modern terms: *Russkiy Mir*, the Russian World.

The Russian World is a sketchy yet undoubtedly divisive ideology of what Russia is (or at least pretends to be). As a political concept, it is vague and imprecise. It is a sacralised view of Russian national identity. It asserts that Russia has the mission to expand its influence and authority until it dominates the Eurasian lands by means of a strong, centralised Russian state aligned with the Russian Orthodox Church. Based on the idea of a "clash of civilisations," Russian Christian civilisation is opposed to Western liberalism, which is equated with barbarism.[35]

Patriarch Kirill's Easter message also addresses his flock in Ukraine, the Ukrainian Orthodox Church of the Moscow Patriarchate, and aims to include them and preferably all Orthodox believers in Ukraine in the imagined community of the Russian World. Ukraine should not exist as an own nation. The Patriarch's political theology around Christ the Warrior is built on the logic of victory and defeat.[36]

What kind of messages are the Ukrainian church leaders sending? Patriarch Filaret (Denisenko) of the Ukrainian Orthodox Church of the Kiev Patriarchate (one of the independent Orthodox churches in Ukraine) matches his Moscow colleague's militant tone and nationalist worldview. He says: "we firmly believe that soon the Lord will send us victory over the aggressor, for where the truth is, there are God and victory."[37] The image of hope is the speedy

---

[34] In her response to the paper, Elena Volkova called these messages "Jihad-like sermons."

[35] Paul Coyer, "Putin's Holy War and the Disintegration of the 'Russian World'," 4 June 2015. (http://www.forbes.com/sites/paulcoyer/2015/06/04/putins-holy-war-and-the-disintegration-of-the-russian-world, 1 November 2015); "Appeal by Metropolitan Hilarion on the Celebration of the 1,025th Anniversary of the Baptism of Rus," 19 June 2013. (http://www.synod.com/synod/eng2013/20130619_enmhappeal1025.html, 1 November 2015)

[36] An excellent analysis of this new civic religion in Russia is offered by Andrei Desnitsky, "Die Orthodoxie und die 'Religion des Sieges' in Russland," in: *Religion & Gesellschaft in Ost und West* 34 (2015) 8, 14-16.

[37] "Church Leaders' Easter Messages to Ukrainians," 8 April 2015. (http://risu.org.ua/en/index/all_news/culture/religious_holidays/59674, 1 November 2015)

victory over the enemy. There is no doubt that God is on the side of Ukraine. In an interview, Patriarch Filaret declared that "God is on the side of truth, and since Putin and the Kremlin committed an act of falsehood, they will be defeated by God."[38] His patriotic theology is clearly black-and-white, building on the oppositions of good and evil, truth and lie, victory and defeat. Is there any room for a future relationship with the enemy?

Patriarch Sviatoslav (Shevchuk)[39] of the Ukrainian Greek-Catholic Church proclaims that "[C]elebrating Easter during war is being able to see the Risen Christ in our victory today."[40] Here again we hear a story of sacrifice, heroism, and victory, though first of all of a spiritual kind. When it comes to attitudes toward the enemy, "those who let themselves be deceived by insatiable imperial ideology of lie and violence" – the foreign aggressor Russia but also the pro-Russian rebels in the Donbas – Patriarch Sviatoslav makes efforts to speak in a nuanced way. The Truth of Christ does not simply refer to the "truth" of the Ukrainian position. He states that the Truth of Christ comes to the fore where people speak and show the truth about what is happening in Ukraine. This nuance is significant. It keeps open the possibility that the truth might be inconvenient. Such people, according to the Patriarch, can become the true apostles of the gospel of peace and love. He insists that we debunk the propaganda that deceives the minds of many Europeans. We should not perceive the conflict as a civil war, or as a war between two nationalisms; it is a conflict between an authoritarian state system and a statehood built on free and responsible citizenship.

Cult of the Heavenly Hundred

The Cult of the Heavenly Hundred (*Nebesna Sotnia*) is a symbol for the political theology of Ukrainian churches. This is the glorious title for the more than one hundred people (among them three women) who were killed by snipers during the bloody attack of 19-20 February 2014. It was the gruesome end of the Revolution of Dignity.

---

[38] Interview in *Den'*, the Day newspaper, 1 April 2014. (http://www.day.kiev.ua/en/article/society/church-not-silent, 1 November 2015)

[39] Officially the ecclesial title is: Major Archbishop of the Ukrainian Greek-Catholic Church. For the Greek -Catholic faithful, in everyday speech, he is their patriarch. In its ecclesiology, the UGCC claims the title of patriarchate, according to the tradition of the Eastern churches, but so far the Holy Father refused to give the blessing. Antoine Arjakovsky, *Conversations with Lubomyr Cardinal Husar. Towards a Post-Confessional Christianity* (Ukrainian Catholic University Press: Lviv 2007), 139-152.

[40] "Church Leaders' Easter Messages to Ukrainians."

On the first anniversary of the massacre, Patriarch Sviatoslav said: "Someone will think of victims of Maidan, another will talk about a fusillade at Maidan. But we Christians realise something much deeper here. We talk about an Easter sacrifice of the Heavenly Hundred."[41] Their free-willed sacrifice is a beginning of new life for the nation. With their "holy blood" they sanctified the freedom of Ukraine.

Searching for a shared, inspiring national narrative, Patriarch Sviatoslav does not back a narrow nationalism. The national unity of Ukraine should be inclusive, like the community of the Heavenly Hundred, some of whom were "sons of Belarus and Armenia." Nevertheless, the outcome is a sacralisation of events and victims. The Heavenly Hundred are viewed as the celestial patrons who invisibly guard Ukraine. Chapels are built in memory of the *Nebesna Sotnia*. They are the subject of an entire iconostasis (by Roman Bonchuk, Ivano Frankivsk).[42] And the Ukrainian state has installed An Order of the Heaven's Hundred Heroes.

I wish to question this growing cult of the Heavenly Hundred. Elevating them to the status of an Easter sacrifice makes their individual stories, motives, and dreams invisible and impalpable, and reduces them to a single story. Does honouring the risk they took automatically mean that I agree with each of them? The sacralisation makes it impossible to criticise the narrative behind the cult. Does the Gospel compel one to love one's own country above everything else? Is a violent death in a people's protest life-giving or perhaps sometimes or many times just tragic, without sense, a reason to cry to God in despair?

Patriotic Religion and War on Gender

Military War and War on Gender

In the midst of the military war with Russia, a war on gender, led by churches and right-wing organisations, has restarted in Ukraine with fresh energy.[43] How can this simultaneity be explained?

---

[41] "The Head of the UGCC: 'A Victim of the Heavenly Hundred Is an Easter Sacrifice'," 23 February 2015. (http://news.ugcc.ua/en/news/the_head_of_the_ugcc_a_victim_of_the_heavenly_hundred_is_an_easter_sacrifice_73043.html, 20 May 2016)

[42] http://ahamot.org/en/celestial-sotnya-heroes-never-die/, 6 November 2015.

[43] For this term and phenomenon, see Heinrich Boell Stiftung, *Anti-Gender Movements on the Rise? Strategising for Gender Equality in Central and Eastern Europe* (Heinrich Boell Stiftung: Berlin 2015); Jadranka Rebeka Anić, "Anti-Gender Bewegung: Ein Beitrag zur Bewertung

The anti-gender movement has some history in Ukraine. I would like to mention two events to illustrate this. In April 2012, the Dognal Group, a break-away sect that calls itself the "Ukrainian Orthodox Greek-Catholic Church,"[44] held a public manifestation. A group of about 30 people had gathered in front of the city hall in Lviv, carrying billboards with pictures and slogans against homosexuality, abortion, and juvenile justice reform. In the centre of the stage there was an act of performance art: a hangman entirely clothed in black and with a black hood, held a scythe in his hand while sitting on a coffin. On his chest was a sandwich board with only one big word painted in red: GENDER. It was a perfect visual illustration of the idea that gender ideology is the "culture of death." Though the Dognal group has very few supporters in Ukrainian society, with this anti-gender campaign they play on sentiments and fears that are widespread among Ukrainian people.

Later, on 27 November 2012, a conference seminar on "Gender Theory" took place at the Ukrainian Catholic University, organised by the "Institute of Marriage and Family." The invited keynote speaker was Italian Professor Maria Luisa Di Pietro (endocrinologist and specialist in bioethics), who warned against the dangers of gender ideology. The head of the Theology Department of the Ukrainian Greek-Catholic Church [UGCC], Bishop Yaroslav Pryriz, commented on that occasion:

> Until recently, the term 'gender' was completely unknown by the general public, not only in Ukraine but throughout the whole world. But suddenly it became one of the leading principles of certain ideologies. The aim of gender ideology is to create a new type of man who is endowed with the freedom to choose and imple-ment his sexual identity, regardless of biological sex. It is clear that such a position is unacceptable from the point of view of Christian morality. But even more disturb-ing is that gender ideology is protected by national and multinational institutions, and traditional moral values are discriminated against and persecuted. If its further

---

des Phänomens," in this volume; Rita Perintfalvi, "The True Face of the 'Gender Ideology' Discourse: Religious Fundamentalism, or Questioning the Principle of Democracy?" in this volume.

[44] Named after their leader, the Czech Republic citizen Antonin Dognal, the group consists of fundamentalist Catholic clerics and nuns, and its activities are characterised by aggressive actions and an anti-European Union agenda. The group is suspected of having allegiances to Moscow. Andrew Higgins, "Ukrainian Church Faces Obscure Pro-Russia Revolt in Its Own Ranks," in: *New York Times*, 21 June 2014. (http://risu.org.ua/en/index/monitoring/society_ digest/56840/, 6 November 2015)

movement is not stopped, then soon Christians and all those who follow the eternal moral precepts risk becoming delinquents.[45]

Battle for Traditional Values

Oksana Kis calls gender a litmus test for Ukrainian democracy. Already in 2013 she wrote, "the sharpness of the conservative reaction was [is] conditioned precisely by the maturity and increasing influence of the women's movement and gender studies, along with the shift in the appropriate legal basis [concerning gender equality]."[46] She comments on the conservative forces, that include the churches:

> Turning to glaring disinformation and manipulation of the Ukrainians' consciousness, exploiting their national and religious sentiment, and homophobic prejudice, they present gender policy as a phenomenon aimed exclusively at propagating homosexuality and subverting traditional family values in Ukraine.[47]

The reason for the current re-emergence of the anti-gender campaign is the intended reform of the Constitution of Ukraine, to bring it in accord with European legislation. In March 2015, the President of Ukraine set up the Constitutional Commission for this purpose. Its Working Group on Human Rights has already made proposals ensuring gender equality and the rights of sexual minorities.

The churches have fiercely opposed these reforms. In general, as Alfons Brüning observes, religiosity in Ukraine, as in other areas of the former Soviet Union, bears characteristics of a post-soviet morality that gives stability preference over freedom.[48] In the current situation, however, this devotion to conservative values takes more militant forms.

The All-Ukrainian Council of Churches and Religious Organisations [AUC-CRO], which played a wonderful, connective, and courageous role during the

---

[45] "Expert from Italy Speaks at UCU about Dangers of Gender Ideology," 1 December 2012. (http://ucu.edu.ua/eng/news/1241, 6 November 2015)

[46] Kis, "Feminism in Contemporary Ukraine"; Tatiana Zhurzhenko, "Gender, Nation, and Reproduction: Demographic Discourses and Politics in Ukraine after the Orange Revolution," in: Olena Hankivsky and Anastasiya Salnykova (eds.), *Gender, Politics, and Society in Ukraine* (University of Toronto Press: Toronto 2012), 131-151.

[47] Kis, "Feminism in Contemporary Ukraine," 10.

[48] Alfons Brüning, "'Project Ukraine' under Threat – Christian Churches in Ukraine and their Relations 1991-2015," in: *The Journal of Eastern Christian Studies* 67 (2015). 1-2, 101-140.

Maidan revolution and in the following months,[49] is now in the forefront of defending the "principles of human relation that are traditional for Ukrainians."[50] They campaign to enshrine in the Constitution the right to life "from conception to natural death" and keep marriage defined as a "family union between a man and a woman." According to the AUCCRO, "justifying such dubious proposals [of the Constitutional Commission] by reference to European experience is irrelevant, because the European Union has opposing views on the issue of anti-discrimination legislation, marriage and family, and legal opportunities for sexual minorities."

Local churches support the campaign of the Council of Churches and Religious Organisations. The rectorate of the Ukrainian Catholic University in Lviv backed the amendments of AUCCRO with an "Appeal to Government Leaders", delivered on 29 July 2015.[51]

In the short introduction the public appeal reads,

> In our opinion the health of the family and the promotion of family values is a real challenge in ensuring the basic rights of Ukrainian citizens. Only in this way is it possible to overcome the practice of abortion and reduce the number of divorces, the level of family violence, the number of children abandoned by their parents, social orphans, the fall in the birth rate [demographic anxiety!], and other severe social problems.

Protection of the traditional patriarchal family is believed to be the panacea for a huge range of social evils. It is shocking that a letter from a public university lacks a modicum of academic reasoning. It is even more painful that the letter reflects un unawareness of the often harmful reality of patriarchal family relations to the lives and rights of women and children.

---

[49] See Heleen Zorgdrager, "Patriotism, Peacebuilding and Patrons in Heaven: The Ukrainian Greek-Catholic Church in Times of War," paper presented at the conference "The Churches and the War in Ukraine," 4 April 2015, Tilburg, Netherlands. (https://pthu.academia.edu/HeleenZorgdrager)

[50] http://risu.org.ua/en/index/all_news/state/legislation/60272, 6 November 2015; http://risu.org.ua/en/index/all_news/confessional/auccro/60611, 6 November 2015.

[51] http://ucu.edu.ua/eng/news/4258. See also Matthew Matuszak, "Ukrainian Catholic University Defends Christian Values," in: The Cardinal Newman Society Issue Bulletin, *Examining Critical Issues in Faithful Catholic Education*, 26 August 2015, 1-7. (http://www.cardinalnewmansociety.org/Portals/0/CENTER/Ukrainian%20Catholic%20U_Issue%20Bulletin%202.pdf, 6 November 2015)

This position does not necessarily reflect the opinion of all members of the university. There are more nuanced voices in the ranks of the Ukrainian Catholic University. Since 2012, the UNWLA Lectorium on Women's Studies has organised lectures that discuss in a more academic and informed way social, historical, political, and religious issues concerning women, men, sexuality, and the family in the Ukrainian context.

On 20 October 2015, the AUCCRO declared once again that the draft proposal of the Constitution (and consecutive legislative initiatives) was unacceptable to them because they believed it would undermine the legal basis of the traditional family and impermissibly violate the rights and freedom of the citizens. AUCCRO stated that the Constitution should be based on the traditional moral values of the Ukrainian people.[52] According to them, these corrections lead to positive discrimination of sexual minorities, propaganda, and discrimination of other parts of society. On 19 November, the target was the bill on amendments to the Labour Code.[53] AUCCRO condemned the bill and asked the President to refrain from signing it. The Council sees the main threat in the introduction of new terms into the legal environment of Ukraine. In particular these terms include the definition of "gender identity" and "sexual orientation" which would, according to the Council, open further way for the implementation of other provisions that are common in Europe: a ban on criticism, introducing quotas in employment, and legalising gay marriage.

The pro-life and traditional values agenda has become the major unifying factor among the churches in Ukraine and shapes their involvement in the public discourse. It is a well-structured and coordinated campaign to misrepresent the concept of gender, to create an enemy image of "gender-ideology," and to introduce a new kind of religious and moral fundamentalism.[54] At the moment of writing, it is still unclear how this battle over the Constitution will end.

To gain a better understanding of the popular concept of the "traditional Ukrainian family," we can consult a schoolbook series of Christian Ethics, in this case one that considers itself modern and even ecumenical: *Osnovy Chrystyanskoyi Etyky* [Foundations of Christian Ethics], published in 2010.[55]

---

[52] http://risu.org.ua/ua/index/all_news/state/church_state_relations/61448, 1 November 2015.

[53] http://risu.org.ua/en/index/all_news/community/religion_and_society/61734, 26 November 2015.

[54] See Anić, "Anti-Gender-Bewegung," and Perintfalvi, "The True Face," in this volume.

[55] Halyna Dobosh, *Zhivu i navtchayus' u rodyni*, Osnovy Christianskoyi Etyky 2 (Svit: Lviv 2010).

The title of volume two is "Live and learn in the family." It reads, in Chapter 4:

> The father is the head of the family. He protects the family. He rules and is respected always as head of the family. The word of the father is always and for everyone important. The saying is: 'Father knows how to educate, and mother how to caress.' [...] We call God Father. We honour our fathers because they represent God on earth.[56]

Then, some chapters later, we find the saying "as the family, so the nation."[57] Family and nation are both declared patriarchal and sacrosanct institutions, according to this Christian textbook intended for primary school pupils.

Homophobia

It is difficult to assess whether homophobia has increased since Maidan. Favourable factors for the strengthening of domestic homophobia include the further radicalisation and militarisation of the society as well as the economic and social dislocations caused by the political crisis. Nazariy Boyarsky, of the "Coalition against discrimination in Ukraine," states that Ukrainian society idealises the supporters of the radical right-wing organisations, who carried out attacks on the members of the LGBT community in the past, as "Defenders" and "Warriors of Light" as a result of their involvement in the revolutionary events and ATO. At the same time, "the law enforcement agencies do not pay enough attention to the activities of such [homophobic] organizations... and compared to other countries Ukrainian society treats it [homophobic activities] more passively."[58]

The gay pride rally in Kiev was allowed to take place on 6 June 2015. Although for the first time in history it was guarded by the police, several dozen assailants attacked the police and the participants.[59]

On 12 August 2015, the leaders of churches in Odessa appealed to the city authorities not to allow a gay pride festival "for the sake of peace among residents and visitors."[60] The churches that foment the hatred and intolerance

---

[56] Ibid., 14 (my translation from Ukranian).

[57] Ibid., 55 (my translation from Ukranian).

[58] "Homophobia in Ukraine after EuroMaidan: research", 30 May 2015. (http://upogau.org/eng/inform/ourview/ourview_2292.html, 6 November 2015)

[59] http://www.bbc.com/news/world-europe-33034247, 6 November 2015.

[60] http://risu.org.ua/ua/index/all_news/community/religion_and_society/60806, 6 November 2015 (my translation from Ukranian).

against LGBT people, now hypocritically refer to possible violence as an argument to prohibit the gay pride event. The district court in Odessa has banned the rally and one of its arguments for doing so is "for the sake of national security."[61]

The "heroic narrative" that emerged from Maidan might also influence the perception of homosexuality in society. In a highly militarised society, homosexuality is considered and condemned as "emasculated masculinity." Homosexual males do not fit the image of a hero-warrior. Another example of how the heroic narrative can merge with the traditional values discourse is illustrated by a poster presented in the centre of Lviv shortly after Maidan. It pictured a sweet baby and the text read: "In order to become a hero, one first has to be born. Do not commit abortion." The city council of Lviv is mentioned as one of the sponsors of the pro-life campaign.[62]

Towards a Feminist Political Theology in the Ukrainian Context

I wish to contribute to Aristotle Papanikolaou's attempt at designing an Orthodox (and profoundly ecumenical) political theology that goes beyond nationalist, anti-Western, and imperial schemes.[63] In his book *The Mystical as Political: Democracy and Non-Radical Orthodoxy* (2012), Papanikolaou lays the groundwork for an Orthodox political theology that endorses democratic principles. The guiding theological concept in his proposal is divine-human communion, or *theosis*. In Papanikolaou's understanding, *theosis* is far from the individualised goal of moral self-perfection. Deification as a mystical principle refers to creation's and human beings' eternal capacity for transformation. They are meant to grow into the all-encompassing divine-human communion. Politics, for Papanikolaou, is the practice of learning, despite all difficulties and conflicts of interest, to love the neighbour/the stranger.

According to Papanikolaou, the Orthodox attitude toward modern democracy is half-hearted. Orthodox churches in post-Communist countries never unequivocally support democratic forms of government and democratic values,

---

[61] http://upogau.org/eng/inform/uanews/worldnews_2618.html, 6 November 2015.

[62] Picture of the poster in Heleen Zorgdrager's photo-archive.

[63] Aristotle Papanikolaou, *The Mystical as Political: Democracy and Non-Radical Orthodoxy* (University of Notre Dame Press: Notre Dame 2012). A critical political theology in Ukrainian context is also envisioned by Cyryl Hovorun, "Political Orthodoxy: an Ideology? a Civil Religion? a Heresy?" paper dated 28 May 2015 (https://www.academia.edu/12662544/Political_Orthodoxy_an_Ideology_a_Civil_Religion_a_Heresy, 6 November 2015); see also Cyryl Hovorun, "Christian Duty in Ukraine," in: *First Things*, August 2015 (https://www.firstthings.com/article/2015/08/christian-duty-in-ukraine, 6 November 2015).

but are always pushing to ensure their own cultural hegemony. For Papani-kolaou and also for Pantelis Kalaitzidis,[64] democracy and human rights are not a threat to the Orthodox spiritual ideal, but rather conditions necessary for achieving *theosis*.

From a feminist perspective, we can contribute to the concept and praxis of a different political theology. There is a rich source of feminist liberation theology, developed from Latin America to South Africa and Indonesia, to connect with and to draw on. We can also connect with the design of a feminist public theology that emphasises the deeply hybrid and ambiguous representations of female religious agency in the post-secular world (Anne-Marie Korte).[65]

I propose the following elements as important building blocks for a feminist public theology in the Ukrainian (and Russian) context:

1. **Truth-telling about the patriarchal ideology and power relations in state, society, and church as well as truth-telling about what is happening on the ground**
   Women must claim the right of freedom of speech in the churches, and extend the space and rights of civil society into the walls of the church itself. Today, in Ukraine, there is no public discussion in the churches or theological institutions about women's rights, reproductive rights, or the rights of sexual minorities. The teaching of the church is unidirectional: from the church that "possesses the truth" to the people in society. Women and men do not feel free to express their doubts and various opinions.

2. **Deconstruction of heroic narratives and of salvation framed in the logic of victory and defeat, and the creation of alternative salvific images like "human rights Mariology" (Elena Volkova)[66] and divinisation as the path of the cross and the sword (Maria Skobtsova)**
   We must continue to collect post-heroic narratives of grassroots heroes that reveal the truth in a more human, tentative, provisional form. Interestingly, a research in the U.S. has shown that real heroes adhere to a broad definition

---

[64] Pantelis Kalaitzidis, *Orthodoxy and Political Theology* (World Council of Churches: Geneva 2012).

[65] Anne-Marie Korte, "Pussy Riot's *Punk Prayer* as a Case of/for Feminist Public Theology," in: Ulrike Auga, Sigridur Gudmarsdottir, Stefanie Knauss, Sivia Martínez Cano (eds.), *Resistance and Visions – Postcolonial, Post-secular and Queer Contributions to Theology and the Study of Religions*, Journal of the ESWTR, 22 (Peeters: Leuven/Paris/Walpole 2014), 31-54.

[66] Volkova, "Every Son's Mother," in this volume.

of the "in group". Most people only include relatives, friends, and colleagues, but the potential hero considers all humanity to be his/her neighbour.[67] That would be a great starting point for alternative concepts of heroism. It could begin by showing how the Gospel is misrepresented when church leaders limit the meaning of John 15:13 to the sacrifice of the soldier for his Fatherland.

The imagery of the "cross and sword" of Maria Skobtsova can be inspiring here.[68] For Skobtsova, two images symbolise – on an equal basis – the love of the neighbour: the path of the Mother and the path of the Son. The Son symbolises the active sacrificial service to the world, while the Mother/ Mary symbolises the path of compassion, co-suffering, co-bearing the other's pain. Skobtsova calls it "the way of the cross" and "the way of the sword." She explains that the soul of every religious person walks both the path of the Mother and the path of the Son. This opens up an alternative kind of spiritual heroism. The sword that pierced the soul of the Mother (we are all mothers of all of humanity) becomes the cross, leading to acts involving suffering and sacrifice.

3. Rethinking the relation between feminism and patriotism

How can women contribute to "good forms" of patriotism and to "inclusive expressions" of national identity? What can we learn here from the experiences of Central and Eastern European women and their studies of the past and present? How does a philosopher like Hannah Arendt reflect on the relation of the individual to the nation and state, from the perspective of statelessness?

4. Clearly opting for a model of the Church in partnership with (and not as the moral voice of) civil society

The attitude of Orthodox churches towards modern democracy is ambivalent, as Papanikolaou shows.[69] There is never unequivocal support for democratic forms of government over other options, while the churches express a clear concern for maintaining or re-establishing a cultural hegemony. This

---

[67] Tonie Mudde, "Heldenbrein" [Brains of Heroes], column in *Volkskrant*, 25 april 2015.

[68] "De l'imitation de la Mère de Dieu" (1939), in: Hélène Arjakovsky-Klepinine (ed.), *Mère Marie Skobtsov (1891-1945), Le sacrement du frère* (Editions du Cerf: Paris 2001), 175-190. It is important to note that the symbols – the cross and the sword – are found in the poem "Snow Maiden" of Aleksandr Blok, dated 17 October 1907.

[69] Papanikolaou, *The Mystical as Political*, 50-52.

cultural hegemony is manifested in the claim of a privileged status of traditional churches in public education and legislation. All-male church leadership presents itself as the moral voice of society in its aggressive policy to shape public morality on issues such as family, abortion, and homosexuality from supposed and non-disputable moral Christian principles. As long as the Church is not open to dialogue with liberal parts of society and to partner with other social organisations on the basis of equality, it will not be able to fulfil a truly constructive, peacebuilding role in society.[70]

5. Building postcolonial alliances

Alliances between Ukrainian and Russian women, and relationships with other European women, are needed to unravel geopolitical conflicts and the impact they have on women, motherhood, human relations, reproductive rights, and so on. It is also necessary to influence the social teachings of churches by coordinated action and to work through transnational networks and ecumenical organisations to pursue women's goals and objectives. Women who are in leadership positions in the World Council of Churches should raise their voices and urge the WCC to openly condemn the misuse of religion in this war for imperialistic goals, and the severe violation of the rights of religious communities in Crimea and Donbas. The WCC should end its Moscow-friendly policy.

6. Acknowledging that reconciliation begins here and now, and consists of the not-so-glorious work of practicing hope according to a recovery model of long-term care[71]

Reconciliation is supported by the face-to-face encounters of common women and men and of symbolic figures of the contesting groups. Reconciliation is practiced by everyone who does not give up in a situation of despair and tries to remain human. I put my hope in my Ukrainian students, who do not only act for the wellbeing of fellow Ukrainians, but also let the question of forgiveness of the enemy torment their hearts and souls.

---

[70] Compare Viktor Yelenski, Церква повинна вступати у дискусію з ліберальною частиною суспільства [Church must enter into a dialogue with liberal part of society], 31 December 2015. (http://risu.org.ua/ua/index/all_news/community/religion_and_society/62097, 14 March 2016).

[71] Laura J. Shepherd, "The Road to (and from) Recovery: A Multidisciplinary Feminist Approach to Peacekeeping and Peacebuilding," in: Gina Heathcote and Dianne Otto (eds.), *Rethinking Peacekeeping, Gender Equality, and Collective Security*, (Palgrave Macmillan: London 2014), 99-117.

Based on interviews with Ukrainian students and dialogue with Russian and Ukrainian scholars, this paper aims to investigate the roles of Ukrainian women in the current society of Ukraine in the light of the current "war on gender." Whereas men and women participated in near equal numbers in the Maidan movement, the militarism now seems to sharpen gender dichotomies. The ideology of "man-making" serves the – in theory – absolute separation of military and civilian worlds of the battlefield and the home front. This paper shows how this propagated dichotomy is broken down by various women who challenge the alleged barrier between the home front and the battlefield. In the midst of the military war with Russia, however, Ukraine also faces a renewed war on gender, led by churches and right-wing organisations. This consists of a well-structured campaign to misrepresent the concept of gender, creating an enemy image of "gender-ideology." Both the Russian Orthodox Church and the Ukrainian Orthodox Church of the Kiev Patriarchate build upon an enemy image in their political theology based on a divisive ideology of victory and defeat, whereas the Ukrainian Greek-Catholic Church shows a more ambivalent perspective. It applies to all these churches, however, that in times of military and ideological war, family and nation are represented as patriarchal and sacrosanct institutions, leading to paternalistic, pro-life, and homophobic tendencies. In conclusion, this paper seeks to contribute to an Orthodox (and profoundly ecumenical) political theology that goes beyond nationalist, anti-Western, and imperial schemes, proposing several building blocks for a feminist political theology in the context of the Russian-Ukrainian conflict.

Dieser Artikel, der auf Interviews mit ukrainischen Studierenden und dem Dialog russischer und ukrainischer Wissenschaftlerinnen basiert, untersucht die Rolle der ukrainischen Frauen in der heutigen Gesellschaft der Ukraine im Lichte des aktuellen "Genderkrieges". Während Männer und Frauen fast gleichbeteiligt waren an der Maidan Bewegung, scheint der Militarismus die Gender-Dichotomien jetzt zu verschärfen. Die Ideologie des "Man-making"s dient der – theoretisch – absoluten Trennung von der militärischen und zivilen Welt und dem Unterschied zwischen Schlachtfeld und Heimatfront. Dieser Artikel zeigt wie diese propagierte Dichotomie von mehreren Frauen in Frage gestellt und abgelehnt wird ist. Mitten im militärischen Krieg mit Russland sieht sich die Ukraine zusätzlich einem erneuten Genderkrieg ausgesetzt, angeführt von Kirchen und rechts-politischen Organisationen. Mithilfe einer gut strukturierten Kampagne wird ein Feindbild der „Gender-Ideologie" geschaffen. Sowohl die Russisch-Orthodoxe Kirche als auch die Ukrainisch-Orthodoxe Kirche und das Kiewer Patriarchat bauen ihre politische Theologie von einer trennenden Ideologie von Sieg und Niederlage auf einem Feindbild auf. Die Ukrainische Griechisch-Katholische Kirche dagegen, zeigt eine ambivalente Perspektive. All diese Kirchen aber erklären in der Zeit des militärischen und ideologischen Krieges sowohl Familie als auch Nation zu patriarchalischen und sakrosankten Institutionen. Hierdurch entstehen paternalistische, Pro-Life und homophobe Tendenzen.

Abschließend soll dieses Papier zu einer orthodoxen (und zutiefst ökumenischen) politischen Theologie beitragen, die über nationalistische, anti-westliche und imperialistische Ideologien hinausgeht. Dazu werden mehrere Bausteine für eine feministische politische Theologie im Rahmen des russisch-ukrainischen Konfliktes benannt.

Heleen Zorgdrager is professor of Systematic Theology and Gender-Studies at the Protestant Theological University, Amsterdam, The Netherlands, and visiting lecturer to the Ukrainian Catholic University in Lviv, Ukraine, since 2005. Her current research is on theology and sexuality, public theology from a feminist perspective in post-Soviet space, and the concept of theosis/deification in ecumenical theology. Email: hezorgdrager@pthu.nl

Journal of the European Society of Women in Theological Research 24 (2016) 107-119.
doi: 10.2143/ESWTR.24.0.3170028

Larissa Hrotkó

Jüdisch-christlicher Dialog als Beitrag zur geopolitischen und geokulturellen Balance in Europa

Vorwort

Dieses Vorwort entstand erst nach der Konferenz von Kolymbari, als der Beitrag selbst im Wesentlichen schon fertig war. Der Grund, warum ich es doch ergänzen wollte, war das mangelnde Interesse für mein Thema, das mich beunruhigte.

In Kolymbari sprach ich über die Erfahrungen des ungarischen jüdisch-christlichen Dialogs auf jüdischer Seite. Dabei analysierte ich die lokalen Formen des Dialogs aus gesellschaftlicher und theologischer Sicht und fasste einige Gedanken zu dessen Zukunft zusammen. Dass das kaum jemand hören wollte, machte mich nachdenklich.

Spricht das Thema des jüdisch-christlichen Dialogs die Wissenschaftlerinnen nicht an? Oder könnte die Diskussion zum moslemisch-christlichen Dialog angesichts aktueller Geschehnisse in Europa vom größeren Interesse sein?

Kurz vor der ESWTR-Konferenz auf Kreta erlebte ich doch etwas anderes. Es war in Wien. Im März 2015 fand dort eine Konferenz zum Abschluss des Grazer FWF-Projekts P24782 „Die Hebräische Bibel im jüdisch-christlichen Dialog in Österreich und Deutschland nach 1945", statt, die vom Institut für Alttestamentliche Bibelwissenschaft der Katholisch-Theologischen Fakultät der Grazer Karl-Franzens-Universität unter Leitung Prof. Dr. Irmtraud Fischer und dem Institut für Judaistik der Wiener Universität organisiert wurde. Unterstützt wurde diese Konferenz durch den Fonds zur Förderung der wissenschaftlichen Forschung. Während der Tagung erlebte ich das unglaubliche Engagement der christlichen Theologinnen und Forscherinnen, die sich um die Entwicklung des jüdisch-christlichen Gesprächs bemühen. Sie aktualisieren Kenntnisse über die Hebräische Bibel (תנ״ך), christliche Theologie und nicht zuletzt unsere multikulturelle europäische Gesellschaft. Die Frage war nicht, ob das jüdisch-christliche Gespräch noch eine Zukunft hat, sondern viel mehr, wie es lebendiger und wirksamer gestaltet werden soll. Dabei kamen gerade

Larissa Hrotko
Jüdisch-christlicher Dialog als Beitrag zur geopolitischen und
geokulturellen Balance in Europa

von den christlichen Theologinnen neue Initiativen, wie die Hebräische Bibel den Christinnen näher gebracht werden kann, ohne dass sie dabei jedes Mal „christianisiert" wird.

In meinem Referat in Wien erwähnte ich die multikulturelle Mitgliedschaft der ESWTR als Vorbild erfolgreicher Zusammenarbeit der Frauen aus verschiedenen Religionen und Konfessionen. Doch im August desselben Jahres musste ich zu meinem Bedauern feststellen, dass die Begeisterung vielleicht zu früh war. Gibt es in den Ländern Europas in Hinblick auf die christlich-jüdischen Beziehungen keine Schwierigkeiten mehr? Die ungarische Gesellschaft und das Judentum Ungarns empfinden es anders.

Die Ermittlungen des Instituts für Forschung öffentlicher Meinung und Marktforschung „Medián" zeigten, dass 44% der ungarischen Bevölkerung das Jüdische 2014 für ein fremdes gesellschaftliches Element hielten. Verglichen mit den anderen gesellschaftlichen Minderheiten, wie zum Beispiel Skinheads oder Romas, war diese Zahl zwar nicht die höchste, doch erwies sie einen deutlichen Anstieg im Vergleich zu 2013, als 38% der nicht-jüdischen Bevölkerung die jüdische fremd befanden.[1] Die meisten Ungarinnen und Ungarn zeigten jedoch eher Gleichgültigkeit dem Thema gegenüber. Unter den Kriterien der Judenfeindlichkeit wurde in der Ermittlung der Forschenden des oben genannten Instituts der angeblich zu starke jüdische Einfluss auf die Medien, Kultur und ungarische Gesellschaft angeführt. Die zu hohe jüdische Präsenz in einigen wirtschaftlichen und wissenschaftlichen Branchen, sowie die weitverbreitete Meinung, dass die Jüdinnen und Juden von Natur aus zu unsauberen Mitteln im Erreichen ihrer Ziele neigen, gehörten ebenso zu den so genannten jüdischen Eigenschaften, die Anstoß bei den nicht-jüdischen Menschen finden.

Darüber hinaus gibt es noch immer Ungarinnen und Ungarn, die denken, dass sich „die Juden" für den Tod Jesu verantworten müssen, es waren 2014 immerhin 16% der Bevölkerung, was zweimal so viel ist wie 2013! Und 14% der nicht-jüdischen Bevölkerung waren damit einverstanden, dass die jüdischen Einwohnerinnen und Einwohner das Land verlassen sollen. Das sind heute sogar deutlich mehr als 2006 (7%), 2011 (12%) oder 2013 (9%).[2]

---

[1] Vgl. Hahn Endre, Róna Dániel, *Antiszemita előítéletesség a mai magyar társadalomban. Kutatási jelentés.* (Medián Közvélemény- és Piackutató Intézet: Budapest 2015), 1-44, hier:10. (tev.hu/wp-content/uploads/2014/04/Median_TEK_antiszemitizmus-tanulmany_2014_HU.pdf, 9. Oktober 2015)

[2] Vgl. Hahn, *Antiszemita előítéletesség,* 6.

Larissa Hrotkó
Jüdisch-christlicher Dialog als Beitrag zur geopolitischen und
geokulturellen Balance in Europa

Zu den rabbinischen und geokulturellen Voraussetzungen des jüdisch-christlichen Dialogs in Ungarn

Die Frage, ob der jüdisch-christliche Dialog in der ungarischen Gesellschaft noch Zukunft hat, stellte sich Rabbiner Slomó Köves – Schlomo Kövesch – im Vortrag zu den theologischen Ansätzen des Antisemitismus an der Evangelischen Religionswissenschaftlichen Universität zu Budapest. Im Vorfeld zum Vortrag konstatierte der orthodoxe Rabbiner der *hasidischen* Bewegung *Chabad Lubavitsch*, dass die jüdische Bevölkerung seitens der ungarischen Gesellschaft noch immer überwiegend im Kontext des Antisemitismus wahrgenommen wird.[3]

Der oben zitierte Bericht des Meinungsforschungsinstituts „Medián" enthält weitere relevante Angaben, die die Verbindung zwischen dem antisemitischen Verhalten und der Zugehörigkeit zu einer Konfession oder Religion aufdecken. 22% der Personen, die sich antisemitisch verhielten (insgesamt 21% der Bevölkerung), bekannten sich zu einer Konfession. Lediglich 66% der Gläubigen konnten als nicht antisemitisch eingestuft werden. Die höchste Anzahl sich nicht antisemitisch verhaltender Personen zeigte diejenige Gruppe, die als nicht-religiös eingestuft wurde.

Trotzdem behauptet die Forschung, dass das Jüdische für die meisten Ungarn lediglich ein Symbol des Andersseins bedeutete. Ihre Antipathie, so die These, richte sich nicht nur gegen jüdische Mitmenschen, sondern auch gegen alle anderen religiösen und ethnischen Minderheiten des Landes. Es wird außerdem behauptet, dass gesellschaftlicher Status von Menschen und Judenfeindlichkeit nicht miteinander in Verbindung gebracht werden können. Weder das Vermögen noch die Ausbildung oder das Lebensalter hängen phänomenologisch mit der Einstellung der Judenfeindlichkeit zusammen. Bemerkenswert ist jedoch, dass es sowohl unter der männlichen Bevölkerung, als auch unter den politisch aktiven oder passiven Anhängern der rechtsradikalen Partei „Jobbik" mehr Personen gab, die judenfeindliche Gefühle äußerten. Die Judenfeindlichkeit wird vermutlich durch nationalistische, ordnungs- und autoritätsorientierte Attitüden gefördert, die Abneigung gegen alle Formen des Andersseins, inklusive Homosexualität generieren.

Als ich einen *neologen* Rabbiner bat, ein paar Fragen zum interreligiösen Dialog zu beantworten, war er sofort bereit, darüber zu sprechen. Es ist bekannt, dass der nicht nur in der Öffentlichkeit geführte Dialog in der ungarisch-jüdischen

---

[3] Köves Slomó, *Az antiszemitizmus, mint teológiai és társadalmi probléma. Az antiszemitizmus zsidó szemmel.* (http://www.youtube.com/watch?v=RgeuX3Gfi0M, 12.Oktober 2015)

Larissa Hrotko
Jüdisch-christlicher Dialog als Beitrag zur geopolitischen und
geokulturellen Balance in Europa

Neologie zur traditionellen rabbinischen Tätigkeit gehört.[4] „Warum macht ihr
das?" – fragte ich den Rabbiner. „Es ist unsere Pflicht, die wir von Abraham
überliefert bekommen haben." „Wozu? Ergibt es einen Sinn? Die Umgebung
bleibt uns gegenüber weiterhin misstrauisch…" „Die Stimmung und die Zeiten ändern sich", antwortete er, „doch niemand hat uns entlastet. Du kennst
doch diese Stelle aus Talmud, wo es heißt, dass im Heiligtum jeden *Sukkot*
70 Opfer für die Völker der Welt gebracht worden sind. Darum müssen wir
uns weiterhin um die Aufrechterhaltung der jüdisch-christlichen Beziehungen
bemühen und dafür in der Öffentlichkeit auftreten. Ich glaube fest daran, dass
diese Auflage vom Ewigen kommt."[5]

Den Befehl des Ewigen, der Umgebung Respekt zu erweisen und für die
anderen Völker der Welt an einem der größten jüdischen Pilgerfest zu beten,
ist übrigens auch im 4. Buch Mose (*Bamidbar* oder *Numeri*, Kapitel 29) zu
lesen. Die Weisen Israels sahen daran die Verbindung zu Israels Priesterrolle.
Nach Rabbi Elasar entspricht die Zahl der geopferten Stiere den 70 Nationen
der Welt, symbolisch werden sie für alle Völker der Welt geopfert.[6]

So sei Judentum nicht nur ein Sammelbegriff für die einzelnen jüdischen
Menschen, sondern auch eine geprägte Lebensform, setzte der Rabbiner fort.
Stolz mischte sich in seiner Antwort mit dem großen Respekt den nicht-jüdi-
schen Gläubigen gegenüber. Bewusste Identität und gegenseitiger Respekt
bilden wohl die eigentliche theologische Voraussetzung für das erfolgreiche
Gespräch der Religionen in einer Gesellschaft.

Die ungarische Kultur ist heute nach wie vor auf jene nationale Einheit
ausgerichtet, die sich als traditionelles Christentum zeigt. Die jüdische Bevölkerung – und ich meine damit alle jüdischen Religionsrichtungen und Gemeinschaften Ungarns — besteht heute viel eindeutiger auf ihrer jüdischen Identität als vor *Schoa*. Diese Diskrepanz zwischen dem Nationalen und Partikularen
erschwert die jüdisch-christliche Kommunikation, deren größte Aufgabe die
Gestaltung der geopolitischen Balance ist. Da wir in einer europäischen

---

[4] *Neologie* ist die typisch ungarische jüdische Religionsgemeinschaft, die moderne Lebensweise
bevorzugt, bei den Ritualen und Gottesdienst jedoch auf der rabbinischen Tradition besteht.
Die jüdischen *Neologen* nutzten die Möglichkeiten der Integration und lieferten dem ungarischen Staat berühmte Komponisten, Schriftsteller und Wissenschaftler.

[5] Aus dem Interview vom 8. November 2014 mit Rabbiner des Rabbinerseminars und Jüdischer
Universität István Darvas. Das Interview wurde ursprünglich auf Ungarisch aufgenommen und
von der Autorin ins Deutsche übersetzt.

[6] תלמוד בבלי-מסכת סוכה פרק ה דף נה, *Talmud Bawli, Sukka* 55b. (http://www.mechon-mamre.
org/b/l/12605.htm, 1. März 2016)

Larissa Hrotkó
Jüdisch-christlicher Dialog als Beitrag zur geopolitischen und
geokulturellen Balance in Europa

Gesellschaft leben, die eindeutig als postsäkular zu bezeichnen ist, haben beide Religionen, Christentum wie Judentum, zu dieser geopolitischen Balance beizubringen. Sie haben ihre Sprache auf Toleranz zu überprüfen und neue Formen für die religiösen Überzeugungen zu finden, um ihre Anhängerinnen und Mitglieder nicht zu fanatisieren. Das Letztere ist vor allem die Aufgabe der Religionswissenschaftlerinnen und -wissenschafter sowie der Theologinnen und Theologen, die ihre eigene religiöse Überlieferung noch tiefer und vielleicht auch kritischer – im wissenschaftlichen Wortsinn – erforschen sollten.

Mit mangelhaftem Wissen erklären die Rabbiner des *neologen* Judentums Ungarns den Ursprung des ungarischen Antisemitismus. In diesem Punkt schließt sich ihnen die *Chabad Lubavitsch* an.[7] Meiner Ansicht nach ist das aber zu stark verallgemeinert, denn mangelhafte Kenntnisse sind nicht die einzige Ursache des antisemitischen Verhaltens.

Die ungarischen Formen des jüdisch-christlichen Dialogs von heute

Unter den aktuellen Formen des Dialogs ist vor allem die sogenannte politische Tischrunde zu erwähnen, ein Gespräch, an dem sich höhere Politiker beider Seiten beteiligen. Im Hintergrund stehen Interessen größerer jüdischer und christlicher Gemeinschaften. Diese politische Runde ist für beide Seiten existenziell wichtig, doch wurde sie bisher nicht professionell genug realisiert. Die Verhandelnden taten so, als wären die Voraussetzungen des Zusammenlebens von verschiedenen ethnisch-religiösen Gruppen in der Natur des Landes bereits gegeben und also vorhanden. Es scheint als hätten sie übersehen, dass diese Voraussetzungen doch erst erschaffen werden sollen und müssen!

Die führenden jüdischen Kreise Ungarns streben nach wie vor nach Aufklärung der nicht-jüdischen Bevölkerung. Obwohl es nicht die einzige Form des Dialogs ist, kann man sie sicher als die bekannteste bezeichnen.

Je nach dem gesellschaftlichen Stand der Beteiligten kann der Dialog als offiziell oder informell bezeichnet werden. Der offizielle jüdisch-christliche Dialog wird von Rabbinern und jüdischen Religionsgelehrten einerseits und von den christlichen Priestern und ihren begeisterten Volontären andererseits realisiert. Unter den jüngsten beispielhaften Veranstaltungen auf dieser Ebene

---

7   *Chabad Lubavitsch* ist eine der *hasidischen* Religionsrichtungen im Judentum, die sich selbst heute als charismatische Bewegung bezeichnet. In Budapest wird *Chabad* von drei Gemeinschaften vertreten, von denen eine als Kultur- und Lehranstalt dient. Trotz aller Bemühungen wurde *Chabad* nicht zur führenden jüdischen Gemeinschaft Ungarns. Ungarisch-jüdische *Neologie* entwickelt sich zurzeit eher in Richtung der religiösen Vielfältigkeit und Toleranz.

Larissa Hrotko
Jüdisch-christlicher Dialog als Beitrag zur geopolitischen und
geokulturellen Balance in Europa

ist die wissenschaftliche Tagung am Rabbinerseminar zu Budapest hervorzuheben. Sie fand im Andenken an einen Professor des Rabbinerseminars statt, der auch an der nicht jüdischen Universität des Heiligen Stephans von Ungarn unterrichtete. Der Hauptgedanke dieser Veranstaltung war, dass die Wissenschaft keine Religionsgrenzen kennt. Diese Idee prägte die jüdische Gesellschaft schon vor *Schoa*, doch wurde sie später als naiv und unbrauchbar insbesondere von den Israelis ungarischer Herkunft kritisiert.

Die Suche nach der gemeinsamen theologischen Sprache prägt die jährlichen biblischen Konferenzen von Segedin im Süden Ungarns, an denen Vertretungen aller Konfessionen und Religionsgemeinschaften Ungarns teilnehmen. Man denkt, die Heilige Schrift könnte die Wissenschaftler und Wissenschaftlerinnen verschiedener Konfessionen vereinigen. Doch das ist nicht immer der Fall. Die traditionellen theologischen Auslegungen stehen manchmal dem Dialog im Wege.

Unter rabbinisch-zivilen Initiativen muss vor allem der so genannte „Marsch des Lebens"[8] genannt werden, der jedes Jahr als eine großdimensionierte Veranstaltung in Budapest stattfindet. Darüber hinaus gibt es auch die Ausstellungen und Gedenk-Feiern, wie zum Bespiel die Veranstaltungen „Holokaust-2014"[9]. Allerdings wurde dieses Programm von der *neologen* jüdischen Gemeinde Ungarns aus politischen Gründen teilweise boykottiert, was auf die mangelhafte Zusammenarbeit der politischen jüdisch-christlichen Tischrunden zurückzuführen war.

Die sogenannte jüdisch-christliche Gesellschaft von Budapest hat eine halb-informelle Struktur. Sie fungiert zwar unter dem Schirm der Jüdischen Universität in Budapest, doch muss sich finanziell selbst tragen. Diese Gesellschaft wurde vom ersten Rektor der Universität und des Rabbinerseminars in der Nachkriegszeit, Prof. Dr. Sandor Scheiber gegründet.[10] Sie verdankt der Autorität dieses Namens, dass sie noch immer besteht. Bemerkenswert ist, dass sich Scheiber diese Gesellschaft als eine Gruppe vorgestellt, die eher auf

---

[8] Dieses Jahr soll der Marsch am 17. April um 16 Uhr an der Großen Synagoge in der Dohány-Straße beginnen und zu dem Stephans-Dom von Budapest führen. Das Motto dieses Jahres lautet: „Im Zeichen des jüdisch-christlichen Zusammenlebens in der Gesellschaft." (http://www.eletmenete.hu, 28. Februar 2016).

[9] Unter diesem Namen sind offizielle Veranstaltungen zu verstehen, die von der Regierung finanziert wurden. Die meisten jüdischen Gemeinschaften lehnten die finanzielle Unterstützung der Regierung ab, weil die der Meinung und den Vorschlägen jüdischer Seite zur Gestaltung des Programms über längere Zeit nicht zugehört hat.

[10] Keresztény Zsidó Társaság, (http://www.kzst.hu, 28. Februar 2016).

Larissa Hrotkó
Jüdisch-christlicher Dialog als Beitrag zur geopolitischen und
geokulturellen Balance in Europa

die Arbeit als auf gemeinsames öffentliches Auftreten ausgerichtet ist. Aus dieser Idee entwickelte sich die Gesellschaft von jüdischen und christlichen Autoritäten und Laien, die monatlich Konferenzen, Vorlesungen und Konzerte zusammen veranstalten und die in Verbindung mit den internationalen Partner-Organisationen stehen. Die Tagespolitik wird an diesen Veranstaltungen streng vermieden. Als Beispiel der Veranstaltungen dieser Gesellschaft ist die Konferenz zur Mystik zu erwähnen, bei der ich als jüdische Religionswissenschaftlerin einen Vortrag über die jüdischen Wurzeln der Mystik der Heiligen Theresa von Avil gehalten habe. Stattgefunden hat diese Konferenz in einem Raum der katholischen Kirche der heiligen Mystikerin am Rand des historischen jüdischen Viertels von Budapest.

Informell soll die christliche Initiative der „Katholischen Gemeinschaft der Seligpreisungen" eine der Formen des Dialogs genannt werden. Die Schwestern dieser Gemeinschaft betrachten sich als jüdische Jüngerinnen Jesu. Deshalb passen sie ihre eigene Liturgie an die jüdischen Feste und Bibellesungen an. *Schabat* ist für sie heilig. Doch das Fasten am Donnerstag und das Feiern der Sonntage – und nicht nur das, versteht sich – zeigt, dass sie sich ihrer katholischen Identität klar bewusst bleiben. Zu den jüdischen Festen, kommen die Schwestern in die Synagoge. Sie sind dann in Begleitung von Jugendlichen aus den Bezirken der Stadt, die für ihre antisemitische Tradition besonders bekannt sind. Auf der jüdischen Seite können sie dann mit der schon fast professionellen Toleranz der Gemeinde der Budaer Synagoge „Frankel" rechnen. Die katholischen Schwestern sind immer, auch am *Jom-Kipur*, herzlich willkommen. Sie kennen jüdische Gebete und beten auf *Ivrit*. Die gemeinsame Gebetssprache entwickelt das Vertrauen. Doch weder die Katholikinnen, noch die Jüdinnen aus der Synagoge suchen nach Medienpräsenz. Für sie ist das gemeinsame Beten etwas Innerliches und Selbstverständliches.

Es gibt in Ungarn auch solche private Initiativen, die sehr professionell funktionieren. Eine der Initiativen wurde von der, als Kirche nicht anerkannten „Ungarischen Brüderschaft des Evangeliums" aufgenommen. Sie wird vom ehemaligen Abgeordneten des Parlaments und Seelsorger Gábor Iványi geführt, der auch dafür bekannt ist, dass er die Eheschließung von Präsident Viktor Orbán vollzog. Die Initiative an der Theologischen Hochschule der Brüderschaft arrangiert sich wie ein Podiumsgespräch, bei dem verschiedene Fragen des Zusammenlebens besprochen werden: beispielsweise die des Philosemitismus und seiner Gefahren, oder Fragen zu gemischten Ehen.

Als weitere alternative Form des jüdisch-christlichen Gesprächs ist die Zusammenarbeit im Ökumenischen Verein der Theologinnen Ungarns, MTÖE,

Larissa Hrotko
*Jüdisch-christlicher Dialog als Beitrag zur geopolitischen und
geokulturellen Balance in Europa*

zu erwähnen. Die sehr verschiedenen Mitgliedsfrauen dieses Vereins[11] haben das gemeinsame Ziel der gesellschaftlichen und individuellen Emanzipation der Frauen in der Religion.

„Der Ökumenische Verein der Theologinnen Ungarns (MTÖE) respektiert die Würde des nach dem Gottesbild erschaffenen Menschen, unabhängig vom Geschlecht, der Herkunft, Religion oder sexueller Orientierung.

Wir halten den gesellschaftlichen Dialog im Interesse sozialer Gleichberechtigung von Frauen und Männern und gegenseitiger religiöser Toleranz für unentbehrlich.

Als eine der wichtigsten theologischen Aufgaben betrachten wir die Förderung des inklusiven Denkens in unseren Kirchen, Gemeinschaften und im gesellschaftlichen Leben unseres Landes. Deshalb arbeiten wir gerne mit allen religiösen und säkularen Organisationen zusammen, die die Menschenwürde, den gerechten Umgang mit allen Mitgliedern der Gesellschaft, die Ökumene und den zwischenreligiösen Dialog für relevant halten und sich nach der Realisierung dieses Dialogs streben."[12]

Aus der Geschichte interreligiöser Kommunikation der Frauen Europas

Die Geschichte europäischer Kommunikation beweist, dass Frauen sich von Anfang an aktiv daran beteiligten. Ein aussagekräftiges Beispiel ist der Hamburger „Soziale Frauenverein zur Ausgleichung confessioneller Unterschiede". Er funktionierte 1848 in Hamburg als Verein jüdischer und katholischer Frauen zur Verwirklichung gemeinsamer sozialer Projekte. Die Initiative des Vereins kam von der jüdischen Seite.[13]

Johanna Goldschmidt (1806-1884) gehörte zum Hamburger Reform-Judentum. Schon früh lernte sie die pädagogischen Ansichten von Rousseau und Pestalozzi kennen und wurde zur begeisterten Anhängerin von Friedrich Fröbel. Neben der pädagogischen Tätigkeit bemühte sie sich um die Annäherung der Jüdinnen und Katholikinnen in ihrer Heimatstadt.[14]

Seine Gründung verdankte der katholisch-jüdische „Soziale Frauenverein" nicht zuletzt dem Roman von Goldschmidt, der 1848 unter dem Titel „Rebekka

---

[11] Sie sind zugleich Mitglieder der ESWTR.

[12] Eigene Übersetzung der Autorin (http://www.teologusnok.hu,12. Oktober 2015).

[13] Vgl. Inka Le-Huu, „Johanna Goldschmidts Beitrag zur Begegnung jüdischer und christlicher Frauen in Hamburg (1847-1849)" in: *Salondamen und Dienstboten. Jüdisches Bürgertum um 1800 aus weiblicher Sicht,* (Juden in Mitteleuropa, Wien: 2009), 40-48.

[14] Vgl. Inka Le-Huu, *Johanna Goldschmidts Beitrag,* 40.

Larissa Hrotkó
Jüdisch-christlicher Dialog als Beitrag zur geopolitischen und
geokulturellen Balance in Europa

und Amalia. Briefwechsel zwischen einer Israelitin und einer Adeligen über Zeit- und Lebensfragen" bei F. A. Brockhaus in Leipzig anonym erschien.[15] Dieser Roman war nicht nur spannend, sondern vor allem aufschlussreich. Im Vorwort beschrieb die Autorin die benachteiligte Situation der Jüdinnen und ihre existenziellen Ängste. Die gesellschaftlichen Vorurteile gehörten zum Alltag der jüdischen Frauen in Hamburg. Die Zurückhaltung der Jüdinnen wurde von den Christinnen oftmals sehr falsch als Stolz interpretiert, was die Kommunikation zum Teil erschwerte.[16]

Goldschmidt erzählt in diesem Buch von der religiösen Erziehung in den jüdischen Familien und äußerte ihre Meinung zum formal nicht möglichen Austritt aus dem Judentum. „Johanna Goldschmidt verortet die Religion im Privaten, in der Familie und nicht in der Öffentlichkeit oder in geweihten Stätten. Die Religiosität eines Menschen werde während der Kindheit in der Familie geprägt, weshalb sie eine Konversion im Erwachsenenalter kritisch beurteilt, denn zu diesem Zeitpunkt sei der Weg der emotionalen Annäherung an die Religion bereits versperrt und nur eine intellektuelle Auseinandersetzung möglich."[17]

Ganz konkrete Ideen äußerte die Autorin über die gemeinsame Arbeit in einem Frauenverein. In dieser Form der gesellschaftlichen Kommunikation konnten die Frauen einander stärken und ihr oft vernachlässigtes intellektuelles Potenzial entwickeln. Dabei überschritten sie die Grenzen ihrer Konfessionen.

Das gemeinsame Ziel der jüdischen und katholischen Mitgliedsfrauen des Vereins war die Emanzipation der Gesellschaft. Das ermöglichte es ihnen, Unterschiede und Vorurteile zu überwinden. Die Frauen arbeiteten auf dem Gebiet der Erziehung, Bildung und Kultur zusammen. Im Vordergrund dominierten zwar die bekannten Ideen der Aufklärung, doch galt der Frauenverein gerade wegen der gelungenen interreligiösen Kommunikation als eine gesellschaftliche Innovation. Allerdings war die Initiative von Goldschmidt innerhalb des damaligen Judentums nicht unumstritten.[18]

Der Verein funktionierte nur über kurze Zeit, doch der Grund dafür lag nicht in den religiösen Unterschieden. Echte Differenzen entstanden im beruflichen

---

[15] Vgl. Inka Le-Huu, *Johanna Goldschmidts Beitrag*, 40-41.
[16] Vgl. Inka Le-Huu, *Johanna Goldschmidts Beitrag*, 42.
[17] Inka Le-Huu, *Johanna Goldschmidts Beitrag*, 43.
[18] Vgl. Annette Mehlhorn, „Gleich und doch verschieden – getrennt verschieden oder gemeinsam? Intrareligiöse Debatten und interreligiöser Dialog im Wechselverhältnis zwischen Religion, Politik und Gender" in: *Jahrbuch der Europäischen Gesellschaft für theologische Forschung von Frauen* 17 (2009), 29-40.

Larissa Hrotko
Jüdisch-christlicher Dialog als Beitrag zur geopolitischen und
geokulturellen Balance in Europa

Bereich. Ein Teil der Mitglieder unterstützte das Programm Friedrich Fröbels und die Errichtung der Kindergärten, während die anderen die Pläne von Carl Fröbel und Stiftung der Hochschule bevorzugten. Die primären Grundziele wurden aber 1849 bereits erreicht. Danach trennten sich die Wege der Stifterinnen. Der kurzlebige Hamburger Frauenverein zeigte aber weitgehende Möglichkeiten gegenseitiger Bereicherung der Frauen aus verschiedenen Konfessionen.

Beispiele von Stiftungen interkonfessioneller Frauenvereine gibt es auch in der ungarischen Frauenkultur.[19] So existierte beispielswese in Arad ein Frauenverein des Roten Kreuzes, dessen jüdische und christliche Mitglieder zusammen die verwundeten Soldaten des I. Weltkrieges pflegten.[20]

Die Fakten der Vergangenheit beweisen, dass die Frauen auch auf dem Gebiet des gesellschaftlichen Dialogs der Religionen kreativ wirken können, obwohl diese Arbeit nur selten analysiert und veröffentlicht wird.

Der Ausblick in die Zukunft als Zusammenfassung

Bei den Gesprächen mit den Rabbinern der größten Gemeinschaft Ungarns konnte festgestellt werden, dass der jüdisch-christliche Dialog fortgesetzt werden soll. Ganz unabhängig voneinander neigten die Gesprächspartner zur Unterstützung „privater" Formen des Dialogs, mit deren Hilfe das Gespräch aus den „oberen", das heißt den offiziellen und klerikalen Etagen der Gesellschaft, auf die Ebene der Mitgliedschaft erweitert wird.

An Stelle größerer Gesellschaften können kleinere Stiftungen gebildet werden, die sich kurzfristige konkrete Ziele setzten: seien es eine Ausstellung oder wissenschaftliche Tagungen oder auch ein gemeinsames soziales Projekt. Diese Form des Dialogs entbehrt der Regelmäßigkeit, doch kann sie zu den tieferen Veränderungen in allen Schichten der Gesellschaften beitragen.

Die theologischen Grundlagen des interreligiösen Dialogs sind zwar weiterhin angefragt, doch sollten sie sich vor allem in Richtung einer so genannten inklusiven Religionstheologie entwickeln, die sowohl die Soziologie als auch die Philologie der Kultur des zwischenreligiösen Dialogs integriert. Die Aufgabe dieser Wissenschaft ist es, die gesellschaftlichen Voraussetzungen zu

---

[19] Vgl. Larissza Hrotko, „Ungarische Frauen im Aufbruch zwischen Religion(en) und Politik. Ein Überblick über die Entwicklung der ungarischen Frauenbewegung." in: *Jahrbuch der Europäischen Gesellschaft für theologische Forschung von Frauen* 17 (2009), 153-164.

[20] Lippai Dezső, „Az aradi nők háborús munkássága", in: *Egyenlőség. A magyar zsidóság politikai hetilapja*, (August 1917), 5-6, hier 5.

Larissa Hrotkó
Jüdisch-christlicher Dialog als Beitrag zur geopolitischen und
geokulturellen Balance in Europa

beschreiben und die Sprache des Dialogs zu bilden. Dabei ist folgendes zu beachten:

– Die am Dialog Beteiligten müssen ihre eigene Religionskultur und Tradition kennen, um Prioritäten setzen zu können. So entwickelt sich religiöse Toleranz als gute Strategie bei den interreligiösen theologischen Gesprächen.

– Die Soziologie des Dialogs lehrt, wie wir als Teile einer Weltgeschichte agieren,

– Ehrlichkeit und Toleranz müssen in der Sprache präsent sein. So braucht es neue Formen, um Vertrauen den anderen gegenüber zu entwickeln, um Kritik ertragen und sie in angemessener Sprache formulieren zu können. Solche Kommunikationsregeln sollen beachtet und Erpressungen aller Art auf jeden Fall vermieden werden.

Oben sind Kapitel 29 des 4. Buches Mose (*Bamidbar*) und Traktat *Sukka* des Babylonischen Talmuds als biblische Grundlage des jüdisch-christlichen Dialogs von jüdischer Seite erwähnt. Eine klarere Zusammenfassung theologischer Anknüpfungspunkte jüdischer und christlicher Religionstradition ist kaum möglich. Ein Grund dafür ist, dass die jüdische Religionswissenschaft – mindestens in Ungarn – den Begriff einer Theologie nach der *Schoa* ablehnt. Es wird erklärt, dass es im Judaismus nicht um die Systematisierung unserer Kenntnisse über G-tt geht, sondern grundsätzlich darum, die Verbindung zwischen dem Ewigen und den Menschen wahrzunehmen und zu bewahren, sowie das Verhalten des Einzelnen und der Gemeinschaft der Individuen im Sinne göttlicher Gebote zu gestalten.

Als inklusive Religionstheologie könnte feministische Theologie dazu dienen, nach erfolgter kritischer Analyse jüdischer und christlicher Religionstraditionen gemeinsame Ausgangspunkte zu finden. Der theologische Feminismus kann bei der kritischen Analyse der institutionellen Religion insofern Hilfestellung leisten, als die von einigen Theologinnen „Hermeneutik des Verdachts"[21] genannte Kategorie erneut Anwendung fände. Die feministischen Theologinnen kritisieren damit nicht nur die negativen Seiten der Religionen, sondern eruieren neue Konfliktlösungsstrategien in den interreligiösen Beziehungen. Als befreiende Theologie unterstützt die feministische Religionswissenschaft die Teilnehmerinnen des Dialogs bei der Beseitigung von Vorurteilen, die die

---

[21] Helene Egnell, „The Messiness of Actual Existence" in: *Jahrbuch der Europäischen Gesellschaft für theologische Forschung von Frauen* 17 (2009), 13-27, hier 17.

Larissa Hrotko
*Jüdisch-christlicher Dialog als Beitrag zur geopolitischen und
geokulturellen Balance in Europa*

Offenheit dem und den Anderen gegenüber behindern. Wegen des allbekann-
ten christlichen Habitus, den patriarchalen G-tt des Alten Testaments dem
feministischen Jesus gegenüberzustellen, verliert der jüdisch-christliche Dialog
an Ehrlichkeit, wenn er diese These zu seiner Grundlage macht.[22] Denn die
alten Gewohnheiten, die tief in unseren Traditionen wurzeln, können erneut
und versteckt zu Formen des Anti-Judaismus führen.

Die letzte, doch nicht unbedeutende Bemerkung betrifft die Rolle der Frauen
im gesellschaftlichen Dialog zwischen den Religionen. In Ungarn dominieren
die Männer auf diesem Gebiet. Sie übernehmen die Führung. Frauen werden
die Ausführenden, die „Macherinnen". Das ist nicht nur für die religiöse
Emanzipation der Frauen ungünstig, sondern wirkt sich ganz negativ auf die
Anzahl der Beteiligten aus. Auch in dieser Richtung kann vieles unternommen
werden, indem man beispielsweise die Geschichte der Beteiligung der Frauen
an der Friedensbewegung und dem Gesellschaftsdialog der feministischen
Theologie in weiteren gesellschaftlichen Kreisen bekannt macht. Die feministischen Theologinnen analysieren und entdecken neue Interpretationen beider
Traditionen.[23]Diese Erfahrungen befördern den jüdisch-christlichen Dialog,
doch leider sind die Arbeiten feministischer Theologinnen in Ungarn kaum
bekannt. Dies bedeutet neue wichtige aufklärende Aufgaben für die feministischen Theologinnen Ungarns auch auf dem Gebiet der interreligiösen und
internationalen Gespräche. Zusammenfassend lässt sich sagen: „Konkret kann
feministische Theologie die Theologie der Religion herausfordern, sich an die
Ränder der religiösen Traditionen zu begeben, wo sich Traditionen im kreati-
ven Grenzbereich verändern und das Chaos realer Existenz greifbar wird."[24]

In der letzten Konferenz der ESWTR in Kolymbari zeigte sich ein mangelndes
Interesse zum Thema des interreligiösen Dialogs. Die Gleichgültigkeit charakteri-
siert auch die meisten Ungarn, wenn sie zu diesem Thema angesprochen werden.
Trotzdem stieg die verbale Judenfeindlichkeit in Ungarn in den letzten zwei Jahren
an. Das ergab sich aus einer sozialen Forschung zum antisemitischen Verhalten. Dieser Anstieg wurde auch unter den christlichen Gläubiger deutlicher. Die ungarischen
Rabbiner versuchen die nichtjüdische Bevölkerung aufzuklären, aber es gibt auch
andere Formen des Dialogs, unter denen die informellen vom besonderen Interesse
sind. Die Beteiligung der Frauen an dem jüdisch-christlichen gesellschaftlichen

---

[22] Vgl. Egnell, *The Messiness*, 17

[23] Vgl. Katharina von Kellenbach, *Anti-Judaism in Feminist Religious Writings* (Scholars Press:
Atlanta 1994)

[24] Egnell, *The Messiness*, 26.

Larissa Hrotkó
Jüdisch-christlicher Dialog als Beitrag zur geopolitischen und
geokulturellen Balance in Europa

Gespräch hat eine lange Geschichte schon, obwohl die führenden Positionen auch auf diesem Gebiet vor allem von Männern besetzt sind.

At the latest meeting of ESWTR, in Kolymbari, no special interest had been given to the topic of interreligious dialogue. Indifference towards this topic is typical of the majority of Hungarians, if addressed, too. Despite this fact, verbal antisemitism has grown in Hungary in the latest years. This is what could be drawn as a consequence from the sociological research of anti-Semitic behaviour. This can also be seen among Christian believers. Rabbis in Hungary are trying to enlighten non-Jewish people about Judaism, although there are other forms of dialogues as well. Among these, informal ways are especially interesting. Women's participation in the Jewish-Christian social dialogue has a long history, although the field also knows men in leading positions. Despite all these, feminist theology may open new ways for women in interreligious relationships and context.

En la última conferencia de ESWTR de Kolymbari se reveló un bajo interés respecto al diálogo interreligioso. Así también ocurre entre los habitantes de Hungría, una situación que se demostró en las investigaciones sociales sobre el comportamiento antisemítico de ese país, donde la mayoría de ellos y ellas también presentan un cierto desinterés en el tema, aun cuando el antisemitismo verbal aumentó allí en los último años, incluso, entre los cristianos y cristianas manifestándose con mayor frecuencia esta conducta. Los rabinos de Hungría informan a los y las ciudadanas no judías y no judíos respecto de la cultura y religión judía entre otras formas de dialogar acerca del tema en cuestión, sin embargo, es en el ámbito informal donde se despierta un mayor interés. Desde hace muchos años, el género femenino ha participado en el diálogo judeo-cristiano, no obstante, es el género masculino quienes han ocupado los cargos directivos en esta área; dado este contexto, creemos que la teología feminista puede abrir nuevos caminos para el diálogo interreligioso y una mayor visibilización del trabajo femenino.

Larissa Hrotkó ist Philologin, Theologin und jüdische Kulturhistorikerin. Sie wurde Judaismus an Rabbinnischen-Jüdischen Universität von Budapest promoviert. Ihre Arbeitsfelder umfassen jüdische Liturgie sowie Auslegung von Thora-und Talmud-texten und Publikation über die Hebräische Bibel. Ihre letzte Publikation „Ilona Gold-zieher, ein Name aus der Geschichte jüdischer Frauenbildung Ungarns" erschien in dem Konferenzband der Universität János Selye in Komarno (Slowakei).

Journal of the European Society of Women in Theological Research 24 (2016) 121-132.
doi: 10.2143/ESWTR.24.0.3170029

Dzintra Iliško

A Hopeful Vision of a Just World: Ecofeminist Agenda

Women in the Baltic Countries in Times of Transitions

The ideals of equality formulated in the Soviet Union formally granted equality to both men and women. Still, the Soviet promises for women's emancipation were hindering the majority of women from gaining liberation in daily life. Formally, women were granted equal rights with males. But women as a group had no real political power while male priorities prevailed. It was less costly to promote a few Soviet women than to elevate women as a group, thus women's unpaid work remained invisible.

During the transition to a new democracy, women's equal participation in the overall changes in the society was not high on the agenda, as social networks did not exist. Although all the legislation supports gender equality, men earn higher salaries. Stereotypes of "woman/men professions" are introduced already at school, teaching housekeeping for girls and technically based subjects for boys. During the Soviet period, religion was underground and was a matter of private life of individuals, mostly preserved and practiced by women. Increasingly, however, it became politicised in the hands of men at the national and regional levels and is being manipulated in accordance with, or in reaction to, new realities and the old gender arrangements.

The current situation of gender equality reflects quite an optimistic picture: the employment of women in the Latvian labor market is 60.8%, higher than the European Union [EU] average (58.5%); College/university (tertiary education) degree of Latvian women is 29.9%, significantly higher than EU average (24.8%) – but the challenge is how to motivate students to choose gender atypical fields of study.[1] Still, it is necessary to motivate graduates to enter gender atypical sectors and occupations.[2]

---

[1] European Commission, Directorate-General Justice, Unit D2 "Gender Equality", *The Current Situation of Equality in Latvia – Country Profile* (2012). (http://ec.europa.eu/justice/gender-equality/files/epo_campaign/130911_epo_country_profile_latvia.pdf, 9 June 2015)

[2] Ibid.

Latvia has joined the United Nation's [UN] "Convention on the Elimination of All Forms of discrimination Against Women" in 1992.[3] On 13 June 2014 the European Institute for Gender Equality published the new "Gender Equality Index" in which Latvia occupies the 15th place on the EU list. The index reflects six main domains – work, money, power, knowledge, time, and health – in which gender gaps may be observed. Latvian women hold high positions in the parliament, they served as Ministers in various spheres (foreign affairs, welfare, culture, public health, military) and once as president of the state; women have were also been candidates for the EU commissioner post. In 2013, both Latvia and Lithuania, part of the Organisation for Economic Cooperation and Development [OECD], adopted the OECD Gender Recommendation, which sets guidelines for achieving gender equality in education and employment and mainstreams gender equality via monitoring the progress of gender equality.[4]

Cimdiņa warns us about the negative stereotyping of women as housewives, prostitutes, and permanent consumers of cosmetics and fashion that still prevails in the mass media and societal norms and reality.[5] Women are not represented as potential equals in profession, business, social, and political life. A certain asymmetry and gender inequality persist and present a real challenge to struggle for.

A Recently observed phenomenon in Latvia, and more se in Estonia and Lithuania, is that women, alongside their belonging to an organised form of religion, are practicing spirituality which supports the ideals of equality. Many people are (re)embracing the ancient, nature-based spirituality which is in line with ecofeminist spirituality. Their efforts lie in envisioning possibilities for a more holistic and just life and freedom. They are looking for a spirituality that is embodied and joy-oriented.

The practice of differing religious faiths without clear national origins was one of the manifestations of post-socialist transnationalism. The religious realm was overtaken by various religious churches. Catholicism, Protestantism, and the Orthodox Churches were no longer the only religions to be discovered. The transnationalisation of faith led to the emergence of a religious market.

---

[3]   UN, *The Convention on the Elimination of All Forms of Discrimination against Women and its Optional Protocol* (2003). (http://www.ipu.org/PDF/publications/cedaw_en.pdf, 9 June 2015)

[4]   OECD, *Recommendation of the Council on Gender Equality in Education, Employment, and Enterpreneurship* (2013).(http://www.oecd.org/gender/C-MIN(2013)5-ENG.pdf, 9 June 2015)

[5]   Ausma Cimdiņa, *Enlargement, Gender and Governance* (EGG). EU Framework 5, Project No: HPSE-CT-2002-00115(Executive summary) (University of Latvia: 2002).

Catholic and Protestant Churches started losing their monopoly.[6] The religious faith of many women may be described as "an extra-institutional, resolutely individualistic and often highly eclectic personal theology self-consciously resistant to dogma."[7] Religious fellowship becomes institutionally decentralised, or, as Harding puts it, "without pope, without Rome, without costly denominational bureaucracies [...] managed by loose, fragmentary pastoral networks."[8] The national faith was not always as meaningful or morally effective as many expected it to be. Lamanauskas asserts that women felt their beliefs to be dysfunctional, incoherent, shallow, and unfulfilling within the institutionalised religion.[9] Therefore, women in Latvia autonomously determine their religious identity on the basis of what is available in the religious supermarket. Classic religious traditions are easily being combined with other traditions and elements of new religious movements. The religious supermarket involves esoterism, new religious movements, and syncretism. The availability of classic religious options in Latvia expands alongside other ancient traditions, earth religions, and new religious movements which seem so attractive to women.

The Sustainability Agenda for a Just World: High Priority in a Political Agenda

Inequality still affects many people. This simple fact was stated in leading forums and conferences on sustainable development, such as the World Conference on Education for Sustainable Development held in Bonn in 2009 and an International conference held in Nagoya, Japan in 2014.

Several UNESCO-issued documents and declarations emphasise that global crises reflect the reality of unsustainable economic developments based on short-term gains, and that unsustainable consumption patterns threaten future generations.[10] A number of significant international documents further

---

6   Gediminas Lamanauskas, "On the Charisma, Civility, and Practical Goodness of 'Modern' Christianity in Post-Soviet Lithuania," in: *Focaal: European Journal of Anthropology* 51 (2008), 93-112.

7   Bradford Verter, "Spiritual Capital: Theorizing Religion with Bourdieu against Bourdieu," in: *Sociological Theory* 21, 2 (2003), 150-174, here 158.

8   Susan Harding, *The Book of Jerry Falwell: Fundamentalist Language and Politics* (Princeton University Press: Princeton 2000), 273.

9   Lamanauskas, "On the Charisma," 96.

10 UNESCO, *Bonn Declaration* (2009). (http://unesdoc.unesco.org/images/0018/001887/188799e. pdf, 5 June 2015); UNESCO, *Shaping the Future We Want* (UNESCO: Paris 2014). *(http:// unesdoc.unesco.org/images/0023/002303/230302e.pdf, 5 June 2015)*

highlight the ideal of a just and sustainable societal development, among them reports by the United Nations Conference on Environment and Development [UNCDE];[11] Global Action Program on Education for Sustainable Development [GAP on ESD];[12] the final report of the Decade of Education for Sustainable Development, launched and endorsed at the World Conference held in Aichi-Nagoya, Japan, in November 2014, setting the goals of sustainable living in a just world;[13] and the post-2015 document, "Framework for Action Education 2030," adopted at the World Education Forum held in Incheon, Republic of Korea, in 2015.[14] These documents call for the transformative agenda on local and global s in order "to resolve global challenges, and ultimately to call all citizens to become proactive contributors of creating a more just, peaceful, tolerant, inclusive, secure and sustainable world."[15] They stress the role of women as drivers of sustainable development and their full engagement in decision making, policy shaping, and contribution to an agenda of a just world. GAP also contributes to a post-2015 agenda, aiming to fight exclusion and inequality through empowerment of women, stating that sustainability is about adapting to "a new ethic of living on the planet" and "creating a more just society through the fair distribution of social goods and resources."[16] It is a holistic and creative process based on society's always changing worldviews and values. Among the important initiatives and documents, the Incheon Declaration ratified in Korea in 2015 stands out, affording gender equality a high priority by way of supporting gender-sensitive policies and eliminating gender-based discrimination and violence in schools.[17]

Extensive networks like UNESCO, the Baltic and Black Sea Consortium in Educational Research [BBCC], the European Society of Women in Theological Research [ESWTR], Copernicus Alliance, a European network uniting more

---

[11] UN, *Report of the United Nations Conference on Environment and Development* (1992). (http://www.un.org/documents/ga/conf151/aconf15126-1annex1.htm, 6 June 2015)

[12] UNESCO, *Roadmap for Implementing the Global Action Program on Education for Sustainable Development* (UN: Paris 2014). (http://unesdoc.unesco.org/images/0023/002305/230514e. pdf, 8 June 2015)

[13] UNESCO, *Shaping the Future We Want*.

[14] World Education Forum, *Incheon Declaration: Education 2030: Towards Inclusive and Equitable Quality Education and Lifelong Learning for All* (2015). (http://www.uis.unesco.org/ Education/Documents/education_2030_incheon_declaration_en.pdf, 8 June 2015)

[15] UNESCO, *Roadmap for Implementing the Global Action Program*.

[16] Sacha Kagan and Julia Hahn, "Creative Cities and (Un)Sustainability: From Creative Class to Sustainable Creative Cities," in: *Culture and Local Governance* 3, 1-2 (2011), 11-27.

[17] World Education Forum, *Incheon Declaration*.

than 60 institutions committed to higher education for sustainable development, and others played a significant role in reaching the aims set by the UNESCO decade. Women in the west have served in significant leadership positions and pursued a commitment to the ideals of a just world. A Feminist agenda aiming at integrating the principles and practices of a sustainable world in all spheres of life and bringing the ideals of justice into political, economic, social, and cultural spheres of life has also been at work in Latvia. By practicing political leadership, women have made important advances in implementing just and sustainable local policies. Evidence collected by the World Bank clearly shows that when women and men are relatively equal, economies tend to grow faster, the poor move more quickly out of poverty, and the well-being of men, women, and children is enhanced.[18] The report also acknowledges that:

> Respect for both genders encourages fuller participation in the society by all its members and ensures that their perspectives are fully acknowledged and taken into consideration. To understand gender inequity is to recognise expressions of power, privilege and inequity related to gender in the local community and in countries worldwide.[19]

An Ecofeminist Agenda for Healing a Dysfunctional and Disconnected World

An agenda of sustainability cannot be achieved through political agendas and declarations only. It requires changes in thinking. Western ecofeminist theologians and thinkers, such as Gebara,[20] Ruether,[21] McFague,[22] and Christ[23] have laid a strong foundation for raising women's awareness, empowering women to take informed decisions and responsible actions, and setting agenda for a just and sustainable development for the whole Creation. They

---

[18] UNESCO, *Exploring Sustainable Development: A Multiple-Perspective Approach* (UNESCO: Paris 2012). (http://unesdoc.unesco.org/images/0021/002154/215431E.pdf, 8 June 2015)

[19] Ibid., 14.

[20] Ivone Gebara, *Longing for Running Water: Ecofeminism and Liberation* (Fortress Press: Minneapolis 1999).

[21] Rosemary Radford Ruether, "Ecological Theology: Roots in Tradition, Liturgical and Ethical Practice for Today," in: *Journal of Theology* 42, 3 (2003), 226-234; Rosemary Radford Ruether, "Religious Ecofeminism: Healing the Ecological Crises," in: S. R. Gottlieb (ed.), *The Oxford Handbook of Religion and Ecology* (Oxford University Press: New York 2006), 362-375.

[22] Sally McFague, *The Body of God: An Ecological Theology* (Fortress Press: Minneapolis 1993).

[23] Carol Christ, "Ecofeminism and Process Philosophy," in: *Feminist Theology* 14, 3 (2006), 289-310.

have suggested a holistic vision of a whole creation by emphasizing the importance of environmental, social, and economic contexts of sustainable development.[24] They point to growing unsustainability as a current state of humankind, characterised by a growing ecological crisis and high levels of consumption resulting in waste, pollution, and a growing number of poor populations. They emphasise the evident signs of injustice, characterised by the underrepresentation of women in the political sphere, forced prostitution, and other forms of discrimination in many Asian countries.[25]

Although there is no one "correct" version of ecofeminism, most eco-feminists would agree with the core perception that the domination of women and the domination of nature are fundamentally connected. In other words, violence against the Earth becomes intertwined with a desire to control women. Both oppressions were created and are perpetuated by an ideology called "patriarchy". The experience of exclusion and marginalisation of Eastern women slightly differs from the one described by Western ecofeminist theology, and makes feminism more fluid and potentially more incoherent in the context of the former. Therefore, the Western discourse needs to be contextualised for the Baltic states in order to define the relevant valid and viable frames and mechanisms for seeking justice.

Many ecofeminist writers state that women are better than men in initiating changes, by challenging and changing the structures that reflect a patriarchal mode of thinking. Ecofeminism seeks to discover the interrelatedness of the exploitation of women and the natural world. This connectedness is based on "conceptual connections", or, as Warren asserts, a construction of a notion of women and nature in male-biased ways that fosters all sorts of value dualisms, such as body/mind, emotion/reason, and women/men where, historically, women, nature, body are considered to be inferior in comparison with man, mind, reason.[26] This dichotomy is expanded to conceptual dualisms described as "-isms of domination, like sexism and classicism," which has reinforced men's power over both, women and nature.[27] Spretnak argues that this dualistic structure was promoted in the Greek world, perpetuated by Christianity, and

---

[24] McFague, *The Body of God;* Ruether, "Religious Ecofeminism."

[25] Rosemary Radford Ruether, *Integrating Ecofeminism Globalisation and World Religions* (Rowman and Littlefield Publishers: Lanham 2005).

[26] Karen Warren, "The Power and the Promise of Ecological Feminism," in: *Environmental Ethics* 12, 2 (1990), 125-146.

[27] Ibid., 127.

reinforced by the scientific revolution.[28] Ecofeminists encourage deconstructing human/nature and male/female dualisms that will later lead to alleviating leadership potential for both men and women. Warren reflects on ecofeminist struggles to challenge mainstream views on reason, rationality, knowledge, and the nature of the knower as separate and disconnected from nature.[29] This involves challenging both the social domination of women and the ecological domination of the Earth. By challenging "political connections", ecofeminists attempt to build up grassroots activism and to analyse the domination patterns that guide praxis.

Holistic Vision of the Earth: Embodiment of Sustainable Solutions

One of the most illustrative examples of a person's relatedness to Nature is described in Shel Silverstein's children's classics, The Giving Tree.[30] This poem can be read as a metaphor of men's abusive relationships to women. It may also be seen as a powerful metaphor of the Western patriarchal exploitation of the Earth. Or, as Berry comments, one reject one's role as an integral member of the Earth community in favor of a radical anthropocentric attitude towards life.[31]

Ecofeminist theologians and thinkers suggest a holistic and inclusive vision of the Creation, which is not hierarchical in its essence.[32] Chittister argues that the Earth itself has been treated as a pyramid by the humans, "it was cut in pieces, dominated, destroyed, and doomed to struggle for its own existence and the survival."[33] This model of Earth and Creation based on patterns of domination reigns from the beginning of scriptural history and became a legitimising foundation for Christian patriarchy which presents quite a destructive and dysfunctional cosmology embodied in the Baltic context as well. Chittister holds that ladders and pyramids assume a division of society into groups and casts, while circles describe a community of equals. Ecofeminist thinkers propose values of stewardship, responsibility, and equality. They reject a mechanistic model of the world and offer a cosmology of the world as an

---

28 Charlene Spretnak, "Ecofeminism: Our Roots and Our Flowering," in: I. Diamond et al (ed.), *Reweaving the World: The Emergence of Ecofeminism* (Sierra Club Books: San Francisco 1990).
29 Warren, "The power and the promise."
30 Shel Silverstein, *The Giving Tree* (Harper Collins: New York 1992).
31 Thomas Berry, *Befriending the Earth. A Theology of Reconciliation Between Humans and Earth* (Twenty Third Publications: Connecticut 1991).
32 Gebara, *Longing for Running Water*; McFague, *The Body of God*; Ruether, "Ecological Theology."
33 Joan Chittister, *Heart of Flesh. A Feminist Spirituality for Women and Men* (Eerdmans Publishing Company: UK 1998), 161.

interconnected unity. Gaard argues that ecofeminists express an image of self "interconnected with all life".[34] In this model, all humans are treated in an equal way regardless of their sex, age, sexual orientation, religion, or mental ability. It includes a profound respect for all species and ecosystems. This model is based on a holistic and ecological worldview as well as an ethics of care. Ecofeminist inspired by this philosophy assert that each person has the creativity and agency to be a co-creator of an ever changing and evolving universe. They suggest Creation Spirituality and a vision of New Creation and a transformed society with transformed relationships celebrating women's experience and creativity. Their vision recognises the need of all people for liberation in reawakening their consciousness. Creation spirituality considers seriously cosmological and feminist Scriptural texts known as Wisdom Literature which predates Christianity.[35] In this Christological vision, Christ is "the paradigmatic manifestation of cosmic wisdom and goodness."[36]

Ruether calls for transformed societies. She argues that social hierarchies of men over women need to be transformed into egalitarian societies which recognise the fullness of humanity in each human person.[37] She calls for a major restructuring of the relations of humans and the nonhuman world, and, like other ecofeminist thinkers, urges the overcoming of a culture of "competitive alienation,"[38] an emerging paradigm in Eastern Europe and the Baltic states. A distinct Biblical call for rediscovering the community of equals appears when the system of victimisers and victims, of rich and poor, is dismantled.

Ecofeminist epistemology recognises a variety of human's experiences. Ecofeminists reject reductionist theories of knowledge and highlight the interdependency of everything. Therefore, Gebara encourages us to begin by recognising that the Bible and all theology is a social construct and calls for deconstructing theology.[39] It is each individual's task to participate in imaginative work and the construction of systems of interpretation by developing

---

[34] Greta Gaard, "Living Interconnections with Animals and Nature," in: Greta Gaard (ed.), *Ecofeminism: Women, Animals and Nature* (Temple University Press: Philadelphia 1993), 1.

[35] Matthew Fox, *Creation Spirituality. Liberating Gifts for the Peoples of the Earth* (HarperSanFrancisco: San Francisco 1991), 108.

[36] Rosemary Radford Reuther, *Gaia and God: An Ecofeminist Theology of Earth Healing* (SCM Press: London 1992), 149-153.

[37] Reuther, *Integrating Ecofeminism*.

[38] Rosemary Radford Ruether, *Unmasking the Powers: Invisible Forces that Determine Human Existence* (Augsburg Fortress Press: Minneapolis 1986), 201.

[39] Gebara, *Longing for Running Water*.

awareness to the ways in which the own constructing of stories validates the exertion of power over others.

Ecofeminist theology is relevant for the Baltic context since it offers various approaches for gaining agency and intersubjectivity through developing multiple points of view, multiple ways of thinking and of talking, and multiple experiences of the world expressed through interactions rather than as univocal propositions. The vision proposed by the ecofeminists is open for shared disposition to dialogue, meditation, communication, power sharing, self-organisation, and self-correction.

The Use of Imaginative Work

Ecofeminists engage in re-imaginative work in order to portray a current state of being. One such powerful metaphor used by Steinbeck in *The Grapes of Wrath* is the metaphor of rape.[40] Steinbeck talks about the acts of violence and exploitation of the Earth by humankind in terms of rape and portrays women as Earth mothers, with Earth itself as "our" Mother. McFague argues for the understanding of God as neither feminine nor masculine, but encompassing all genders.[41] A feminine personification of Creation leads to a more balanced connection between God and all of Creation. McFague suggests the metaphor of "God's body", building up an interdependence of all life, for understanding God and Creation.[42] She encourages the rethinking of theological language. Images of God in the Scriptures are very diverse: God as liberator, friend, mother, father, rock, lover, brother. These images point to the quality of relationship that is possible with God. Johnson asserts that a female imagery of God has a capacity for representing God not only as nurturing, but also as powerful, initiating, and victorious.[43]

Reimagining God's images has the power to transform a dualistic understanding of God and the World. For women in Eastern Europe, a reconstruction of selfhood can take place through telling stories that involve the experience of embodiment. These women, seen as a subordinate group defined by patriarchal constructions, need to seek new and empowering ways to talk about themselves as bodily agents. The locatedness of one's body in the margins and

---

[40] John Steinbeck, The Grapes of Wrath (Penguin Books: New York 1992 [1939]).
[41] McFague, *The Body of God.*
[42] Ibid.
[43] Elizabeth Johnson, *She Who is: The Mystery of God in Feminine Theological Discourse* (Crossroads: New York 1992).

its journey into existence constitute a moral imperative for women in the Baltic states. Graham views the body as a fundamental point of departure in defining very diverse embodied experiences.[44] She challenges any ontological division of bodily experiences that only polarise and distort lived experiences. She encourages us to appreciate the complexity and diversity of bodily experiences and suggests ways for empowering the creative potential of women.

In contrast to classical theism that separated between God and the Earth, and a pantheism that merges God and the World, Johnson emphasises that "the relationships created by mutual indwelling, while non-hierarchical and reciprocal, they are not symmetrical, since the world is dependent on God, that generates freedom, self-transcendence, and the future in the interconnected whole."[45]

Reclaiming the body is an important focus for ecofeminist writers, since human identity had been previously equated with the mind and reason only. The body has been feminised, reduced in value, and seen as inferior. Feminists assert that women seek a spiritual vision in which women and the female body are celebrated as an image of God. They criticise androcentric traditions in which women are viewed as less than fully human, secondary, or subordinate to Christ.[46]

Ruether invites one to an imaginative work of reconstructing the images of God. She argues that the creation of a patriarchal God reflects the desire of men to control the Universe.[47] The concept of God is a projection of masculine desire for absolute power and domination. Ecofeminist theology constructs God as more immanent to the world. McFague asserts that a patriarchal God is distant from the World, relates only to the human world, and controls it through domination.[48] The attempts to reimagine images of God point at the otherness of God as well as the intimacy of God in Creation.

Conclusions

Gender equality is hard to impose from above as it has been reinforced during the Soviet period (women of the Soviet Bloc worked roughly 70 hours a week compared to 15-20 hours less in the West); at the same time, it cannot

---

[44] Elaine Graham, *Transforming Practice: Pastoral Theology in an Age of Uncertainty* (Mowbray: London 1996).
[45] Johnson, *She Who is*, 45.
[46] Carol Christ, *She Who Changes: Re-imagining the Divine in the World* (Palgrave MacMillan: New York 2003).
[47] Ruether, *Unmasking the Powers*.
[48] McFague, *The Body of God*.

develop totally by itself.[49] Strive towards this ideal requires political will, understanding, and efforts to implement it by both males and females. The younger generation of women in Latvia has grown up without an experience of Western liberation movements. Therefore, introducing Western feminists' grand narratives of emancipation does not seem appealing to them. They are alienated from an organised religion and seek spirituality outside of it.

Ecofeminist thinkers propose a new paradigm that challenges the place and role of human beings in the Universe, They offer an alternative paradigm, in which humans are located as an organic and integrated part of the Universe and the role of women is to become agents of change and bring along sustainable changes. They propose systemic thinking as a common frame for looking at things and the Earth. Being part of a pluralistic movement, they draw upon diverse ideologies, such as postmodern philosophy, social constructivism, deep ecology, and eco-spirituality. These ideologies are holistic rather than dualistic in nature, and women from the Eastern European find them more relevant and appropriate.

Ecofeminists suggest applying a systemic approach for envisioning sustainable future by offering a multi-vocal, dialogical, non-linear, contextually situated practice of being in the world. Ecofeminists encourage the reimagining of just communities and societies, of relationships and networks rather than retreating into more complicated discourses based on distance from the Earth. Ecofeminists suggest a conceptual map for moving forward in a holistic and integrative way by promoting long-term systemic thinking and situatedness of one's practices within a global framework of justice. Still, this discourse proposed by the Western, middle-class well-educated women theologians may obtain its validity only if it is translated into women's experiences in local contexts. Women's specific experience should be made into the starting point, since different women have different needs and different experiences of injustice. Western feminist discourse should be seen as contextually bound and located, allowing a fluidity of the possibilities of justice.

Feminist thinkers call for working both within the system and outside of it in order to make critical choices and make the world a better place, in which Western discourses may be perceived as an inspiration for the local justice-seeking frameworks.

---

[49] Witold Maciejewski, "The Baltic Sea Region Cultures, Politics, Societies," in: Witold Maciejewski (ed.), *Social Conditions. Women and Gender in History in the Baltic Region* (The Baltic University Press: Uppsala 2002), 542.

The article elaborates on the ecofeminist vision of a just world and the role of women and men in it, and explores conceptual, symbolic, religious, epistemological, experiential, theoretical, and linguistic connection between the domination of women and nature by questioning the existing social structures. The discourse of environmental justice means giving voice to those who have been excluded from the participation in decision-making processes and allocating rights to the non-human world. The commitment to ensure women's empowerment and agency is also pronounced in the ecofeminist agenda relevant to the Latvian context. Ecofeminism is a heterogeneous movement, presenting a wide spectrum of thoughts and plurality of positions. However, it needs to be contextualised for Latvia in order for bringing a vision of a just society alive. **Key words**: just and sustainable world, ecofeminist agenda, equality.

Die Autorin analysiert die Auffassung ökofeministischer Theologinnen von einer gerechteren Welt und konzentriert sich dabei auf die Erörterung konzeptueller, symbolischer, epistemologischer und theoretischer Kontextkombinationen. Im Artikel werden die Ansichten ökofeministischer Denkerinnen über die Ausbeutung in Bezug auf Frau und Umgebung, sowie über nicht-nachhaltige Beziehungen „Mensch-Mensch" und „Mensch-Natur" betrachtet. Die Autorin erörtert ebenso den Gerechtigkeitsdiskurs im Kontext Lettlands. Der Fokus in den Arbeiten ökofeministischer Theologinnen, Philosophinnen und Theoretikerinnen liegt in der legitimen Beteiligung der ausgeschlossenen Gruppen am Alltag, an der Gesellschaft und an der Verwaltung, sowie in der Förderung ihrer aktiven Teilnahme an Ausgestaltung und Sicherung einer gerechteren Welt. Die ökofeministische Bewegung ist vielfältig und heterogen. Doch sie erhebt keinen Anspruch auf eine gemeinsame Vision und Perspektive. Sie bietet die Möglichkeit, Visionen bei Beachtung lokaler soziowirtschaftlicher Besonderheiten zu kontextualisieren. Theologinnen weisen darauf hin, dass vieles in den Kategorien „Natur" und „Frau" soziale Konstruktionen sind. Vordergründig ist aber immer bestehende Möglichkeit für Veränderungen im Gestalten einer nachhaltigen Welt.

Dzintra Iliško, PhD, is an associate professor at Daugavpils University, Latvia. She is the head of the Center of Sustainable Education at the Institute of Humanities and Social Sciences at Daugavpils University. She is a member of several International organisations, such as the European Society of Women in Theological Research [ESWTR] and the International Society of Religious Education and Values [ISREV]. Her research interests include sustainable education, gender studies, and inclusive education. She takes part in a number of international projects, such as Lifelong Learning Programme [LLP] or Erasmus+, University Educators for Sustainable Development [UE4SD], Nord plus Horizontal No. NPHZ-2014/10085: "Baltic Sea Region Network on Education for Sustainable Development," and the UNESCO/UNITWIN project.

Journal of the European Society of Women in Theological Research 24 (2016) 133-154.
doi: 10.2143/ESWTR.24.0.3170030

Anne-Claire Mulder

Religious Authority, Religious Leadership, or Leadership of a Religious Organisation – Same Difference? An effort in Clarification.[1]

In 2014 I started working on a research project called "Processes of attribution of religious authority and the role of gender in these processes". This project originates in – and is a development of – my long standing interest in questions such as "how do the voice, the (religious and theological) ideas, and the religious and theological worldview of women become authoritative, especially those that are perceived as new, unheard of, other, or different." "How do they become tradition, passed on from one generation to the other?" Or "Why do words spoken by the one become canonical and the words from another person do not."[2] These questions illuminate my intention to approach the issue of "religious authority" from a sexual-difference perspective, with a special focus on the deployment of a "horizon", an "objective" to offer orientation and direction to the realisation of the irreducible difference of female-feminine subjectivity. This tendency can be explained by the influence brought about by my long study of the work of Luce Irigaray.[3] However, the issues are also

---

[1] I want to thank the members of the Onderzoeksseminar of the PTHU-Groningen for their comments upon earlier versions of this text, the ABC-Autorinnen for inspiring discussions in which I learned much, and especially Magda Misset-van de Weg for her encouragements during the different stages of the development of this research project.

[2] On the issue of (religious) authority, see Anne-Claire Mulder, "Introduction,"" in: *Yearbook of the European Society of Women in Theological Research (Peeters: Leuven 2004)*, 12, 5-11; Anne-Claire Mulder et al., "De weg van de aanbeveling... Exploratief onderzoek naar de doorwerking van de aanbevelingen van de oecumenische vrouwensynodes". (unpublished document); Anne-Claire Mulder, Mathilde van Dijk, and Angela Berlis, "Gender in Theology and Religion: a Success-Story?! Report from a Conference," in: *Journal of the European Society for Women in Theological Research* (Peeters: Leuven 2013), 21, 99-117.

[3] See for instance Anne-Claire Mulder, *Divine Flesh, Embodied Word. "Incarnation" as a Hermeneutical Key to a Feminist Theologian's Reading of Luce Irigaray's Work* (Amsterdam University Press: Amsterdam 2006); Anne-Claire Mulder, "An Ethics of the In-Between: A condition of Possibility of Being and Living Together," in: Pamela Sue Anderson (ed.), *New*

pertinent for the acknowledgement and recognition of queer and/or post-colonial voices, actually for all those voices that struggle to be heard when they speak of their religious ideas, their faith; the voices of those who struggle to become acknowledged and recognised as speaking (of) God.[4]

The questions raised in the first lines of this introduction illuminate that I understand granting someone authority as a dynamic process at work in a relation between two persons or a person and a religious text or religious body. The research project mentioned shall focus on the dynamics within this process through empirical research, in an attempt to find out what forms of expression this process of granting authority can take, what motivates persons to attribute religious authority to a person or text, what are the circumstances in which this happens, what is the length of the authority relation between the one and the other, et cetera.

Granted, speaking of the attribution of (religious) authority and depicting this as a relational process is the effect of a certain interpretation of the term "religious authority". Preliminary discussions of the research plans made it clear that many people do not associate the term "religious authority" with a relational process, but rather with the assignment of the leader of a religious organisation – be it ordained or not – to lead the community spiritually. Thus, "religious authority" was understood to refer to "religious leadership". Others associated the term "religious authority" with the power to command or exact obedience which goes hand in hand with the leadership of a religious organi-sation; it was then connected with hierarchical relationships, especially with relations of domination.[5]

This paper aims to show the distinctions and similarities between these dif-ferent interpretations of the term "religious authority". The first part maps the different sources that contributed to the understanding of the term "religious authority" as a relational process in which authority is attributed. The second part presents a description of the genealogy of religious authority associated with the leadership of a religious organisation. The conclusion then delineates

---

Topics in Feminist Philosophy of Religion. Contestations and Transcendence Incarnate (Fem-inist Philosophy Collection) (Springer: Dordrecht/ London 2010), 297-318.

[4] See Ina Praetorius, „Von Gott Sprechen. Als Frau. Nach der Aufklärung," in: *Yearbook of the European Society of Women in Theological Research* (Peeters: Leuven 2004), 12, 77-90.

[5] These interpretations of "religious authority" were also voiced in two group discussions held at two different occasions with members of the ESWTR, first in May 2015, with members of the Romanian section of the ESWTR living in and nearby Cluj, and second with participants of the 16th International Conference of the ESWTR held in Crete in August 2015.

the relevance of this exercise in clarification of the two interpretations of religious authority for the understanding of issues of authority and leadership *per se*, and of the role of gender in these issues.

"Religious Authority" as a Relational Concept

Authority
A number of texts and passages have been very influential for the interpretation of religious authority as a dynamic and relational process presented here. One of the most influential texts has been "Female Voice, Written Word: Women and Authority in Hebrew Scripture," by Claudia Camp.[6] Here, authority is not understood as *power over* others, but as something "*freely* granted" by someone to a person or a book.[7] This means that no one loses her or his freedom in an authority relation.

A second text which piqued my interest was an interview with Luce Irigaray, in which the praxis of *affidamento* or "entrustment", a praxis of cultivating the relations of women among themselves, was discussed.[8] This praxis is further discussed in a book published by The Milan Women's Bookstore Collective, dealing with their own political praxis and reflections.[9] In this book, members of the Collective describe how through the reading and discussing of literary classics by women authors in their women's groups, inequalities within the group were discovered: the voice and ideas of one or several women within the group were favored over those of others. These voices were granted authority because the ideas were thought more important, more fruitful than others. Reflecting upon the nature of this "more", they discovered that these interpretations touched the desire or yearning of those present for (a certain form of) female subjectivity, and/or that they offered some orientation.[10] From this discovery, they developed a praxis of entrustment, of entrusting oneself to the authority of another woman, "who thus becomes guide, mentor, or point

---

6   Claudia V. Camp, "Female Voice, Written Word: Women and Authority in Hebrew Scripture," in: Paula M. Cooey, Sharon A. Farmer, and Mary Ellen Ross (eds.), *Embodied Love. Sensuality and Relationship as Feminist Values* (Harper and Row: San Francisco 1987), 97-113.

7   Camp, "Female Voice, Written Word," 98 (emphasis in the original).

8   Luce Irigaray, *Zur Geschlechterdifferenz. Interviews und Vorträge.* (Wiener Frauenverlag: Wien 1987), Frauenforsuchung Band 5, 118-137, here 124-130.

9   The Milan's Bookstore Collective, *Sexual Difference. A Theory of Social-Symbolic Practice,* (Indiana University Press: Bloomington 1990).

10   Milan Women's Bookstore Collective, *Sexual Difference*, 108-113.

of reference – in short – a figure of mediation between her and the world."[11] As one of the examples of this praxis of *affidamento,* they refer to Ruth and Naomi. Ruth "decided to entrust herself to Naomi and Naomi, after trying to dissuade her, accepted her."[12]

A third important source of this view of authority is the entry on "authority" in the *ABC des guten Lebens* [the ABC of the good Life], the first draft of which was discussed by the collective of ABC-Autorinnen.[13] This text is closely related to the ideas of the Italian philosophers discussed above, as the authors have been engaged in reading, translating, and commenting upon the work of a number of Italian feminist philosophers, some of whom also belong to the Milan Women's Bookstore Collective.[14] This text describes authority as follows:

> Autorität ist eine Qualität, die innerhalb von Beziehungen zirkuliert. Autorität ent-steht immer dann, wenn jemand die Worte oder Anregungen einer anderen Person bedeutsam findet und ihnen Wert zumisst. Ob jemand für mich Autorität hat, erkenne ich daran, dass ihr oder sein Urteil mir wichtig ist, auch wenn ich damit nicht übereinstimme [...] Autorität folgt nicht zwangsläufig aus einer bestimmten Eigenschaft – etwa objektiver Sachkenntnis oder besonderen Fähigkeiten – sondern sie korrespondiert mit dem Begehren derjenigen, die sie anerkennt. Das ist in der Regel dann der Fall, wenn das, was jemand sagt (oder tut oder schreibt) dabei hilft, dem eigenen Begehren zu folgen. Wer Autorität hat, inspiriert, bringt auf neue Ideen, fordert heraus, ermutigt oder zeigt bisher unbekannte Möglichkeiten auf. Genau deshalb kann Autorität große Wirksamkeit entfalten, denn sie bewegt Menschen dazu, sich zu verändern, etwas Neues anzufangen, ihre bisherigen Standpunkte zu überdenken und sich weiterzuentwickeln.[15]

---

[11] Ibid., 8/9.

[12] Ibid., 119.

[13] Ursula Knecht et al., *ABC des guten Lebens* (Christel Göttert Verlag: Rüsselsheim 2012), 25-27. (also found at https://abcdesgutenlebens.wordpress.com. The authors of this *ABC* now call themselves the ABC-Autorinnen.

[14] From the ABC-Autorinnen, Antje Schrupp and Dorothee Markert-Knüfer in particular are important mediators of the thoughts of Italian philosophers as translators and commentators. See for instance Diotima, *Jenseits der Gleichheit. Über Macht und die weiblichen Wurzeln der Autorität* (Ulrike Helmer Verlag: Königstein/Taunus 1999).

[15] Knecht et al., *ABC*, 25/26. "Authority is a quality that circulates within relationships. Authority comes about in those instances when someone considers the words or suggestions of another person to be meaningful and valuable. I realise whether someone has authority for me by the fact that her or his judgement is important to me, even if I do not agree [...] Authority does not follow necessarily from a certain characteristic – like objective expertise or special skills –

This description emphasises that authority is an aspect or dimension of a relation, between two persons or between a person and the words or the life of another person. Thus, an authority – someone who helps to follow one's yearning – can also present itself in the form of a text or an exemplary life. The last possibility explains the turn to female mystics as Teresa von Avila or Hildegard von Bingen in the context of discussing female authority.[16] It also illuminates that the relational exchanges are not focussed on the relation itself, but that it is directed at the development of the one who entrusts herself to the judgement of the other, to her intellectual and spiritual growth, her growth in self-confidence.

The dynamics of this authority relation between two persons is thus that the one seen as an authority for the other constitutes a reference point; a "voice" offering direction and authorising the one who entrusts herself to this reference point in her enterprises: offering her the energy to straighten her back, to step out of her comfort zone in an as yet unknown territory, in the knowledge that she has the backing of the other, thus "realizing what she (or he) is capable of being," to use an expression of Luce Irigaray.[17] That does not mean that she has to follow this authority in her (or his) footsteps.[18] For this relationship

---

it corresponds rather with the yearning (or desire) of the person, that acknowledges this authority. That is usually the case when that what someone says (or does or writes), helps to follow one's own yearning/desire. The one who has authority inspires, evokes new ideas, prompts, encourages or shows hitherto unknown possibilities. Precisely for that reason authority can be greatly effective, because it moves persons to change themselves, to start something new, to rethink their current views or standpoints and to develop themselves further" (My translation here and henceforth).

[16] See for instance Diana Sartori, "Warum Teresa," in: Diotima und andere, *Die Welt zur Welt Bringen. Politik, Geschlechterdifferenz und die Arbeit am Symbolischen* (Ulrike Helmer Verlag: Königstein/Taunus 1999), 87-118; Andrea Günter, "Weibliche Autorität dank Durchsetzungskraft, prophetische Begabung und leidenschaftlicher Gottes- und Weltliebe – Mystekerinnen als Denkerinnen von Frauenpolitik am Beispiel Hildegard von Bingen," in: Andrea Güter, *Weibliche Autorität, Freiheit und Geschlechterdifferenz. Bausteine einer feministischen politischen Theorie* (Ulrike Helmer Verlag: Königstein/Taunus 1996), 107-129. See also Andrea Günter, *Frauen vor Bilder, FrauenVorbilder. Die Weibliche Suche nach Orientierung* (Christel Göttert Verlag: Rüsselsheim 2003).

[17] Luce Irigaray, *Sexes and Genealogies* (Columbia University Press: New York 1993), 61.

[18] I insert here the words "or he" between brackets, because I came across a quote from Luisa Muraro, one of the theoreticians of the *affidamento*-relation, in an internet article by Dorothee Markert, in which Muraro writes that this kind of relation was already present in the relations between men and between many women and men, but that these kinds of relations between women were rare. Dorothee Markert, „Affidamento – sich dem Urteil einer anderen Frau

does not rob her of her freedom or responsibility to decide for herself what course to follow. But as they are in this *affidamento* relation, she will only do that after careful consideration of what the other is saying.[19] This illuminates that in entrusting oneself to the direction or judgement of the other, one cannot expect "to receive only affirmation, support or encouragement" but occasionally also critical questioning of what one is doing.[20] And this in turn shows that the one who is entrusted with the trust of the other in her judgement and direction, who thus has become the authority in this relation, must "be ready to take up the authority that is attributed to her and to risk passing judgement or give direction."[21]

This description of the dynamic of authority relations also illuminates what this relation asks for, namely "reflexive practitioners". To live up to its basic characteristic, notably enabling the practitioners "to grow", it asks for careful reflection upon the inner dynamic of the relations: for instance upon the thin line between "authority" and undue influence or the exertion of power from the one in the position of authority; or– upon the thin line between taking the other as authority – for example upon a path to realise something one wants to realise oneself – and idealising this other, longing to imitate her, to become like her. When these lines are crossed, when "authority" has become the exertion of power, when "authority" becomes an object of desire or envy, when authority relation no longer stimulates the growth of the practitioners, then "the fundamental interconnectedness between true authority and the giving of life" is broken.[22]

Religious Authority

Words such as "growth", "life-giving", "thriving", or "flourishing" give expression to an ideal, an image of a life in dignity and peace, an image of the good life. This particular ideal or image of the horizon is expressed or

---

anvertrauen." (http://www.bzw-weiterdenken.de/2011/04/affidamento-sich-dem-urteil-einer-anderen-frau-anvertrauen, 31 October 2015). This remark by Muraro affirmed my own intuition that the process of attribution of authority can be studied not only in relations between women, but in all kind of relations.

[19] For an example of this dynamic, see Dorothee Markert, *Wachsen Am MEHR Anderer Frauen. Vorträge über Begehren, Dankbarkeit und Politik* (Christel Göttert Verlag: Rüsselsheim 2002), 202-205.

[20] Knecht et al., *ABC*, 27.

[21] Ibid.

[22] Camp, "Female Voice, Written Word," 111.

embedded in a wealth of texts, pictures and practices, a narrative matrix,[23] and as such constitutes a living tradition as well as a standard by which to adjudicate the experiences and conditions of everyday life. It can also be understood as transcending the here and now as well as the quotidian, in the sense that it points beyond the experiences of the everyday life towards different options to live the good life.

Following Luce Irigaray's picture of the notion of "horizon", this (image on the) horizon is both an objective and an object of this political process. As an objective, it constitutes the goal that offers direction to the political process. As an object, it is the object of exchange, the "third" in the communication between the one and the other; that which connects them as the object of their communication and that which separates them or differentiate them from each other, as in the case of disagreement about what good life would look like.[24] Irigaray also points out that the image on the horizon that mobilises our individual or collective yearning or desire to realise this can be called "divine", because it constitutes "the absolute" or "ultimate" for us, the essence of our existence. As such this horizon is religious, even when the words "God" or "divine" are not used as the *chiffre* for this absolute and ultimate. For it offers both sense and meaning to the disparate experiences of this lived existence and a standard by which to examine again what is happening and to discover what is good or bad.[25]

However, this sense of what constitutes the absolute and ultimate of our existence must be re-examined and actualised time and again. This implies a conscientious re-examination of the traditions in which this image of the divine of us and for us is embedded. This re-examination can produce new, different, unheard-of images of the divine especially when the stories-we-live-by are re-examined from a location in the margins. This process generates or "authors" a different order or cohesion in the disparate experiences of human

---

[23] Knecht et al., «Matrix», *ABC*, 98-100.

[24] Irigaray, *Sexes and Genealogies*, 57-72. For an interpretation of Luce Irigaray's notion of "horizon" see Mulder, *Divine Flesh, Embodied Word*, 167-174.

[25] This interpretation of "religion" is inspired by Irmgard Busch's two etymological interpretations of the word. According to Busch, religion understood as "binding together" goes back to the Latin verb *religare,* but "religion can also be traced back to the Latin verb *relegere* which renders an interpretation of religion as 'conscientious', as knowing and discovering what is good and bad." See Irmgard Busch, "Religie," in: Hedy D'Ancona et al. (eds.), *Vrouwenlexicon. Tweehonderd jaar emancipatie van A tot Z* (Het Spectrum: Utrecht 1989), 324-325.

existence, a different picture of what is the meaning and value of life and how to live it.

The outcome of this process needs to be "authorised" however to become (part of) a living and life-giving tradition; in other words, this image of the absolute and ultimate needs to be recognised, acknowledged and affirmed as "authoritative", as a true and to-be-trusted (religious) point of orientation. This raises the question "who is responsible for this authorising?" Or, to formulate the question differently, "who is the religious authority authorising an image of the divine of and for us as true or trustworthy?"

The picture of "authority" described above does not provide such a clear-cut answer to this question, because what goes for "authority", also goes for "religious authority". Religious authority is also attributed to someone whose words or ideas are experienced as meaningful and valuable by someone else. In this case it concerns her or his "speaking (of) God", or her or his words or ideas about the absolute or ultimate of human existence. This process of attributing religious authority to her or his words and ideas places her or him in the position of religious authority, makes her or him a religious authority, someone turned to for advice when needing to judge a situation in light of the religious tradition. This means that religious authority is dynamic and not fixed, circulating and not limited to (persons in) certain positions or to the ordained.

This interpretation of religious authority is different, however, from the dominant one, in which it is indeed seen as fixed and limited to certain positions, most often the position of the leader of a religious organisation, be it ordained or not. The following part shall present an account of the coming about of this understanding of religious authority.

Religious Authority: Leader of a Religious Organisation?

In mapping the genealogy of the recurrent identification of religious authority with leadership of a religious organisation, Hannah Arendt's text "What is Authority" is a good starting point.[26] This text has been influential for the women of the Milan Women's Bookstore Collective, Kathleen Jones, the ABC-Autorinnen, and other writers.[27] Arendt's text is relevant because she

---

[26] Hannah Arendt, "What is Authority?" in: Hannah Arendt, *Between Past and Future, Eight Exercises in Political Thought. With an introduction by Jerome Kohn* (Penguin Classic: New York 1961/2006), 91-141.

[27] See for example Paul Verhaeghe, *Autoriteit* (De Bezige Bij: Amsterdam 2015).

describes the authoritarian relation that dominates our thinking about authority and argues that this particular form of authoritarian relation is mediated through the ages by the teachings of the Church and has thus influenced the present understanding of religious authority. This last argument brings to mind the description of the development and tensions in the history of ordination mentioned in an article by Barbara Brown Zikmund.[28] Another book is *Compassionate Authority* by Kathleen Jones.[29] Whereas Arendt describes the development of the concept of authority from antiquity to modernity, Jones' description of authority starts with modernity. Taken together, their books give a broad historical sketch of the genealogy of our contemporary thoughts on authority and leadership.

In a marked distinction from Jones' book on authority, Arendt's text does not address the gendered nature of the political theories on authority she discusses, although it becomes clear from the picture she paints that the form of authority she discusses is "patriarchal authority" or "the authority of the fathers". A similar remark can be made with respect to the history of ordination described by Brown Zikmund. In her depiction of this history, the gendered nature of the different steps in the development is not discussed, but presupposed. It is then addressed in the rest of her text, where she discusses how first and second generation ordained female ministers relate to this history of ordination and change the dominant understanding of the ordained ministry.

Hannah Arendt on Authority

In "What is Authority," Arendt discusses the crisis, even the loss of authority in the political realm. She opens her text with the thesis that: "[...] authority has vanished from the modern world."[30] She moderates this thesis by explaining that it is a specific form of authority that we have lost; one which has been valid in the Western world throughout a long time.[31] One of the manifestations of this loss is that authority is often misunderstood as the exertion of power

---

[28] Barbara Brown Zikmund, "Ministry of Word and Sacrament: Women and Changing understandings of Ordination," in: Milton J. Coater, John M. Mulder, and Louis B. Weeks (eds.), *The Presbyterian predicament: Six Perspectives* (Westminster/John Knox Press: Louisville Kentucky 1990), 134-159.

[29] Kathleen B. Jones, *Compassionate Authority. Democracy and the Representation of Women* (Routledge: New York 1993).

[30] Arendt, "What is authority," 91.

[31] Ibid., 92. Although Arendt does not say it, one can assume from her description that it is precisely the patriarchal form of authority that is disappearing. See also Verhaeghe, *Autoriteit*, 58.

over others, and is thus connected with obedience through coercion. Arendt, however, writes that "the authoritarian relation between the one who commands and the one who obeys rests neither on common reason nor on the power of the one who commands; what they have in common is the hierarchy itself, whose rightness and legitimacy both recognise and where both have their predetermined stable place."[32]

Thus, what has got lost is the recognition of the rightness and legitimacy of this hierarchy; a loss Arendt attributes to the general doubt that was introduced in modernity, and which first undermined tradition, subsequently religion, and now has entered the political realm.[33]

In order to clarify the political discussions on authority held in the 1950s, in which, according to Arendt, important distinctions between authoritarian, dictatorial and totalitarian were blurred, she draws a genealogy of the origins of this lost concept of authority. Her genealogy starts with Plato's reflection upon the way in which the political process of negotiation about the general interest among free men could be ordered. Plato introduced "the laws" as a way of governing the *polis*. These represent an authority that can be obeyed while free men retain their freedom. Plato considered these laws to be an expression of Reason, and presented the philosophers as best suited to govern the *polis* due to their philosophical and reflective expertise, their contemplation of Reason and concomitant ideas of the good and the true. Implicit in this presentation of the laws is that the law's authority is rooted in their transcendent character: they are presented as part of the world of the ideas, and as such, as a measure of the good and the true.[34] This is offered as the reason that the citizens of the *polis* should obey the laws. However, to solve the dilemma that not all citizens (can) contemplate Reason and thus obey its laws out of their reasonable acquiescence, Plato introduced in *The Republic* a myth of rewards and punishments in an hereafter, or a form of hell.[35] What becomes clear from this description is that Plato's idea of the authority of the law goes hand in hand with a dichotomy between seers, theoreticians, thinkers, and/or authorities – experts – and doers, those who obey the authorities, which happen to be all those who are responsible for the continuity of life itself and the life of the

---

[32] Ibid., 93.
[33] Ibid.
[34] Ibid., 109.
[35] Ibid., 108.

polis – the members of the household of free men, women, children, slaves as well as the artisans and craftsmen.[36]

Aristotle reinforced the hierarchy within the authority relation which Plato introduced, by invoking the "natural" difference between younger and older persons as a justification of the difference between those who rule and those who obey.[37]

The thoughts of Plato and Aristotle on authority in a political context, notably their conception of authority as a structure of obedience to laws and institutes by both authorities and subjects, are still influential in contemporary thinking, due to the fact that the Romans made them into "ancestors" when "[they] felt they needed *founding* fathers and authoritative examples in matters of thought and ideas," and thus preserved their thoughts and theories as an authoritative tradition."[38]

According to Arendt, the Romans based authority in the political realm in the tradition of the foundation of their city and connected it with the religious reverence of the (guidance of the) ancestors. She writes: "At the heart of Roman politics [...] stands the conviction of the sacredness of *foundation,* in the sense that once something was founded it remains binding, for all future generations."[39] This means that the Roman political enterprise was directed at preserving this foundation and bringing this founded city to prosperity, to augmentation. This political enterprise was also a religious one, in the etymological sense of the word *religare,* "binding back". For the preservation and augmentation of the foundation was conceived as tying the present back to this past, for instance through practices as the consultation of the ancestors, the founders of the city, with respect to course and events of the present. These ancestors were asked by the eldest, the Senate, for guidance, for direction in the present and for a standard with respect to what would contribute to the prosperity of the city.[40] They were given this authority because of their connection with the ancestors. Thus, their authority in voicing the offered guidance and direction in the present was rooted in the past, in particular in the authority of the ancestors. This picture of the place of authority and of those in or with authority in the Roman political life, illuminates that authority

---

[36] Ibid., 115.
[37] Ibid., 116.
[38] Ibid., 124 (my emphasis).
[39] Ibid., 120.
[40] Ibid., 121-123.

is closely connected with "tradition" and "religion". As Arendt writes, "to act without authority and tradition, without accepted, time-honored standards and models, without the help of the wisdom of the founding fathers, was inconceivable."[41]

According to Arendt, this Roman matrix of thought about the relevance and authority of tradition for the present, with the concomitant effort to actualise the past in the present or to interpret the present by turning to the past and to tradition, has been preserved in and by the Christian Church from the decline of the Roman Empire until far into modernity, when general doubt undermined first tradition and religion, and eventually authority. Arendt describes how the structure of the Roman tradition of thinking about authority was replicated in the Church after Constantine. The death and resurrection of Christ took the place of the sacred foundation. This foundational event was preserved in the testimony of the apostles who would become "'the founding fathers' of the Church, from whom she would derive her own authority as long as she handed down their testimony by way of tradition from generation to generation".[42] Plato's influence was preserved in the idea that the source of the authority of ideas and rules concerning what was good and true – both in terms of conduct and conviction – was transcendent to the concrete and mundane, and revealed by revelation.[43] It was also preserved in the idea that obedience to (the religious and) political authority could be enforced with the threat of hell, with eternal suffering in the hereafter, which kept everyone in line until doubt undermined the belief in (this) hell.[44]

Arendt's depiction of the way in which the Roman matrix of thought about authority was continued in the Church's thoughts and practices of authority is illuminating regarding the question of why we identify religious authority with "exerting power over". It brings to mind the spiritual power wielded by ecclesial authorities over the psychological well-being of the faithful; a power that would bring them to obedience, to remain within the realm of tradition.

Arendt's depiction also sheds light on the picture drawn by US theologian Barbara Brown Zikmund of the historical development of the ordained ministry and the way in which religious authority has become identical with ordained ministry. In her text "Ministry of Word and Sacrament: Women and Changing

---

[41] Ibid., 124.
[42] Ibid., 125/126.
[43] Ibid., 127.
[44] Ibid., 128-135.

Understandings of Ordination," she describes six developments or tensions in the history of ordination as a backdrop to her arguments about the way the ministry of women changes the understandings of ordination.[45]

Brown Zikmund first explains that the practice by which the churches ordain their ministers, notably "the laying of hands", was a common practice in the postexilic synagogue. Existing leaders laid on hands to bless a new generation of elders who were chosen, or set apart, for a special office. This practice was also used in the first church communities. These church communities, however, used the pattern of the patriarchal household to organise themselves, thus they had local leaders and followed local practices of organizing their "household", and also received travelling apostles, evangelists and others. By the end of the second century, leadership of the church was consolidated around local elders and the bishop. Authority became a more formal matter. This consolidation marked the end of the previous situation in which local leadership was tempered by these travelling apostles, evangelists, and ambassadors, and there was a variety in the way leadership was organised.

Second, "ordination became a formal means of preserving the link between the apostolic witness (those who knew Jesus firsthand) and the ongoing institutional Church."[46] At first, the apostolic witness was not linked to the leadership of the (local) church but to the gospel itself or to the way the community lived its life in the light of the gospel from generation to generation, or it was recognised as an aspect of the leadership of certain leaders. But after several centuries, an "apostolic succession" of ordained leaders was established to preserve apostolic witness.

This is an example of the manner in which the Church followed the Roman matrix of thinking about tradition and authority. Here, the sacredness of the foundational moment is preserved by making sure that the present witness is linked back to the witness of the founding fathers. Ordination authorises the words and acts of this leader as words and acts that actualise the apostolic witness for the present. The importance of this step in thinking about ordination and authority is explained by the following development.

---

[45] Brown Zikmund, "Ministry of Word and Sacrament," 137- 143. Brown Zikmund writes that this reconstruction is based upon the work of Edward Schillebeekx, *The Church with a Human Face: A New and Expanded Theology of Ministry* (Crossroad Publishing & Co: New York 1985), 137 + 177 note 2.

[46] Brown Zikmund, "Ministry of Word and Sacrament," 138.

145

For, third, "ordination was meant to protect the Church from heresy".[47] The ministry of teaching and preaching thus became invested in the ordained leaders of the community. Using Arendt's ideas on authority, this meant that "apostolic succession" became not only a formal means to preserve the link to the founding fathers. It was also used to distinguish between "true" and "false" witness, or to determine which actualisation of the witness of the fathers was directed at the augmentation of the faith of the community and which actualisations could not be authorised, should not be obeyed or followed, should even be labelled "heresy" with the concomitant threat of hell.

A fourth step in the development of the ordained ministry was linked to the civic responsibilities the Church obtained in the centuries after the decline of the Roman Empire.[48] Thus the ecclesiastical hierarchy not only kept the faith in times of unrest but upheld the stability of society in the face of chaos. Arendt acknowledges this political power of the Church and attributes it to its authority to threaten with excommunication or eternal suffering.

The other developments by which ordained ministers were the only ones who could celebrate the sacraments, especially the Eucharist, or forgive sins, set them further apart from the laity. This "setting apart" was theologically justified by explaining that through the laying of hands the priests received a special power, whereupon "through him the mysteries of the faith found expression."[49]

The protestant Reformation challenged the power and the tradition of the institutional Church and rejected, among others, the special status of the clergy, emphasising instead the priesthood of all believers.[50] Luther foregrounded moreover the faith of the individual believer as well as the Bible as sole authoritative source of the faith. Both positions imply a breach from the idea that only the clergy had knowledge of what was true and good, or that they were the only ones who stood in direct line with the Apostles, and could determine what was apostolic witness and what was heretical.

With respect to the status of the ordained ministry, the Reformers were ambiguous, however. They rejected this special status of the priesthood on the one hand, but held on to the idea that the offices were also divinely ordained. Thus, Calvin advocated that it was the congregation that invested the ministers with the authority to preach and minister the sacraments. This meant that the

---

[47] Ibid.
[48] Ibid., 139.
[49] Ibid.
[50] Ibid., 141-143.

local faith community was given power over the minister, (although ordination in a local congregation is also understood as an affirmation of God's call to the ministry by the call of a local faith community). On the other hand, Calvin seems to hold onto the special status of the ordained minister when he writes that after ordination "[a minister] was no longer his own master but devoted to the service of God and the Church. As ordained servant of the divine Word he no longer speaks or acts in his own name but in the name of God," or as a representative of Christ.[51]

Thus, ordination sets the minister apart from the community, or places him in a position across from the faith community, a fact symbolised by the position of the preacher in the pulpit facing the community from up high. Using Arendt's analysis of the foundation of authority and power clarifies, that Calvin's view of the power and authority of the ordained implies a shift from the idea that the authority of the ordained is based upon his place in the unbroken chain of apostolic witnesses towards the idea that the authority of the ordained minister lies in a transcendent power calling this person to serve it by representing it in person.

The Authority of the Leader

Arendt's picture of the genealogy of the notion of authority clarifies that authority was thought to be legitimised by God. In this discourse, secular and religious rulers could understand themselves as servants or representatives of the divine Authority, including the power to threaten with hell and damnation in order to enforce obedience to their authority. This legitimation of the authority of the religious authorities is still present in the reflection on ordained ministry. In secular life, however, this discourse of the divinely ordained order of authority, whereby a King could understand his power as legitimised by divine Law, has lost its power in favour of a discourse about the strong leader.

The beginning of this discourse of the strong leader can be traced back to Thomas Hobbes, the philosopher of the social contract theory. Hobbes' point of departure was the contention that it was only possible to live together peacefully when everyone surrenders his (or her) freedom to pursue their own

---

[51] Calvin, *Institutes*, 4.3.16; quoted in Brown Zikmund, "Ministry of Word and Sacrament," 142. Calvin's formulation is oddly reminiscent of Plato's description of the relation between the ruler and the law: "The law is the despot of the ruler, and the ruler is the slave of the law." See Arendt, "What is Authority," 106.

interest in favour of the welfare of the larger group.[52] A social contract signed by all would be the only way to prevent an all-against-all war. In this social contract, the participants sign away their freedom to realise their own interest to the sovereign, a *Leviathan*. By this contract, the sovereign is invested with the responsibility to take care of the welfare of the subjects as well as with the power to decide what is (in) the interest of all. The sovereign has, moreover, the authority to make sure that (t)his idea is realised, namely, that the subjects really subject themselves to the authority of the sovereign and obey him, or her.[53] Thus, authority is defined in the social contract theory as the exercise of sovereign, social control by legitimate rulers on behalf of the public welfare.[54] The notion of legitimate rulers is important for this theory. The authority of the ruler is not legitimated by divine law or succession lines but from the bottom up, notably by the fact that "the people" have consented to be ruled by this sovereign – be it a single person taking the leadership position or a group of persons who together form a government – because they think that this sovereign will take care of their collective interests. In other words, the subjects subject themselves to the power of the sovereign but they do this consciously; they are not coerced to obey but consent to the authority relation installed between sovereign and subject under the terms of the social contract.

Kathleen Jones gives an interesting analysis of how this theory is permeated with gendered examples, connotations, and presuppositions, which in effect, make the picture of the sovereign gendered in the masculine. This masculinity of the sovereign comes to the fore by the slippages of Hobbes, when he describes the power of the sovereign as the power of the One over the many. Thus Hobbes writes: "A multitude of men are made *one* person, when they are by one man, or one person represented[...] For it is the *unity* of the representer not the *unity* of the represented that maketh the person *one*.".[55] This preference of the One and of Unity over the many can also be interpreted as a marker of masculine desire in discourse or of the phallic character of this

---

[52] This paragraph on the authority of the leader is largely based on Kathleen Jones, who shows that Hobbes describes a state of nature in which the sexes "had the same natural right to claim something as mine." Jones, *Compassionate Authority*, 45.

[53] It is noteworthy that although the dominant image of the strong leader is male and masculine, the sovereign is a "position" of and in political leadership. As such, this position can be occupied by men and women alike. Jones, *Compassionate Authority*, 46.

[54] Jones, *Compassionate Authority*, 33.

[55] Quoted in Jones, *Compassionate Authority*, 46 (emphasis in the original).

discourse.[56] It can also be seen as a consequence of the dominance of the masculine in grammar, ruling that masculine singular pronouns can be used in the generic – thus referring to and representing "the human subject" – or that a group of five women and one man has to be described using plural masculine pronouns.

Although the connection between authority and leadership can be traced back to social contract theories, it becomes more pronounced in Max Weber's discussion of leadership. Weber distinguishes between traditional, rational, and charismatic leadership. Traditional leadership refers to the kind of leadership that finds its foundation in respect for the tradition and for those who hold this position. Weber thinks of leadership that was inherited by its bearers and accepted by the subjects. One may think of monarchs, for instance, or of children of the founders of family businesses, but also of leaders of religious organisations whose legitimacy is based in the apostolic succession or in the practice of ordination of the religious leader of the local community.

Rational or bureaucratic authority is, according to Weber, grounded in laws and wielded by an administrative structure capable of enforcing clear and consistent rules. It is moreover based on competence and experience and not on inherited positions or family and network relations. It therefore rests "on the belief in the validity of legal statute and functional competence based on rationally created rules."[57] This also implies that leadership is not related to personal characteristics, but rather based upon education, experience, and position in the organisation or group (if leadership is approached from the perspective of group dynamics). The shadowy side is that the leadership of the organisation becomes faceless.

According to Moisés Naím, Weber applauded the rationality of the bureaucratic organisation, its specialisation with detailed job descriptions and its hierarchical structure with a clear chain of command. He also argued that "rational, professionalised, hierarchical and centralised structures were ascendant in every domain, from successful political parties to trade unions, 'ecclesiastical structures' and great universities."[58] The success of bureaucratic

---

[56] See Luce Irigaray, *This sex which is not one* (Cornell University Press: Ithaca, New York 1985), 68-85.

[57] Max Weber, *Economy and Society, An Outline of Interpretive Sociology;* quoted in Moisés Naím, *The End of Power. From Boardrooms to Battlefields and Churches to States, Why Being In Charge Isn't What It Used To Be* (Basic Books: New York 2013), 40.

[58] Naím, *The End of Power*, 41.

organisations lies in their efficiency, predictability, and stability. Procedures ensure equal treatment and control over the unpredictable. But the shadowy side of this kind of organisation is that the kind of knowledge that is deemed necessary for leadership can be described as "technical" and procedural, knowledge which one acquires through experience. This emphasis on techni-cal, rational knowledge – knowledge necessary to ensure a controlled and efficient organisation – constructs all forms other than instrumental knowledge as "irrational". It also contributes to the identification of authority with "the exertion of power over", notably over life as it is lived with its irregularities and surprises.[59] The notion that being an authority has to do with expertise and competence has inspired a movement to professionalise the ordained minister or priest, so that this professional would be more competent in managing the different processes in the religious community and able to offer a (rational) answer to the question "how are we going to do this?"

Although Weber's argument that bureaucratic leadership would affect every domain of organisation has proved to be prophetic, his ideas about charismatic leadership are now most often referred to. This can be seen as the effect of the dominance of rational leadership and of bureaucratic organisations, since the rigid-ity of rational leadership gives rise to a yearning for a different kind of leadership, one that can enforce change or transformation. This is why charismatic leadership is also called transformative leadership. Charismatic leadership can be described as "the power or ability to lead and inspire others solely by means of the persua-sive force of one's personality, so without use of coercion or material reward."[60] This is a rather toned down version of Weber's description of "charisma", which he described as "a certain quality of an individual personality by virtue of which he is considered extraordinary and treated as endowed with supernatural, superhuman or at least specifically exceptional powers or qualities."[61] Weber describes the charismatic leader thus as someone endowed with characteristics or competences that can be seen as special gifts, gifts from God perhaps?[62]

---

[59] Jones, *Compassionate Authority,* 129-130.

[60] H.P.M. Goddijn et al., *Geschiedenis van de Sociologie* (Boom: Meppel 1980), 178; quoted in Hazeleger, "Wat is leiderschap? Wat is leiderschap in de kerk?" in: Jodien van Ark and Henk de Roest (reds.), *De weg van de Groep. Leidinggeven aan groepen in gemeente en parochie* (Meinema: Zoetermeer 2001), 223-232, here 225 (my translation from the Dutch).

[61] Weber, *Economy and Society* (1978), (I) III, iv, 241; quoted in Jones, *Compassionate Authority*, 112.

[62] The word "charismatic" is derived from the Greek word "charisma" meaning gift of/ by grace. In 1 Kor 12: 1-11, Paul makes clear that the members of the Christian community are endowed

This description also illuminates why charismatic leaders are so often associated with heroism, with revolutionary heroes, with prophetic leaders. They think "out of the box," to use a contemporary expression, and they are moreover able to inspire a movement of change. Their extraordinary powers attract people, who listen to their voice and ideas and get inspired to follow these ideas. Their power lies in the fact that they bring about transformation, or engender the new. This implies that they have to prove themselves time and again as leaders worth following, for instance by doing extraordinary things to ensure the (miraculous) change in the lives of those that follow their directions. Although they do not need force to lead those they inspire, it is not easy for charismatic leaders to ensure the continuation of the movement they lead. In effect, their authority or power over their followers is uncertain, and they may turn into different kind of leaders, those who use coercive power to ensure the realisation of their dreams, when they do not accept that their followers turn to someone else.

Religious Authority and Leadership of a Religious Organisation: Same Difference?

Returning to the question of why "religious authority" is so often interpreted as referring to the leadership of a religious organisation, it may be taken to be the effect of the equation of two modes of "being authority" that dominate the discourse on authority: "being an authority" and "being in authority".[63] These two modes are presented as being almost identical, although they are not. The discursive genealogy of the concept "authority" shows that "being an authority" can refer both to someone who is an authority for someone else through a process of attribution of authority, and to someone who is (considered to be) an authority, because of her or his expertise and experience. These two modes of "being an authority" may go hand in hand, but they are not identical. Thus, someone may freely grant authority to someone because she or he inspires, evokes new ideas, prompts, encourages, or shows hitherto unknown possibilities. This person may be an expert due to professional training, but that is not necessary for the process of granting authority to someone else's words or acts. Expertise may be a prerequisite for positions of leadership, but it is not a requirement for getting acknowledged as an authority. For granting

---

with different "charismata", and that all these different charismata are necessary to build up the community.

[63] This distinction is derived from Leslie Green's lemma on "authority," in: *Concise Routledge Encyclopedia of Philosophy* (Routledge: London 2000), 68.

authority to someone else is not bound to the rules for the legitimisation of authority positions. It is a far more contextual and flowing, and perhaps "horizontal" process, even though authority relations between persons can be characterised as asymmetrical.

"Being in authority" refers, however, to the legitimisation of the authority. It asks whether someone is "by rights" in the position to command obedience and/or enforce interpretations, or in the position to govern or lead others. The discourse around the claim to such rights shows that these rights are variously established by an appeal to age old traditions of the founding fathers of state or church, to the invocation of rules, such as those of the social contract or of the bureaucratic organisation, or to the possession of gifts of grace, hence to the authority of the charismatic leader.[64] In everyday discourse, the distinction between "being in authority" and "being an authority" has become blurred, so that someone is thought to "be an authority" because this person is in a leadership position and can command obedience. Calling a leader of an organisation "an authority", however, only illuminates that this person has the position, with the concomitant rewards and responsibility, to take the final decisions. But once again, this being in authority by right does not necessarily mean that one is also seen and acknowledged as an authority *de facto*, as someone whose words or suggestions are thought to be meaningful and valuable to the ones who do the granting of authority. This necessitates that subjects freely grant authority to the one who is an authority – *de jure*.

As already indicated above, this identification of "being an authority" with "being in authority" has left its traces in the discourse about religious authority and about ordination. The dominant tradition identifies "being an authority" – understood as speaking authoritative words and giving directions to live according to the gospel – with being in the rightful position to speak authoritative words or with giving The one, authoritative interpretation. This equation has had very negative effects on the understanding of "being a religious authority". It has reduced religious authority to the power of the one who is in leadership position to enforce his or her interpretation of the situation, of the scriptures. Thus, it channelled religious authority in such a way that it became invested in one person or in one tradition at the expense of the voices and interpretations of the many. It has also limited the attribution of being a religious authority by right to the professionals, the experts, and the ordained.

---

[64] Jones, *Compassionate Authority*, 107.

This interpretation veils the many other relations in which authority is at work, not as an exertion of power over people, but as the transmission of tradition and affording orientation by interpreting tradition in light of the questions of the present – such everyday activities as raising children, coaching, mentoring, teaching, and keeping a network of people – or a faith community – together.

But why is it so important to make the distinction between "being an authority" and "being in authority"? My answer would be that it would make it possible to shift the focus from issues of leadership and the necessary capabilities for leaders of religious organisations, to the practices in everyday life in which authority is at work. In other words, it would enable a shift from authority *de jure* to authority *de facto,* and therefore to practices such as mentioned above in order to look for that that is meaningful and valuable in the words and gestures of the one who is granted authority in these everyday practices. This would imply that it would no longer be the prerogative of the one in authority to speak authoritative words, but that this would be determined by the many different practices of attribution of authority. It would also open up the floor for the authoritative words of those speaking from different locations in life and from different experiences about what might be understood as the word of God.

Attention to these practices may shed a new light upon what listeners and followers experience as words that "inspire, evoke new ideas, prompt, encourage and shows hitherto unknown possibilities."[65] In other words, it may shed light on which words and practices are understood to be authoritative about the good life *coram Deo* or experienced to be oriented towards growth, to be life giving, experienced as words that can be trusted and believed in, and hence, as authoritative words of God.

Why is the term "religious authority" often understood as "the leadership of a religious organisation" and not as imparting the authoritative words of God? This is the question explored in this paper. The author first identifies the sources that brought about her understanding of authority as a relational and dynamic concept, having to do with imparting words which inspire the other to grow, to realise what she or he may be capable of being. She then explains that this interpretation of authority comes close to an understanding of religious authority when connected with Luce Irigaray's notion of a divine horizon offering orientation for this process of growth. A religious authority would thus be someone imparting orientation through words valued as authoritative. This interpretation differs from the dominant interpretation of both

---

[65] Knecht et al., *ABC*, 25.

(a) authority as the power to command or enforce one's views, and (b) religious authority as referring to the leadership of religious organisations. Based on Hannah Arendt's text "What is authority?" and several other sources, the author traces the origin of this understanding of religious authority from the classical period to modernity. She concludes that the understanding of religious authority as the leadership of a religious organisation is the effect of equating "being in authority" with "being an authority". Whereas the former refers to the legitimation of authority and therefore the legitimation of the power to command, the latter presents authority as a relational and dynamic process that is not affixed to a position, but located in everyday life. Authority is freely granted to someone imparting orientation through words that can be trusted and believed in because they are life giving.

Warum wird der Begriff „religiöse Autorität" oft als „Leitung einer religiösen Institution" verstanden, nicht als autoritatives Sprechen göttlicher Worte? Dieser Frage wird in diesem Artikel nachgegangen. Dabei werden zunächst die Quellen identifiziert, die die Autorin dazu geführt haben, Autorität als ein relationales und dynamisches Konzept zu verstehen, das andere dazu inspiriert, die eigenen Potentiale wahrzunehmen und mit ihnen zu wachsen. Es wird gezeigt, dass diese Interpretation von Autorität im Dialog mitLuce Irigarays Begriff eines göttlichen Horizontes religiöse Autorität als einen Begriff erklärt, der Orientierungen für diesen Wachstumsprozess bietet. Eine religiöse Autorität ist, so verstanden, jemand, der oder die in Worten eine Orientierung vorgibt, die als autoritativ gewertet werden kann. Diese Verstehensweise unterscheidet sich von der vorherrschenden Interpretation, Autorität als eine Macht zu verstehen, die befiehlt oder die eigenen Sichtweisen durchsetzt, und Autorität als Leitung religiöser Organisationen versteht. Hannah Arendts Text „Was ist Autorität?" nutzend, zeigt die Autorin die historische Entwicklung dieses Autoritäts-verständnisses von der Aufklärung bis in die Moderne. Daraus zieht sie den Schluss, dass religiöse Autorität, verstanden als Leitung einer religiösen Organisation, das Resultat einer Gleichsetzung ist. „Eine Position inne haben, die qua Amt Autorität hat" ist identisch mit „eine Autorität sein" ist. Während die erste Interpretation sich auf die Legitimierung von Autorität und Befehlsgewalt bezieht, stellt die zweite Autorität einen relationalen und dynamischen Prozess dar, der nicht an eine Position gebunden ist. Er ist im Alltag verortet. Autorität wird hier in aller Freiheit einer Person zugesprochen, die mit Worten sagt, in was vertraut werden kann, Worte, die geglaubt werden können, weil sie Leben ermöglichen.

Anne-Claire Mulder coaches students during their training for the ministry and teaches women- and gender-studies- theology at the Protestant Theological University in Groningen, The Netherlands. Her PhD focused on the work of Luce Irigaray, and she has also written about dialogue, domestic violence, and human dignity. She is one of the ABC-Autorinnen. Her current research project deals with the role of gender in the various processes of the attribution of religious authority.

Journal of the European Society of Women in Theological Research 24 (2016) 155-167.
doi: 10.2143/ESWTR.24.0.3170031

Roberta Nikšić

Sociopolitical Engagement of Women Theologians in Bosnia-Herzegovina and Croatia

Postcard from Bosnia-Herzegovina

If I could send you a postcard from Bosnia-Herzegovina, it would be very colourful and bright, full of multi-religious and multicultural monuments. But reality is not so bright. Bosnia-Herzegovina has had a turbulent history. Populated since Bronze Age, Illyrian, Romans, Slavs, and Ottomans left their traces in mythology, folk tales, faith, art, and architecture. It was also in-between Catholic West and Orthodox East civilisation, and in some part of its history part of Ottoman civilisation, which had a great impact on its cultural and confessional character.[1]

Today Bosnia-Herzegovina is a post-war, post-socialist and ethnically divided country. Living in the Bosnian post-war reality for the last two decades has not been easy: it is an everyday struggle for a better life, for hope and peace. A negative peace, or the absence of war, has been achieved, but with unviable state institutions and ethnic divisions imposed by the Constitution coined in frame of the Dayton Agreement. The establishment of Dayton Bosnia-Herzegovina in the autumn of 1995, with its division of Bosnia-Herzegovina into the so-called two entities – *Republika Srpska* (The Republic of Srpska), which arose on war crime against Bosniaks and Croats, and the Bosniak-Croat Federation of Bosnia-Herzegovina and acomplicated Dayton Constitution, has so far proved itself damaging for the economy of Bosnia-Herzegovina and its cultural and political life in general. The constitutional framework of Bosnia-Herzegovina imposes and reifies ethnic divisions. Furthermore, the ethno-nationalist political parties have not done much to make the changes necessary to improve the social and economic well-being of their impoverished people. The Bosnian society is dealing with various problems: economic poverty, an enormous gap between pour citizens and rich war profiteers, ethno-confessional

---

[1] See Noel Malcolm, *Bosnia. A Short History* (New York University Press: New York 1994).

ideology, a status of permanent innocent victimhood among all nations, sanctification of the nation, wartime mass graves that are still being dug, and political marriage of religion and corrupted politicians.

Three ethnic groups reside in Bosnia-Herzegovina: Bosniaks, Croats, and Serbs, defined in the Constitution of Bosnia-Herzegovina as "constitutive nations" and not as national majorities and minorities. Their contemporary standard languages rest on a common linguistic foundation and are mutually very close. In spite of their linguistic closeness, they are mutually differentiated by separate cultural and political identities, and have different national narratives. Each of these narratives emphasises the originality of one's own ethnic group in Bosnia-Herzegovina's territory and projects it into the distant past, while the presence of the remaining two ethnic groups is more or less marginalised and viewed as an import from the outside, or the product of centuries-old foreign influences in Bosnia-Herzegovina.[2] Their God is their nation, to which everything is subdued, even their religion.

Religion is an important part of ethnic/national identity in Bosnia-Herzegovina for all three major ethnic groups. As religion and ethnicity overlap, it is perfectly clear and normal for the majority of people in Bosnia-Herzegovina that the Croat God has to be Catholic, and if you are not a Catholic, you can not be a true Croat. In much the same way, if you are a Serb you are Orthodox, and if you are Bosniak you are a Muslim. This coalescence of ethnicity and religion at the beginning of 1990s resulted in the harsh reality of the war, in which religion was used both as a tool in the empowerment of ethno-national agendas and goals, and to increase distance between the three ethnic groups. Scholarship dealing with the Balkan region in the last two decades shows an enormous politicisation of religion as well as a nationalisation of religion and God that reduced religions to mere nationalised symbols, celebrating a God who loves and prefers one nation over others and who assists in others' defeat. Some religious authorities went so far as to bless warring activities that resulted in persecution and killing, and most were silent about crimes committed in the name of their ethnic and religious groups.[3]

---

[2] See Srećko M. Džaja, "The Bosnian-Herzegovinian Croats: A Historical-Cultural Profile," in: *Croatian Studies Review* 8 (2012), 63-90, here 63-87.

[3] See Paul Mojzes, *Balkan Genocides. Holocaust and Ethnic Cleansing in the Twentieth Century* (Rowman and Littlefield: Lanham MD 2011); Zilka Spahić Šiljak, "Nation, Religion and Gender," in: *Politicization of Religion. The Case of Ex-Yugoslavia and its Successor States* (Palgrave Macmillan: London 2014), 185-210; Andjelic Neven, *Bosnia and Herzegovina, the*

It is only when people emphasise core common values, such as social justice, compassion, empathy, that they are able to transcend ethno-national divisions. Such was the case of a mass protest against a weak and corrupted government.[4] Bosnia-Herzegovina is blessed with cultural and religious diversity and a capital city praised as a European Jerusalem, but the country is also cursed with prejudices towards the different and the other. Bosnians are constantly building some bridges toward that other but at the same time fearcrossing these bridges.

What good can come from this small divided country? Is there hope for its inhabitants and the next generation? This blasphemed question has haunted me for years and years, and the subject of this paper is a hopeful attempt in answering it. All of our searching comes from our deep and emotional personal stories, and mine is no different, deeply affected by Bosnia-Herzegovina's recent past-war and war past. I was born in *Mrkonjić Grad*, a town in northern Bosnia-Herzegovina, today part of *Republika Srpska*. There was a time when three religious communities, Catholics, Orthodox, and Muslims lived there peacefully. Every year on Christmas and Easter, people from other religious communities and atheists came to our Catholic Church of Saint Jacob and Philip to listen to the choir. But suddenly, this friendly tradition stopped and members of the choir, along with other renowned and important Croat and Bosniak citizens endowed with a rich cultural and social heritage, became unwanted others. In those days, when religion was used in political scheming and war games, they became pawns. They experienced torture, humiliation, exodus, death. People from *Mrkonjić Grad*, all these heavenly voices from the choir and of my childhood memories were expelled from their hometown. Some of them died as victims of war, in forced exile, or in war camps. Some

---

End of a Legacy (Frank Cass: London 2003); Mitja Velikonja, *Religious Separation & Political Intolerance in Bosnia-Herzegovina* (University Press: Texas 2003).

4   February 2014 will be remembered for some of the most turbulent protests in the history of Bosnia-Herzegovina, when thousands of citizens in major cities took to the streets to speak out against economic hardship and systematic corruption. Most of the protests, during which several municipal buildings and the state presidency office were set on fire, took place in the mainly Bosniak and Croat Federation. Bosnian Serb political leaders went into overdrive trying to stir up bad memories of the 1990s conflict in a bid to undermine the protests and stop them spilling over into the Serb-led *Republika Srpska*. Much of the Federation-based media meanwhile focused on the destructive consequences of the unrest, labeling the protesters hooligans, rather than exploring their root causes in the country's problems with economic decay, deprivation, and corruption.

still live in exile. A few have returned to their homes and live as first Christians, silent and invisible, for they are unwanted there. Today, twenty years later, they are still the forgotten and unwanted others.

A similar story can be told of other religious and national communities in Bosnia. No one was spared in that war, and all suffered being the unwanted others in the eyes of the others. The war in Bosnia was stopped twenty years ago, but its inhabitants maintain a feeling of an unfinished war because nationalism, fundamentalism, and homophobia are present in the society – through the media, in schools and their educational system, even in religious communities, among Catholics, among Orthodox, among Muslims, without any difference. Nowadays, my motherland and hometown is a war victim, a widow, a beggar, a raped woman, a starved orphan, a mighty war criminal and profiteer, and a land of sorrow, familiar with suffering. The leper at the gates of Europe. Even if the story of my motherland has no form or charm to attract us nowadays, I wanted to hear her prophetic voices, so that she can be a prophet to me, to others, to us, so that we can all learn from her unresolved past, her unreconciled present. She, with her "face inhumanly disfigured" can teach us something: How can we possibly live with the burden of nationalism, fundamentalism and homo-phobia. Even when both my memories and views, and the prevailing public media discourse regarding Bosnia-Herzegovina, depict past crimes and current prosecutions, corruption, ethnic tensions, and ethno-nationalistic rhetoric, pro-phetic voices among women thelogians of different religious and ethnic back-grounds tell of a Bosnia-Herzegovina as a privileged place of Godly presence.

Voices of Women Theologians in Bosnia-Herzegovina

Some women theologians in Bosnia-Herzegovina have preserved hope at the time of enormous destruction and hopelessness of war. They did not vacil-late, hoping that good would prevail; they tried to give a voice to the voiceless, to help those in need, to promote women's human rights, to foster dialogue, and above all, to provide a "safe space" for telling stories and healing traumas. They had a vision of how to re-establish relationships between friends and neighbours in a divided and impoverished post-war society, as well as how to establish new ones for the sake of peace and reconciliation. They had been actively involved in peace-building in divided post-war communities.[5] Knowledge

---

[5] Zilka Spahić Šiljak, "Women, Religion and Peace Leadership in Bosnia and Herzegovina," in: *EWI Fellowship programme.* (http://www.eiz.hr/who-we-work-with/meet-the-local-partners/fellows/?lang=en/&lang=en, 1 February 2015)

and skills have been gained through formal and informal learning, for example in basic conflict resolution training and communication skills, peace building, non-violent communication, mediation, inter-religious dialogue, inter-ethnic and inter-religious relations, and peace training. Women theologians have also established several women's empowerment fund to raise resources as well as consciousness to the violence and injustice women face on the one hand, and the unique opportunities women have as key actors in their own development on the other. Women theologians also headed NGOs in the post-war period which supported multiple psycho-social projects for women across the region. They have enticed many people to walk the paths of peace as their intents were to bring hope and relief back to the life of returnees, women and children who had experienced various forms of violence during and after the war. They wanted to enable women's and young people's political and economic empowerment and to find systematic solutions to gender equality issues through laws, policies and mechanisms within state institutions. These women inspired many to join them on their journey toward peace, even though they were neglected by the media and in the political, national, and religious discourse.[6] Grassroots organisations were the only way for them to reach marginalised person at that time, and those were made of women mostly, because the state was too weak and preoccupied with nationalist agendas and feminism was considered "very fancy and unnecessary" in comparison with the "real problems".[7] They were faced with many other challenges when establishing their NGOs, because foreign donors sought partners among secular civil and human rights organisations and not among faith-based organisations established by theologians and religious communities. This may be due to the politicisation of religion, the involvement of religious authorities in blessing war criminals, the silence of religious authorities regarding crimes, and the close collaboration between ethno-national political parties and religious communities and churches in pursing their common agendas.

After the year 2000, the scenario changed, and faith-based organisations began receiving foreign funding for their activities, primarily through the offices of the Inter-religious Council of Bosnia-Herzegovina. One such case is that of the nongovernmental organisation Medica, headed by Sabiha Husić,

---

[6] Zilka Spahić Šiljak, *Sjaj ljudskosti. Životne priče mirotvorki u Bosni i Hercegovini* (TPO Fondacija: Sarajevo 2013), 328, here 6-7.

[7] See Elissa Helms, *Innocence and Victimhood. Gender, Nation, and Women's Activism in Postwar Bosnia-Herzegovina* (University of Wisconsin Press: Madison, WI 2013).

a psychotherapist, Islamic theologian and interreligious peace-builder. Medica is an experts' NGO that continuously offers psychosocial and medical support to women and children who are victims of war and post war violence, including war rapes and other forms of torture, sexual violence in general, and domestic violence survivors, as well as victims of trafficking in human beings.[8]

Sabiha first learned of the organisation while displaced from her hometown of *Vitez* to the city of *Zenica*, where she and her family had to walk in the course of thirteen nights in 1993 during the war. Medica was working in the refugee camps, and Sabiha recalls that "the approach toward women which I saw there gave me the reason to live, and my willingness to help other people was even bigger."[9] She became a volunteer, working directly with women survivors in areas where rape was used as a deliberate tactic in the war, oftentimes at great personal risk. It is estimated that 20,000 women were subjected to rape and other forms of sexual violence during the 1992-1995 war in Bosnia-Herzegovina. The survivors suffer from a sense of fear, depression, powerlessness, insecurity, and serious health conditions, with continuous recurring flashback.[10] In the Bosnian post-war climate, Husić urges reconciliation, bringing together women from all communities for workshops on stress and trauma, dialogue and conflict resolution. Along with its direct work with victims of war trauma and post-war violence, Medica implements a variety of educational, research and publishing projects focused on the promotion and protection of human rights, and the prevention and rehabilitation from war trauma, sexual and domestic violence. For example, approximately 7,500 women participated at Medica's trainings on trauma, gender-based violence and human women's rights, non-violent communication and conflict resolution, dialogue, reconciliation, inter-religious peace dialogue and co-existence. Thanks to Medica, women who survived war rapes received a legal status of civil victims of war.

The services provided by Medica include a shelter/safe house (accommodation, psycho-social work, individual and group therapy work, medical support and assistance), a psychological counseling centre, an SOS help-line, a Crisis Intervention Center, a Children's house and Drop-in centre, occupational

---

[8] http://medicazenica.org/uk, 10 February 2015.
[9] "Sabiha Husic of Bosnia-Herzegovina," Joan B. Kroc Institute for Peace and Justice. (https://www.sandiego.edu/peacestudies/institutes/ipj/programs/women-peacemakers/about/sabiha-husic.php, 10 February 2015)
[10] Mirsad Tokača, "Grijeh šutnje i rizik govora" in: *Svjetlo riječi* 340/341 (2011) , 6-59, here 6-9.

therapy, provision of legal aid, and provision of support and assistance to men in psychological counseling centre and on the field. Medica assists clients accommodated in its safe house in making contact with relevant government agencies (police, Social Service centres, the judiciary system, the Prosecutor's Office, Municipality administrations and other institutions) and non-governmental organisations for comprehensively exercising their rights and fulfilling their needs. Sometimes, this kind of mediation is also continued after their leaving the safe house, for example in trying to find a job or fulfilling other needs and exercising their various rights.[11]

In the first ten years of its operation, the main reason for accommodating clients in the Medica *Zenica* safe house was war trauma, whereas in the last ten years the predominant reason was domestic violence. During the past twenty years, it accomodated 1,078 women and 855 children. Unfortunately, this spectrum of different services attests to the fact, that people in Bosnia-Herzegovina have been daily witnesses to human rights violations, of which one of the most severe forms has been against women and children. Medica's experience shows that the most common reasons for women's not reporting violence are fear, fear of judgment, and often rejection of victims/survivors by their family and community. A very important additional factor is the economic dependence of women. For this reason, Medica was the first organisation that organised educational and supportive workshops for women and girls.[12]

Sabiha often collaborates with other women theologians. One such collaborator is her colleague, Zilka Spahić Šiljak, an Islamic feminist theologian, research scholar and public intellectual, with more than a decade of experience in the higher education and nongovernmental sectors in Bosnia-Herzegovina. Šiljak's research and civil activism focus on the nexus of human rights, religion, politics, gender, and peace-building. Her research has been included in such publications as *Contesting Female, Feminist, and Muslim Identities: Post-socialist Context of Bosnia and Herzegovina and Kosovo* (2012); *Women, Religion, and Politics* (2010); *Women Believers and Citizens* (2009); and *Three Monotheistic Voices: Introduction to Judaism, Christianity, and Islam* (2009). She promotes peace-building initiatives in Bosnia-Herzegovina and worldwide as well as peace and political leadership of women. She also offers women's narratives as a tool in peace education and the empowerment of

---

[11] http://medicazenica.org/uk/, 10 February 2015.
[12] Ibid.

women, locally and internationally.[13] Recently, Zilka has completed a book manuscript on women's role in peace-building in Bosnia-Herzegovina.[14] Drawing upon life-story interviews with women peacemakers of multiple ethnic and religious backgrounds, the book explores the sociopolitical and cultural challenges they faced, as well as the successes they achieved, while re-rebuilding peaceful relations in a postwar, ethnically divided society. It documents and analyses their contributions to reconciliation in a postwar, plural democratic society:

> [A]ccounts of these women's humanity can awaken younger generations who live today in ethnically homogenized communities in Bosnia-Herzegovina in ethnically homogenized communities. These young people should be exposed to peace narratives and learn that their next-door neighbor might be actively working on peace issues. The work of these women can serve as a model and inspiration for young people to do something by which new generations will remember them and that will provide meaning to their lives.[15]

Zilka Spahić Šiljak is also the director of Transcultural Psychosocial Organisation [TPO Foundation]. The TPO Foundation contributes to the development of democratic civil society through the promotion of research, psychosocial and intercultural program activities, and the implementation of standards for gender equality through various types of education, alongside raising awareness of these issues in local communities, especially through promoting gender sensitisation in Bosnia-Herzegovina legislation. It also promots intercultural dialogue, peace building and reconciliation in cooperation with relevant NGOs, both national and international. Among its projects one can find the development of the "My Business Idea, My Opportunity" manual, aimed at empowering women in rural and other areas. This is done through education and training, encouraging women to start their own businesses and engage in socio-political activity, such as the joint media campaign "Vote for Women," in order to increase the number of women in political life and state institutions. Recently, the TPO Foundation, in partnership with The Global Ethic Foundation from Tübingen, initiated training for secondary

---

[13] http://gender.stanford.edu/people/zilka-spahic-%C5%A1iljak, 10 February 2015.
[14] Zilka Spahić Šiljak, *Shining Humanity: Life Stories of Women Peacebuilders in Bosnia and Herzegovina* (Cambridge Scholars Publishing: UK, 2014).
[15] Ibid., xx.

school teachers, aiming to acquaint them with global ethic and qualify them to mediate global ethic principles and values to their students.[16]

Zilka and Sabiha promote in their work and lives principle of Islam, meaning that Muslim women should be active in their society, both as citizens and as Muslims. According to the Qur'an's ethic of friendship, women and men are *Hafiz*, friends on the same journey to make this world better place for all. It is their duty and their right.

Women Theologians in Croatia

Croatia is faced with several of the same chalengess faced by Bosnia-Herzegovina and all other ex-Yugoslavia countries: economic decay and deprivation, nationalism and enormous politicisation of religion, gender inequality and anti-gender cultural war, to name a few.[17] During and after the Croatian Homeland War for independence, there was also a need to estasblish a tolerant and peaceful society. This crisis situation inspired Ana Raffai to "work for peace." Raffai is a Catholic theologian born in Zagreb. During the war in Croatia, she took refuge in Switzerland where she became involved with a peace movement. After returning to Croatia, together with her husband Otto Raffai, she continued her engagement with the peace movement and was one of the first to spread the idea of anti-war action and non-violence. Today, Ana and Otto run an association called Regional Address for Nonviolent Action [RAND], through which they educate and promote the values of nonviolent action, combining spirituality, social engagement, and studies for different faith groups in Bosnia-Herzegovina and Croatia. Raffai calls this work a "*shalom* service," since its aim is reconciliation. Programs designed for faith groups raise topics such as Biblical prophets' protests against structural violence. Over the last ten years, more than five hundred people have taken part in these training sessions and workshops. Some of their trainees are now trainers active in peace education themselves. Small non-governmental organisations are of particular interest to Raffai, as she thinks they are like antivirus

---

[16] http://www.tpo.ba/b/ProjektiEN.html, 10 March 2015.

[17] See http://www.reuters.com/article/2014/05/04/croatia-economy-eu-idUSL6N0N827Z20140504, 14 October 2015; Sabrina P. Ramet, "What's Love (of Country) Got To Do with It?" in: Sabrina P. Ramet / Davorka Matić (eds.), *Democratic Transition in Croatia. Value Transformation, Educating & Media* (Texas A&M University Press: Texas 2007), 1; Šiljak, "Nation, Religion and Gender."; Rebeka J. Anić, "Gender, Gender 'Ideology'and Cultural War: Local Consequences of a Global Idea – Croatian Example," in: *Feminist Theology* 24 (2015), 7–22, here 14-22.

programs against war, important for the prevention of possible future conflicts.[18]

In 1994, Raffai was one of the co-organisers of the ecumenical prayers for peace, which took place every month in a different church of a different Christian denominations in Zagreb. In this way, she was able to use her knowledge as a theologian to connect actual peace issues with Christian values. In 2007, she was among the five enthusiasts who formed the Ecumenical Women's Initiative [EWI], a Croatian non-profit women's organisation seeking to support and promote women's active engagement as change-makers in both faith communities and society at large. EWI focuses on women's engagement in promoting women's rights, peace building and reconciliation, and faith-based ecumenical and inter-religious dialogue and cooperation. The EWI strives for a just and peaceful society, in which diversity is seen as a strength and source of creativity, in which women have a dignified place and role in private and public life in harmony with their competence and personal choice, and in which religion promotes and supports full equality between women and men. Local grassroots women activists and women theologians from all over the EWI region (Bosnia-Herzegovina, Kosovo, Croatia, Montenegro, Serbia, and Macedonia) are invited to share their vision of how to bring about change in their societal surroundings, and many of them are awarded EWI grants. Last year, EWI awarded society member Stanka Oršolić and her project, "Raising awareness of religious communities in Croatia on the issue of human trafficking (especially women)".[19]

Economic crises and a growing precariat, which deeply affected the life of women has been the urgent issue inspiring Sister Lilja Lončar, director of the NGO *Zdenac* (Vell), to cope with crisis in her own way. Lončar carries out charitable work with and for children of poor single parents in Croatia and cares for the poor and abandoned elderly. She is inspired by Latino American liberation theologians. Through her work, she strives to raise the level of awareness to the plight of those impoverished in every sense of the word, for instance in the frame of her project, "Education in solidarity and for solidarity," aiming to develop concrete steps on the path of liberation in schools in Croatia and Bosnia-Herzegovina. Through the theology of liberation, Lončar

---

[18] http://word.world-citizenship.org/wp-archive/478, 10 March 2015.
[19] http://www.croatianmemories.org/en/video-archive/ana-raffai/?search=subtitle&val=Raffai, 10 March 2015; http://www.eiz.hr/?lang=en, 11 March 2015.

contemplated and planned a new pastoral practice borne by those marginalised by society and in particular by women.[20]

Times of *kairos* in Times of Crisis

Through the work of grassroots organisations such as those mentioned above, many Bosnian and Croatian women from different religious, ethnic, educational, and economic backgrounds were educated in topics such as peace and non-violent communication, multireligiuos and ecumenic dialogue, and economic and political empowerment of women. Among them were women theologians from different Christian denominations and Muslim women theologians. In addition to the organisations already described, other NGOs run by women theologians include Mozaik, headed by Ismeta Begić and Nahla, headed by Đermana Šeta.

Women theologians are also involved in civil activism. The young Orthodox theologian, Marija Grujić from Serbia, began her study in Bosnia-Herzegovina and combined her scholarly work on themes such as gender, multireligiuos dialogue, modern national identities, and religion with civil activism. Julijana Mladenovska Tešija, an Evangelical theologian, and Sister Rebeka Anić also combined civil activism with scholarly research, especcially in the field of women's human rights, gender based violence and multireligious dialogue.[21] They all share and promote a vision of the social utility of knowledge, and the idea that feminist theological knowledge and civil action can change social surroundings that are unfavorable to women.

As a participant in the "Gender-based violence and multireligious dialogue" training course organised by Medica and the TPO Foundation, I have had the opportunity to hold workshops for women in rural areas as well asmeet women, civil victims of war, who became prophets of peace in their communities. The very fact strikes me: from inocent and silent victims, they became actors of peace and prosperity. Their personal painful experience became a fertile soil for nourishing a better world, a world of compassion, acceptance, and understanding, a world of love and friendship. They became the voice of

---

[20] http://zdenac.org/en/about-zdenac, 8 February 2015.
[21] http://www.fb03.uni-frankfurt.de/48468833/Marija-Grujic-M_Sc_, 8 February 2015; https://endingchildpoverty.org/en/resources/videos/134-end-child-poverty-ismeta-begic-predsjednica-uz-mozaik-za-medureligijski-dijalog, 8 February 2015; http://www.eiz.hr/who-we-work-with/meet-the-local-partners/fellows/?lang=en/&lang=en, 1 February 2015; http://english.nahla.ba/, 1 February 2015.

peace and forgiveness among Gods' children. From neglected, forgotten, unwanted others, they became a voice of empathy for all those in pain and solitude. Having been voiceless, they became a strong voice in the search for justice and understanding for all human beings. Once refugees, they became the builders of new relationships of freedom and safety for those in need. Having been banished from their own homes, they became the builders of new homes of comfort and safety. Without the work of the abovementioned organisations and theologians, this achievement would have been much slower. We can learn from them that times of crisis can be times of *kairos*. They were and still are messengers of hope in a hopeless world.

Christian and Muslim women theologians who have cooperated and worked together on mutual multi-religious projects, have crossed over the regional national borders aiming to increase the influence of women, both in their religious communities and in society in general. And they are still doing that. Their intention was to build and establish a more just and peaceful society. They had no time to think about developing new forms of contextual inter-religious theology nor about developing a regional theology of hope for those who suffer. Yet, they did actually develop such a theology, though they had not put their development in writing. They had worked hard in extremely unfavourable conditions for the marginalised members in their society, for women. And yet, these women theologians themselves were and remain on the margins of society and continue to work from the margin for the benefit of the marginalised!

Women theologians are neglected by the world of academic theological knowledge that is still reserved for men in these two countries, neglected by the prevailing public media, and most of the time neglected by religious authorities as well. For Muslim women theologians, the word *hafiz* became a transformative word of hope in promoting women's human rights within Islam and the society at large. By following this perception of Qur'anic friendship among women and men and their duty to strive and cherish social solidarity and compassion towards the marginalised members of the community, such perception achieved visibility in the above-mentioned work of Muslim women theologians. For Christian women theologians, the word "peace" became a transformative word of hope for a world wounded by war memories and traumas and the poverty and despair of their aftermath. The word "peace", as an evangelical category, became a tool of transformation from war to reconciliation, from poverty and despair to hope and prosperity.

Women theologians in Bosnia-Herzegovina and Croatia give rise to the hope that feminist theological knowledge may serve as a powerful tool in transforming our societies into more just, peaceful, and inclusive societies for all. This refers, in particular, to the theology arising among women, based on concrete experiences of concrete women, in concrete historical contexts. In the current case, this is the context of an impoverished society burdened with war traumas, but at the same time blessed with religious diversity. This ambivalence between religious diversity and exclusivity shaped these women's feminist theological practice. Their work took them across fixed religious boundaries, fixed national boundaries, and obstacles fixed by economic poverty and decay. More importantly, their concrete context shaped their feminist theological practice in such a way, that every single site of human suffering and torture became a site for practicing feminist theological knowledge. In a specific situation of war and post-war climate, they developed a specific form of theological answer to their problems: an inter-religious contextual theology, based and modelled upon the crossroad of inter-religious and cultural contexts of their two respective countries.

This article surveys the life and socio-political work of some of the most prominent Bosnian and Croatian feminist women theologians and their contribution to the culture of peace and hope. They are peacemakers, educators and enlighteners, writers, NGO leaders, civil activist and academics, sharing the vision that feminist theological knowledge can change social surroundings that is unfavorable to women. As theologians, they are dedicated to ecumenism and interfaith dialogue, socio-economic empowerment of women, and women's human rights. In our world coined by nationalism, a patriarchal way of life, socio-economic poverty, and wild capitalism, they present us with a vision of times of crises as the times of *kairos*.

In diesem Artikel haben wir das Leben und sozialpolitischen Arbeit einige der prominentesten Bosnisch und Kroatisch feministische Theologinnen und ihren Beitrag zur Kultur des Friedens und der Hoffnung analysiert. Sie sind Friedensstifter, Pädagogen und Aufklärer, Schriftsteller, NGO-Führern, Bürgerrechtler und Wissenschaftler, mit der Vision, das feministische theologische Wissen kann soziales Umfeld ändern, die für Frauen ungünstig ist. Sie sind für die Ökumene und den interreligiösen Dialog, sozioökonomische Ermächtigung der Frauen und Frauen Menschenrechte gewidmet. In unserer Welt, die durch Nationalismus, Patriarchat, sozioökonomischen Armut und neoliberalen Kapitalismus geprägt ist, sie bringen Vision dass Krisenzeiten die Zeiten der *Kairos* sind.

Mag. Roberta Nikšić is a theologian, civil activist and independent researcher. A student at the Centre for Women Studies in Zagreb, She lives and works in-between Bosnia-Herzegovina and Croatia.

Journal of the European Society of Women in Theological Research 24 (2016) 169-177.
doi: 10.2143/ESWTR.24.0.3170032

Natalia Salas Molina

Violencia de género: El caso de la mujer que mató a su marido

La violencia de género está presente en la actualidad a nivel global en diversos niveles, en Latinoamérica desenmascarar el patriarcado cultural y sus elementos dañinos para el género femenino es enseñar a mantener relaciones equitativas entre hombres y mujeres tanto en el contexto público como privado,[1] tarea difícil que nunca termina, especialmente en el ámbito religioso.[2]

Para ilustrar esto, surgió una noticia que conmocionó el interés nacional y mundial en la opinión pública, respecto a un caso de una mujer que mato y cocino a su marido en Chile, comentando este tema en los diversos grupos de mujeres evangélicas donde participo, se me ocurrió preguntar: ¿Qué hubiese hecho usted en este caso dado los antecedentes de violencia previos al suceso? Yo esperaba como respuesta que todas censuraran a la mujer, sin embargo, mi sorpresa fue grande cuando escuche a varias que me dijeron: "yo también lo habría matado".

Así, comencé a cuestionar esta respuesta, ¿Por qué las mujeres cristianas, que conocen el mandamiento bíblico: "No matarás"[3] manifiestan sin ningún freno que ellas también lo harían? y ¿Cómo podríamos juntas encontrar otras recetas frente a la violencia de género? reflexionando desde algunos textos del Antiguo Testamento relacionados que ilustran la temática del sacrificio como, la historia de Abraham e Isaac, la hija de Jefté y el cumplimiento de la profecía de Deborah a través de Jael matando a Sísara, para que nos iluminarán a mirar nuestros posicionamientos de género oprimido y buscar nuevas posibilidades de respuestas alejadas de la lógica reproductiva de la violencia.

---

[1] En mi rol de pastora, psicóloga y lideresa trabajo con mujeres en diversas iglesias evangélicas y otros espacios hace 25 años, la temática de la violencia aparece constantemente en sus diferentes expresiones, por esta razón intencionó aplicar un enfoque de género en las diversos trabajos que realizó, como por ejemplo, debo recordar y explicar que el feminicidio es una conducta aprendida y una amenaza siempre presente para cada una de nosotras.

[2] Michelle Perrot, *Mujeres en la ciudad* (Editorial Andrés Bello, Santiago 1997), 139.

[3] Éx 20,13; Mt 19,18; Mc 10,19; Lc 18,20.

Género, violencia y religiosidad

La violencia está tejida muchas veces con hilos que van cambiando y perpetuando su trama, las noticias sobre asesinatos son cotidianas lamentablemente, sin embargo este caso en particular nos hace detener la mirada, primero porque está invertida la lógica de género ya que generalmente son los hombres quienes matan a las mujeres y pocas veces estos es al revés; segundo, porque aun cuando se conocen otros casos de una mujer que asesina a su pareja son muy pocas las que cocinan partes de esos cuerpos y tercero, las mujeres que practican estas recetas se encuadran en alguna patología psiquiátrica, sin embargo, la protagonista, Rossana, no es diagnosticada como psicótica.[4]

En este caso particular, como consecuencia de sus actos ella es encarcelada, su condena en primera instancia fue de 6 años, pero posteriormente se redujo a 4 años. En una de las prisiones por donde ella circula, se convierte al cristianismo y comienza a participar de sus cultos evangélicos. En ese lugar donde está recluida,

> Ella comparte poco con sus colegas... Entre sus compañeras, esta otra interna, Gladys, quien participa de este grupo de mujeres evangélicas internas, cuando esta última supo que la condena de Roxana se redujo a 4 años, tuvo un ataque de furia, ya que la condena de Gladys es mayor, doce años sólo por matar y sin cocinar. Su condena tiene más años que la de Rossana porque nunca denunció la violencia que vivía de parte de su pareja y para colmo, sus hijos declararon en su contra.[5]

Revelar una pequeña porción de estos testimonios, permite visualizar la violencia que ha sido aprendida a través de los diversos sistemas en que participamos y que afecta a millones de mujeres, desde la unidad micro como la familia hasta las estructuras institucionales, pasando por los mandatos visibles e invisibles presentes en espacios que consideramos sagrados, Miranda señala que "La historia de la vida o práctica religiosa que concierne a las mujeres es una historia de altibajos, discriminaciones y en muchas ocasiones violencia",[6]

---

[4] Angélica Baeza, "Siquiatra de mujer que descuartizó a su marido asegura que no padece patología", en: *Diario La Tercera* (http://www.latercera.com/noticia/nacional/2015/04/680-626382-9-siquiatra-de-mujer-que-descuartizo-a-su-marido-asegura-que-no-padece-de.shtml, 30 junio 2015).

[5] (Entrevista inédita con Susan Vistozo Alcorta, Pastora, Capellana de Gendarmería de Chile, Centro de Cumplimiento Penitenciario Femenino Talca, de 3. 08. 2015)

[6] Gabriela Miranda García, "Mujeres sacrificadas y violencia religiosa: una discusión sobre el martirio y la religión patriarcal", in: Mireya Baltodano y Gabriela Miranda (Coord.), *Género y Religión: sospechas y aportes para la reflexión* (UBL: San José 2009), 41-58, aquí 49.

que constantemente es difícil considerar porque las mujeres estamos tan inmersas en la desigualdad de género, que este modo de funcionamiento habitual nos parece una práctica legitimada en los diversos ámbitos incluso, en las comunidades de fe, donde uno esperaría una mayor empatía entre las relaciones de género con las diversas jerarquías y pares.

Las mujeres hemos avanzado en nuestros derechos, pero este caso nos invita a reflexionar si la violencia ha salido de nuestro espacio o solo ha cambiado de disfraz, ya que las desigualdades de género persisten porque sus raíces están arraigadas en el tiempo y contexto. Tenemos percepciones que nos muestran posiciones marcadamente diferenciadas entre lo femenino y masculino, originadas desde un consenso donde "hay una marca histórica clara respecto de que el advenimiento del capitalismo y su efecto colonial propició de manera universal la desigualdad de género, legitimadas por el discurso cristiano que acompaño el proceso de expansión colonial", señala Montecino.[7] Las ciencias sociales nos enseñan, que en el periodo precolombino las mujeres por ejemplo, en la etnia mapuche en nuestra región tuvieron distintos posicionamientos, pero nunca sufrieron los niveles de violencia que viven hoy en día.

Desde la construcción simbólica de género podemos dar algunas pistas sobre el origen del desenlace de este caso. Rossana y su pareja compartían sus roles, aparentemente complementarios, por ejemplo: un horario laboral común en su negocio; sin embargo las posiciones en el día cambian, en lo público Rossana es socia del negocio, y está bajo las leyes del código laboral que intentan palear "las iniquidades que el sistema del estatus y su imaginario producen cuando las mujeres 'usurpan' los espacios considerados por este como propios y que otorgan prestigio masculino"[8] aclara Montecino, pero en la noche o en los espacios de ocio, probablemente ella se dedicaba a lo doméstico, cocinar, asear y cuidar de su bebé entre muchas otras tareas, mientras él se dedicaba a gastar las ganancias de ambos, incluso los bienes que sólo le pertenecían a ella según consta en los antecedentes del caso.[9]

---

[7] Sonia Montecino Aguirre, *Relaciones de género y vida privada en Chile. La casa y la calle*, in: Sonia Montecino Aguirre y Carolina Franch Maggiolo (Eds.), *Cuerpo, domesticidades y género: ecos de la alimentación en Chile* (Catalonia: Santiago de Chile 2013), 15-67, aquí 18.

[8] Montecino, *Relaciones de género y vida privada*, 23.

[9] (Entrevista inédita con Isabel Medina, Sargento Primero de Carabineros de Chile, Relacionadora Pública de la Iglesia Evangélica de Carabineros de Chile, Santiago de Chile, de 30.01.2015).

Para entender la dinámica de esta relación de pareja, ejemplo de tantas otras que padecen violencia, debemos mirar entre los estudios de género y ciencias sociales, sabemos que en nuestra geografía, en los pueblos prehispánicos de la zona central, las mujeres se encargaban de la alfarería, lo que permitió la transformación de alimentos crudos a cocidos y que la alimentación también estaba presente en las ceremonias fúnebres. Las relaciones sociales de género presentaban una posible relación de complementariedad, sin embargo ocurrió una mutación hacia el año 1000 a. c. donde las mujeres van a quedar en un nuevo orden de géneros, con una posición diferencial, que más adelante con el cruce del imperio inca acentuó la hegemonía masculina, como así también con los mapuches, y las mujeres van a ubicarse en la reproducción de lo doméstico en la agricultura, preparación de alimentos y utensilios según argumenta Montecino.[10]

Más adelante, la conquista de los españoles en nuestro país y posteriormente los colonos alemanes e ingleses trajeron sus modelos de género y sus religiones – católica y protestante – colocando límites a la esfera pública y privado, donde las mujeres continuarán ubicándose en roles de sometimiento y opresión, ahora dado por la cultura y reforzado por las religiones foráneas y en el último siglo por denominaciones evangélicas autóctonas aclara Salas.[11]

Bajo esta estructura de hilos escondidos bordados en la historia, podemos releer el caso de Rossana, quien junto a su marido sustentaban su familia, sin embargo esta armonía se rompe cuando ella recibe una herencia, que decide usar para comprar una vivienda y/o optimizar su negocio, en su escala social alcanzar una vivienda propia o ser microempresaria tiene que ver con la dignidad de ser mujer, la coloca a ella en un estatus superior frente a su pareja y desestabiliza el patriarcado, que nos dice constantemente que las decisiones de poder público son masculinas y las de poder privado, como la cocina, son femeninas.

Aun cuando algunas mujeres hemos salido al espacio público, la búsqueda de igualdad de géneros no logra romper el desequilibrio de participación en el entramado del poder, ya que en lo público las escalas de prestigio están en el dominio que se basa en estructuras de reputación y poder fundadas en la posesión y acumulación de bienes entonces, las mujeres al salir al espacio público

---

[10] Montecino, *Relaciones de género y vida priva*da., 26-29.
[11] Natalia Salas Molina, *Género y liderazgo religioso en mujeres evangélicas chilenas* (Diss., Universidad de Chile 2015), 29-51.

logran una emancipación explica Amorós.[12] Entonces Rossana al empoderarse en lo público y económico cambia las bases de la dominación existente.

Sin embargo, Claudio – el marido – bajo el orden establecido del patriarcado decide tomar el dinero de Rossana y gastarlo todo en su propio beneficio sin esperar ninguna grave consecuencia por sus actos, ya que para nuestra cultura las mujeres deben permanecer en lo reproductivo, subvalorado, no remunerado, sin patrimonio, idea reforzada cotidianamente por la visión teológica constante del sacrificio y el sometimiento femenino.

Bajo este encuadre, el desenlace de las acciones efectuadas por parte de Rossana a Claudio son un grito desesperado de intentar salir de la asimetría genérica establecida, por eso no basta con dispararle al tronco, sino que debe llevar el cuerpo a ese espacio donde lo doméstico tiene poder y valoración: la cocina. Así, "el cuerpo, la comida, la mesa, los productos alimenticios y sus formas de utilización –entre otros- se ordenan en sistemas de significaciones y sentidos que entregan las herramientas para comprender un mundo cotidiano promotor de discursos que establecen y formulan relaciones sociales"[13] plantea Montecino. Entonces, cuando ella utilizó elementos cotidianos como cuchillos y ollas se permitió ejerce el control femenino, y ubicarse en el polo del dominador, del héroe, del dueño de los cuerpo del sexo contrario, del que infringe castigos, el lugar del padre, realizando por una única vez una receta especial, extremadamente terrorífica, femenina, inesperada e irrepetible.

Nuevas recetas, otras oportunidades

Tras el debate de este caso, desde la mirada de género, intentamos en un grupo de mujeres[14] reconocer algunos imaginarios bíblicos instalados en el género femenino evangélico, entonces utilizamos tres textos bíblicos para discutir la posición de lo masculino-femenino y como se relacionan desde el plano de la violencia con el caso en cuestión.

Uno de los tres relatos que leímos, fue la historia que aparece en Gn 22,10, el relato del no sacrificio de Isaac por parte de Abraham, ("Y extendió Abraham su mano y tomó el cuchillo para degollar a su hijo"), pero recibió el

---

[12] Celia Amorós, "Espacio público, espacio privado y definiciones ideológicas de 'lo masculino' y 'lo femenino'", en: Celia Amorós, *Feminismo, igualdad y diferencia* (UNAM, PUEG: México 1994) (http://es.scribd.com/doc/55107977/Espacio-Publico-Espacio-Privado-Celia-AMOROS, 05 junio 2015).

[13] Montecino, *Relaciones de género y vida privada*, 9.

[14] Academia de Teología Femenina María Magdalena. www.academiadeteologiafemenina.com

mandato de no ejecutar la orden. Esta narración está muy presente en nuestra memoria colectiva y la asociamos al amor y la misericordia de Dios, más nunca hacemos una lectura referente al tema del parricidio, al menos desde nuestro contexto.

El segundo relato revisado fue el pasaje ubicado en Jue 11,30-31.34.39 donde sí se sacrifica a la hija de Jefté, cuando su padre

> le prometió a Dios: "Si me das la victoria sobre los amonitas, yo te ofreceré como sacrificio a la primera persona de mi familia que salga a recibirme" [...]...Cuando Jefté regresó a su casa en Mispá, su única hija salió a recibirlo, bailando y tocando panderetas [...] Pasados los dos meses, regresó a donde estaba su padre, quien cumplió con ella la promesa que había hecho. Y ella murió sin haberse casado.

Una mujer sin nombre, como muchas figuras femeninas en la Biblia, ella es violentada por la conducta verbal del padre que hace un voto, quien a su vez era el hijo bastardo de una mujer que se conoce por su oficio, la prostitución, siendo castigado por ello. Esta narración está envuelta en diferentes formas de violencia, historias que se cruzan donde todos y todas salen dañados, nadie parece ser beneficiado o beneficiada.

Isaac y la hija de Jefté son los corderos elegidos para el sacrificio, sin embargo como explica Navarro, "la hija de Jefté realiza un acto por cuenta propia antes de morir".[15] Isaac y su padre obedecen pero no reciben ninguna consecuencia negativa, al contrario todo es felicidad. Jefté y su hija deben cumplir los mandatos, y ella recibe en su cuerpo la sentencia.

El tercer caso bíblico observado, lo encontramos en Jue 4,21 donde la profeta Deborah llama a Barac y le recuerda que no ha cumplido el mandato de Jehová, así que le ordena atacar al ejército enemigo y derrotar al capitán de ejército Sísara, además proclama una profecía respecto a que su pueblo obtendrá la victoria y terminarán con su líder, pero no sería la gloria para ningún soldado sino que una mujer cumplirá la ejecución: "Y Jael, mujer de Heber, tomó la estaca de la tienda, y poniendo un mazo en su mano, vino a él calladamente, y le metió la estaca por las sienes, y la enclavó en la tierra, pues él estaba cargado de sueño y cansado; y así murió". Este relato muestra que en

---

[15] Mercedes Navarro Puerto, "El sacrificio del cuerpo femenino en la Biblia Hebrea: Jueces 11 (la hija de Jefté) y 19 (la mujer del Levita)", en: Mercedes Arriaga Flores / José Manuel Estévez Saa /Rodrigo Browne Sartori (Eds.), *Cuerpos de mujer en sus (con)textos anglogermánicos, hispánicos y mediterráneos: una aproximación literaria, socio-simbólica y crítico-alegórica* (Arcibel: Sevilla 2005), 227-242, aquí 228.

la Biblia Dios utiliza a ambos géneros para cumplir sus profecías, acá las protagonistas son mujeres, una profetisa y la otra ejecuta, así acontece un asesinato, donde las mujeres no son víctimas sino poseedoras del control espiritual y terrenal.

Estos textos ejemplifican situaciones de violencia legitimada e instalada como modelo de vida. Aun cuando hoy en día, ningún padre o madre sacrificaría a su hijo o hija, o enterraría una estaca a una persona del género opuesto, las relaciones entre los masculino y femenino siguen en una constante tensión. La masculinidad tiene asociada la violencia como un valor positivo, Abraham y Jefté son figuras paternas y bíblicas respetadas, que vienen dadas de un simbolismo que se encuentra en una persona de la trinidad asociada al género masculino, como afirma Roudinesco: "A imagen de Dios, el padre es considerado como la encarnación terrestre de un poder espiritual que trasciende"[16] así también, como principio de autoridad incuestionable y como modelo para los hombres en la tierra. Dado este patrón imaginario, instalamos uno nuevo: Dios es padre y madre o simplemente es Dios, no tiene género asociado, sino atributos.

A su vez, las figuras femeninas con conductas asociadas al polo de lo masculino, como por ejemplo Jael, aun cuando actúan como soldado, y ella es el instrumento para cumplir la profecía, no goza de la misma reputación y jerarquía que los capitanes o generales. Tampoco la hija de Jefté, cuyo relato refuerza la idea que las mujeres deben estar al interior de sus casas, en lo privado, porque si salen a la calle, al dominio público, sufrirán castigos como la negación de la maternidad e incluso la muerte. Entonces ¿Por qué Rossana es condenada sí todas participamos de modelos de vida violentos? y podemos suponer que ¡cualquier mujer dada las circunstancias puede ser Rossana! probablemente no disparando, cercenando y cocinando pero sí actuando la angustia en forma salvaje y desmedida como fruto exacerbado del patriarcado.

No obstante, los elementos de la cultura que se instalan como mandatos pueden ser desinstalados o al menos reflexionados, a través de reformar los afectos explica Segato.[17] El poder de las palabras puede oprimirnos o liberarnos. Estos textos permitieron abrir un debate sobre las posiciones masculinas

---

[16] Elisabeth Roudinesco, *La Familia en desorden*. (Fondo de Cultura Económica: Buenos Aires 2003), 22.

[17] Rita Segato, *Las estructuras elementales de la violencia. Ensayos sobre género entre la antropología, el psicoanálisis y los derechos humanos* (Universidad Nacional de Quilmes: Buenos Aires 2003), 145.

y femeninas en la Biblia, y advertirnos que aun en una cultura misógina plasmada podemos abrir nuevos patrones de relación, por ejemplo, facilitando espacios sociales y eclesiales donde las mujeres aborden sus experiencias de abuso y violencia, dolores y posicionamientos diarios, para que trabajen sus emociones de miedo, tristeza y furia que están en juego, usando lecturas bíblicas con enfoque de género que promuevan alejar sus conductas bajo la lógica de la dominación y la asimetría que ubica lo femenino como inferior y no tengan que repetir recetas de cocina fatales, sino prepara otros platos como una sopa de alegría y un plato fuerte de libertad y equidad con un sabor de mayor complementariedad entre los géneros.

La violencia de género es un flagelo siempre presente para todas las mujeres en los distintos ámbitos donde circulamos, develar las distintas aristas que conlleva este entramado significa destejer y tejer constantemente sus hilos. Aplicar los textos bíblicos como un mecanismo de liberación y no de opresión es lo que intentamos hacer algunas mujeres en el último lugar del mundo. El caso de la mujer que cocino al marido nos ilumina para hablar sobre nuestros propias violencias y mirar nuestras posturas junto a las posibilidades ciertas de avanzar hacia la paridad de género, bajo un paragua misógino y una relectura bíblica con lentes de género, en torno al tema del sacrificio.

Gender violence is an ever-present scourge that presents itself to all women in the many areas we frequent. Unveiling it means unknitting and reknitting its many strings. Applying biblical texts as a mechanism of liberation rather than oppression is what we women in the very end of the world try to do. The case of the woman who killed her husband enlightens us to speak about our own experienced violence and look at our own stance in order to see clear possibilities of advancing towards gender equality in misogynist conditions while applying a biblical rereading focused on gender and centring on the theme of sacrifice.

Geschlechtsspezifische Gewalt ist eine Geißel. Sie ist allgegenwärtig für jede von uns Frau in den unterschiedlichsten Bereichen, in denen wir uns bewegen. Sie wie ein Geflecht, in denen ständig alles miteinander verbunden scheint und die unentwegt neue Fäden spinnt. Dies gilt es zu entwirren und Gewalt zu enthüllen. Biblischen Texte als einen roten Faden der Befreiung hineinzuflechten und sie nicht zu Fallstricken der Unterdrückung zu missbrauchen – das ist des, was wir versuchen, wir Frauen auf den letzten Plätzen und untersten Rängen in dieser Welt. Der Fall der Frau, die ihren Mann tötet, zeigt uns unsere eigene Gewalt. Er gewährt einen Blick auf unsere Positionen im Zusammenspiel mit bestimmten Fortschritten in der Geschlechterparität innerhalb des misogynen Rahmens. Mit einer biblischen

Neuinterpretation unter Berücksichtigung geschlechtsspezifischer Aspekte, finden wir Möglichkeiten das zentrale Thema des Opfers und Opferns neu zu besprechen.

Natalia Salas Molina Magíster en Estudios de Género y cultura, Universidad de Chile. Licenciada en psicología, Universidad Bolivariana. Relacionadora Pública, Universidad Diego Portales. Bachiller en Teología, Comunidad Teológica Evangélica. Pastora Iglesia Metodista Pentecostal San Bernardo-La Portada. Directora administrativa, Academia de Teología Femenina María Magdalena.

Journal of the European Society of Women in Theological Research 24 (2016) 179-188.
doi: 10.2143/ESWTR.24.0.3170033

Jone Salomonsen

Sharing the Theological Hopes of First Wave (Suffrage) Feminists

2011 was an important year to Norwegians – a year of hope and crisis. The Arabic spring took place in Egypt and Tunisia as crowds of young people assembled in the streets, men and women together, demanding equality and democracy. Their peaceful movements pre-figured emancipation (to come) from authoritarian society. Five months later, the Occupy movement took to the financial streets of New York to set up a camp community, organise general assemblies, and by means of direct action, demand reform of the economic and social orders. The Occupy movement rapidly spread – to London, Madrid, Hong Kong, although manifest results of its utopian politics are still to come.

In between events in Cairo and New York, on 22 July 2011, Norway experienced the opposite: a terrorist attack. A white Norwegian took to the streets of Oslo, placed a homemade bomb outside the government building, and then drove his car to fetch a ferry over to the Utøya Island, where almost 600 members of the Social Democratic Party's youth organisation were gathered for summer camp. With his own hands (pistol and gun), Anders Behring Breivik killed 69 kids (77 died altogether, including in the government quarter). The massacre is the biggest attack on Norway since World War II. The perpetrator legitimised his actions by publishing a 1,500 page manifest on the internet. The text contains a critique of liberal democracy as we know it and a plea for a return to a non-democratic, authoritarian, patriarchal, ethnically segregated Christian state. His deeper mission is to save the values of white, Nordic masculinity and the honor of true Norwegian men, who supposedly are threatened by the politics of Muslim labor immigration, multiculturalism, and feminism.[1]

---

[1] For more on the terrorist attack, see REDO project, http://www.tf.uio.no/english/research/projects/redo/, and Jone Salomonsen, "Graced Life After All? Terrorism and Theology on July 22, 2011," in: *Dialog – A Journal of Theology, Vol 54, Issue 3* (9/2015), 249-259. (http://www.

In his critique, Breivik attacks the whole idea of egalitarianism, which in short means that he rebukes the full acceptance of the plurality of human morphology, sexuality, and subjectivity – as specifically felt or integrated into individual bodies – as a human birthright. As a first principle, equality is derived from the belief that all human beings are created in the Image of God and are therefore equalised as God's children. Instead of invoking this heritage line, Breivik returns to populist versions of Aristotle's old ideas that not all are fully human: there are naturally born slaves and there are naturally born women. These creatures are secondary – they are inferior, owned and meant to serve.[2]

Feminism as a social movement, aiming at altering law and custom, is less than 200 years old. Since its inception in the early nineteenth century, it has developed in what is known as "waves," depending on what was at stake, and the various strategies to "mobilise" women from a not-fully-human to an equal human state. Although a backlash on feminism had already been announced in the 1980's, and was followed by the argument that people had had enough, that society could not handle more gender-bending norms without losing sight of the "real" distinction between male and female, nobody could have imagined a backlash in the format of male cries for sheer patriarchy and totalitarianism in combination with violence and terror.

The Norwegian terrorist represents, of course, a tiny minority in our part of the world, and he is an outcast in terms of his methods, his killings. But his dystopian vision of a return to a pre-1848 civil state (revolution of the Paris commune) and a new bondage of women to tradition under the authority of men, is in itself a reason for theologians, as well as the Church. to get reacquainted with the whys and hows of the rise of the early feminist movement. First Wave Feminists struggled for rights which many of us today take for granted. Furthermore, women's fight for their own emancipation was interlinked with the anti-slavery movement, or in fact, historically, grew out of this movement.[3]

First Wave feminism, or suffrage feminism, as a social and political movement, started internationally in the 1830's and 1840's almost simultaneously in the United States, England, France, and Germany. Critique of women's

---

tf.uio.no/english/research/projects/redo/redo-publications/salomonsen-2015-dialog.pdf, 6 May 2016)

[2] Aristotle, *Politiken* (Paul Åströms förlag: Jonsered 1993).

[3] Estelle. B. Freedman (ed.), *The Essential Feminist Reader* (Modern Library: New York 2007).

ontological and social subordination in society and Church had of course been promoted by free-spirit thinkers for centuries, and was, for example, loudly present during the French Revolution. But "the woman question" did not evolve from merely being the topic of individual authors' radical thinking and agitation (or from civilised salon discussions) into an organised political movement until the nation-state became a reality, a form of representative democracy was established, and the bourgeois public became split over the question of who really constituted the people of the democracy: Who was to be included in democracy's vision of an autonomous people? Who belonged to this radically new category, and who did not? Who were free and equal "brothers" and worthy of the vote? Who could rationally represent the whole, the people, in the new democratic representative institutions?

The United States of America was the first modern republic constituted as a democracy, and the "woman question" was from early on an important ingredient in U.S. American debates on democracy and voting rights. Its driving forces were both women and men, many of whom were Quakers, radical Protestants, and religious freethinkers. What distinguished them from the contemporary 19th century Norwegian experience is that most U.S. American suffragists had been active in the struggle against slavery. This experience in itself was an integral part of how and why they turned to feminism.[4]

The U.S. American anti-slavery movement, the so-called abolitionists, became a distinct public voice during the 1770s. It was closely associated with the struggle for independence from British colonial rule and a yearning for new governance, and slowly built a large following. As part of their struggle, the reformers educated the citizenry about what slavery actually was, criticised churches' slave-legitimising Bible interpretation, and appealed to people's conscience to rethink right and wrong. They also organised practical run-away assistance to plantation slaves through the so-called "Underground Railroad".[5] Many U.S. American women got involved in this sometimes dangerous work and learned at the same time to mobilise and advocate for noble political and moral causes in general.

In 1831, the movement was formalised into the "American Anti-Slavery Society". Discussions immediately started over the appropriate roles of women and men, and their proximate relations: Could they belong to the same

---

[4] Sarah Knott and Barbara Taylor (eds.), *Women, Gender and Enlightenment* (Palgrave MacMillan: UK 2005).

[5] Ibid.

association? Was it respectable? Could women speak at general meetings and to the public? Could they vote, hold positions, and act as leaders? A lot of women were radicalised by the resistance they met in these so-called emancipatory circles and began to see a clearer link between slavery, racism, class division, economic exploitation, and their own gendered non-citizenship in a burgeoning new democracy. The first national gathering of women that explicitly addressed the problems was held in Seneca Falls, upstate New York, in 1848.[6]

Why was it so difficult to get rid of slavery? And how were arguments that defended slavery linked with arguments that kept women in place? In both cases, we are confronted with questions about nature and the belief that some people are not fully-human but eternally born with a second-class nature, at least when compared to the adult white male prototype, "the" human person.

If we start by taking a closer look at the concepts and arguments in the United States "Declaration of Independence" from 1776, we must first acknowledge the Declaration's originality. This document is the first repudiation ever of inborn differences between people that had been negotiated as a statement collectively and in public. Also, the Declaration summarised sentiments already manifested in actions.[7] The thirteen British colonies along the Atlantic coast broke their filiations with the British Empire and declared themselves a union of independent states on 4 July 1776. Instead of demanding reform from King George and the unpopular British rule, the colonies breached off and formulated a new representative government by and for the people. But the process had been going on for a long time and was fully in accord with Enlightenment ideals. The Declaration typically started by affirming the right of U.S. Americans to a "separate and equal station to which the Laws of Nature and of Nature's God entitle them." Then, and in respect for "the opinions of mankind," they declared and explained why egalitarianism was a natural right:

> We hold....that all men are created equal, that they are endowed by their Creator with certain unalienable Rights, that among these are Life, Liberty and the pursuit

---

of Happiness. – That to secure these rights, Governments are instituted among Men, deriving their just powers from the consent of the governed, – That whenever any Form of Government becomes destructive of these ends, it is the Right of the People to alter or to abolish it, and to institute new Government.[8]

The freedom to develop a new sort of governance was proclaimed to be the sovereign right of the people since governments obtain all their legitimacy from "the consent of the governed," and not from inherited traditions, nor from any God.

The U.S. American judgment of British colonial power was in 1776 merciless: "The history of the present King of Great Britain is a history of repeated injuries and usurpations, all having in direct object the establishment of an absolute Tyranny over [America]."[9] To prove the claim, a number of "facts" were presented to "a candid world." The aim of these explications was to educate the thinking of individuals and of states, not to offer prayers to a higher power or to God the Almighty. Yet, the British refused to be "educated," and the War of Independence (or the Revolutionary War) lasted for six years. With France's military assistance, the United States of America finally won, and on 30 September 1783, the Paris Agreement was signed. Four years later, on 17 September 1787, and two years before the French Revolution (1789), the "Declaration of Independence" could be replaced by the "US Constitution," and the world's first modern democracy became a reality. Like the Norwegian constitution, it is one of the oldest in the world still in use.

The alternative vision of the founding U.S. American fathers was not a secular instead of a religious one, but rather to conceptualise all forms of authority horizontally instead of vertically. By invoking phenomenological knowledge of "life itself" as can be observed and acknowledged by anyone, the men of the revolution turned the nature argument on its head. Instead of using nature to sort people hierarchically into biologically explained classes and casts, they now used the argument to tear down divides and promote kinship and equality. Being born of female womb equalised being born similarly and equally, and meant to have inherited the same natural rights. Being born was, in other words, the same as being created by God. This allowed for a

---

[8] *The United States Declaration of Independence.* (http://www.archives.gov/exhibits/charters/declaration_transcript.html, 3 April 2016)
[9] Ibid.

radically new anthropology in the conception of the state and gave weight to birthright as a new, legal principle.

Yet, women's freedom requested that even the basics of spiritual brotherly kinship and similitude were challenged. According to political scientist Carole Pateman, liberal democracy means that society is no longer based on a duplication of the house and its clan structures, with a "king" at the top, but is constituted as a contract between equal parties.[10] In liberal thinking, modern society is the result of representative public negotiation, not the power to give orders in a lineage. Democracy's self-understanding is therefore that the "natural" powers of the fathers have given way to brotherhood and its "natural" egalitarianism as society's basic principle. Brotherhood, in other words, is what distinguishes modern from pre-modern societies. The power of Birthright invoked in the United States "Declaration of Independence," where a male person is entitled to his rights regardless of whether he is recognised as the son of a particular father, is thus radically different from, for example, Roman law, where the paterfamilias was the sovereign entity exactly because of his power to decide over a son's life and death.

Yet, contract society did not mean that patriarchy disappeared; only that it took on a new form. Carole Pateman clearly believes that the new distinction between public and private, implicit in a modern contract society, was crucial for the transformation of patriarchy. The distinction makes it possible for a state to have two sets of norms for society at the same time: a democratic, negotiated norm set for public policy on the one hand, and a private, authoritarian norm set for the home sphere on the other. While the brotherhood principle governs the public domain, the authoritarian-father institution of the past can continue its old hegemony in the home (albeit in modified form, as for example when social democratic political legislation interferes in the internal affairs of home and forbids corporal punishment of children).

The additional problem for theology is that it is still unclear whether the Church" or "House of the Lord belongs to the protected private sphere and can continue to be organised as a pre-modern ancestral institution (although it has to accept certain coercive reform elements as demanded by the state in all democratic nations, such as a minimum of employment rights); or if the Church really is a public institution that must change its constitution and be reformed when society reforms.

---

[10] Carole Pateman, *The Sexual Contract* (Stanford University Press: Stanford 1988).

However, the "Women's Rights Convention" in Seneca Falls in 1848 both copied and critiqued the regulatory text of the U.S. constitution. Women critiqued the fact that men in 1776 merely distributed equality between themselves, and that they only applied it to men of a certain race and social standing, that is, to taxpaying men with property and income. However, the prelude to the women's meeting in 1848, and the reason why U.S. American suffragettes organised themselves into a separate political body and movement so quickly, was, in fact, the scandal at the "London Anti-Slavery Convention" in 1840. The two abolitionists, Lucretia Mott and Elizabeth Cady Stanton, met as official U.S. delegates in London, but it turned out that the conference was only for men. The women could therefore neither participate in the assembly nor speak, but had to sit in a special gallery as observers and silently listen to the men's debate. The famous Quaker woman, Lucretia Mott, was finally invited to give her prepared speech in the Unitarian Church. This was unheard news and the church was packed. The experience became a dramatic turning point for many. In her speech, Mott applied the abolitionists' critique of slavery to women's situation and to their lack of basic human birthrights. In doing so, Mott broke the years-long and tacit political agreement among radical anti-slavery reformers that emancipation of slaves had to he reached before freedom for women could become a public concern.[11]

When Lucretia Mott and Elizabeth Cady Stanton reinterpreted the U.S. Declaration of Independence at Seneca Falls in 1848, they simultaneously submitted a feminist version, the "Declaration of Sentiments (and Resolutions)" to the delegates. Way ahead of their time, they consistently used a gender inclusive language and extended their fight for freedom from British tyranny to include freedom from the rule of fathers. Although the text was modeled after the famous Declaration of Independence and systematically applied its famous analysis of human freedom to gender, the women did not call for gender separatism or asked other women to throw off fathers, husbands, brothers, and sons and withdraw to an alternative social world. Rather, they formulated women's rights as reachable within a democratic framework.

In addition to replacing the generic "man" with a more inclusive "women and men," descriptions of Kings' despotism was replaced by patriarchal tyranny.[12] The Declaration of Sentiments reads: "The history of mankind is

---

[11] Malone, *Women and Christianity*.

[12] For the radicality of their thinking, see Elizabeth Cady Stanton, *The Woman's Bible (I-II)*, (1895-1898). (http://www.sacred-texts.com/wmn/wb/, 3 April 2016)

a history of repeated injuries and usurpation on the part of man toward woman, having in direct object the establishment of an absolute tyranny over her."[13] While Kings were tyrants in certain historical periods, men have always ruled over women, was the message. Thus, there is no "empty land" that women can flee to in order to cast off their patriarchal tyrants. Change must take place in the actual society.

To prove that their critique of patriarchy was correct, and also to contribute to the education of "a candid world," the Declaration of Sentiments presented "numerous facts" about men's oppression of women per 1848. It opened by critiquing men for having held back women's "unalienable rights" and for keeping up marriage laws that almost made women a person's property, and therefore "civilly dead." It further expressed that men had monopolised all occupations, shut women out of school and education, given her a subordinate position both in Church and in state, and excluded her from the priesthood:

> He allows her in Church as well as State, but a subordinate position, claiming Apostolic authority for her exclusion from the ministry [...] He has usurped the prerogative of Jehovah himself, claiming it as his right to assign for her a sphere of action, when that belongs to her conscience and to her God.[14]

Like their "founding fathers," and in line with the Protestant traditions, suffrage feminists appealed both to the authority of the heart's inner voice and to the autonomy of conscience, including women's conscience, and demanded that women too must decide which functions and tasks they should have or not have in society. To take up roles ascribed by their brethren and not themselves was considered nothing less than blasphemous. Alas, the equal-rights feminists in Seneca Falls started to criticise the brotherhood's abuse of power by means of theological reinterpretations and referrals to enlightenment ideals. For not only was democracy closed to women, the democratic "person" was in reality constructed as a wealthy white man, against the word of "her God." Slaves and women were perhaps people, partly in need of freedom, but not persons as in the meaning of "brother." Consequently, the Declaration of Independence was critiqued for partiality, and therefore as merely tentative in authority. Of the more than three hundred delegates present in Seneca Falls, 68 women and 32 men signed the new Declaration of Sentiments in protest.

---

[13] *Declaration of Sentiments (and Resolutions)*. (http://ecssba.rutgers.edu/docs/seneca.html, 3 April 2016)
[14] Ibid.

There is intended ambiguity in the Declaration of Independence between the external God-principle invoked to anchor human equality, partly from above, and the internal, creative Human constructed-principle invoked to anchor abolishment and reinstitution of government, fully from below. To vivify the challenges posed by First Wave feminists, still unanswered by a majority of churches, I suggest that, as an exercise, we exchange "men" with "women and men," "government" with "sacred texts" or "spiritual practices,", and "governed" with "worshipping community" in the following famous paragraph of the Declaration of Independence, and see where it takes us:

> We hold... that all men and women [men] are created equal, that they are endowed by their Creator with certain unalienable Rights, that among these are Life, Liberty and the pursuit of Happiness. – That to secure these rights, sacred texts and spiritual practices [Governments] are instituted among men and women [Men], deriving their just powers from the consent of the worshipping community [governed], – That whenever any (ecclesiastical) practice [Form of Government] become destructive of these ends, it is the Right of the worshipping community [People] to alter or to abolish it, and to institute new texts and new practices [Government].[15]

As we can see, the structure and meaning of the constitutional text are not significantly altered by exchanging gender-exclusive for gender-inclusive language, or by substituting all modalities of "govern" with sacred texts, practices or worshipping community, or just by variations of "practice." A new rule of government for institutions beyond the state was clearly thinkable 200 years ago and already structurally embedded as a possibility in this foundational text. For the text may include more issues and embrace a larger representative body without being altered in its core. Therefore, it was the actual tearing down of authoritarian notions of social heads and fathers, and of their material manifestations in the real world, that took courage. The combination of radical thinking and exceptional practical courage is what in the end gave us democracy. And only this combination can change the Church towards a more feminist ethical design.

What would happen in Europe if a democratic political address is extended to include sacred texts and spiritual practices? As we know, ecclesiastical changes are taking place. Texts are retranslated, canons are altered, new liturgies and rituals are emerging, Churches are experimenting with participatory democracy. Yet, this reform work may turn out to be more crucial than what may be fully grasped from the pulpit and the religious classroom. For if a new

---

[15] *Declaration of Independence.* The terms substituted for are shown in brackets.

form of ultraconservative political populism is about to take hold of a growing number of young males in Europe today, tainted with sentiments and death-drives from the Radical Right, the Church is called to radically choose public over private life and to re-cultivate its knowledge of the sociality of God in the collective lives of humans. To govern horizontally and by the inclusion of new sacred texts and practices may turn out to be the best re-skilling gift people can hope to get from Church in our time, at least when it comes to finding community, opening the hearts, and start caring about the fear and pain of others. This is not a call to construct a new anti-slavery movement of old, but a new anti-totalitarianism movement of the present that will guard against throwing women back to a pre-ordained gendered cosmos, race to the centre stage, and civilisation back to hierarchy and violence.

This article discusses the alternative vision of the U.S. American constitution and its early feminist critique, and argues that both vision and critique are relevant in a contemporary European setting. The U.S. 1776 Declaration of Independence conceptualised authority more horizontally and used the nature argument to promote kinship and equality, not division. Being born equalised being created by God, which meant inheriting the same unalienable, natural rights. This allowed for a radically new anthropology and gave weight to birthright as a new, legal principle. The "natural" powers of fathers had to yield to the "natural" egalitarianism of brotherhood as society's basic principle. Yet, patriarchy did not disappear. A new distinction between the public and private spheres made it possible for the state to have two norm-sets for society simultaneously: a democratic, negotiated norm-set for polity and a private, authoritarian norm-set for the home and church. The early feminists critiqued the founding fathers for merely distributing equality to their sons, and argued that women's freedom required that also the basics of spiritual brotherly kinship and similitude were changed. An additional theological problem is whether the Church truly belongs to its assigned private sphere and can continue to be organised as a pre-modern ancestral institution, or whether the Church is a public institution that must be reformed when society reforms. If it is not reformed, how will Church meet the rise of ultraconservative political populism among a growing number of young males in Europe today, and counter their yearning to put women back into place – once again?

Jone Salomonsen, Professor of Theology, is Chair of Interdisciplinary Gender Studies in Theology and Religion, University of Oslo. She holds a joint degree in theology and anthropology, and wrote her ethnographic dissertation Enchanted Feminism (2002) on goddess pagans in San Francisco. Salomonsen currently leads "Reassembling Democracy. Ritual as Cultural Resource", http://www.tf.uio.no/english/research/projects/redo/.

Journal of the European Society of Women in Theological Research 24 (2016) 189-201.
doi: 10.2143/ESWTR.24.0.3170034

Maria Ch. Sidiropoulou

Negotiating Female Identity in the Jewish Community of Thessaloniki: Between Tradition and Modernity

Introduction: The Jewish Presence in Thessaloniki – Historical Background

Exploring the relationship between female and Jewish identity is necessarily a multidisciplinary project, founded on the study of the religious component in the context of academic fields such as anthropology, ethnography of religion, and sociology of religion.[1] As the researcher delves deeper into religious communities, she or he wonders: What is the tripartite relationship between tradition, the female sex, and modernity? In Greece, several theological and sociological approaches to gender issues have been expressed, based on the Orthodox Christian tradition and the Church.[2] But what is the position of women in a Jewish communal world and the Greek context?

This paper discusses the modern identity of women in the Jewish community of Thessaloniki. It aims to investigate the multidimensional presence of Jewish females as agents of the cultivation and transmission of Jewish ethno-religious culture and identity. Is the female voice really heard today, or is it simply listened to? Is this voice heard in an institutional way in the communal setting?

---

[1] For various aspects of the Jewish female identity, see, Mary Neitz, "Gender and Culture: Challenges to the Sociology of Religion," in: *Sociology of Religion* 65/4 (2004), 391-402; Harriet Hartman, Moshe Hartman, "Gender and Jewish Identity," in: *Journal of Contemporary Religion* 18/1 (2003), 37-60; Lori Lefkovitz, "Passing As a Man: Narratives of Jewish Gender Performance," in: *Narrative* 10/1 (2002), 91-103.

[2] For theology, see, indicatively, Dimitra Koukoura, *Η Θέση της Γυναίκας στην Ορθόδοξη Εκκλησία [The Position of Woman in the Orthodox Church]* (Sfakianakis: Thessaloniki 2005). For sociology, see Ioannis Petrou, "Το Ζήτημα των Γυναικών και η Εκκλησιαστική Παράδοση" ["Women Matter and the Ecclesiastical Tradition,"] in: *Scientific Annals of School of Theology A.U.TH.* 10 (2000), 221-237; Ioannis Petrou, "Φύλο, Κοινωνικοί Ρόλοι και Ορθοδοξία στην Ελληνική Πραγματικότητα" ["Gender, Social Roles and Orthodoxy in Greek Reality,"] in: *Scientific Annals of School of Theology A.U.TH.* 11 (2001), 253-263; Niki Papageorgiou, "The Position of Woman in the Orthodox Church," in: Christina Breaban, Sophie Deicha, Eleni Kasselouri-Hatzivassiliadi (eds.), *Women's Voices and Visions of the Church, Reflections of Orthodox Women* (World Council of Churches 2006), 97-104.

What is its collective expression in the religious and communal milieu, and how does it manifest itself within the community and outside of it?

The delineation, highlighting, and interpretation of the unique features of the contemporary female Jewish identity are made possible through observation of their daily lives, including their customs, worship, and communal lives. To achieve this end, this presentation will be based on empirical data from fieldwork conducted as part of an ongoing research.

At the outset of our historical overview of the Jewish presence in Thessaloniki, we should note that despite the initial existence of four ethnic groups of Jews – the Romaniotes (316-140 BCE, from Alexandria, Egypt), the Ashkenazim (1376-1470, from Central Europe), the Italiotes (1536, from Italy) and the Sephardi/Sephardim (1492-93, from the Iberian Peninsula) – the dominant identity is Sephardic, or Judaeo-Spanish.[3]

On 31 March 1492, following the famous Alhambra Decree, the Catholic monarchs of Spain ordered all Jews to leave the country. From the end of the 15th century and into the 16th, Sephardic Jews arrived in the Ottoman Empire, leading to the so-called "golden" period for Thessalonian Judaism, at the intellectual-religious, professional, and economic levels.[4]

In the following centuries, in the Eastern European world – as opposed to the Western European one – female identity was shaped not only within the confines of the house, but also by the local culture, by women's matrimonial status, and by their social class.[5] At the same time, however, indigenous women in the Western European world occupied themselves primarily with activities related to their family and household environment. This includes the extroverted Sephardic newcomers who originated from a different cultural background and, unlike their coreligionists in North Africa, the Near and Middle East, were not bound by an autocratic understanding of their husband's role.[6]

---

[3] See Joseph Nehama, *Ιστορία των Ισραηλιτών της Σαλονίκης [History of the Jews of Salonika]* (University Studio Press: Thessaloniki 2000), A', 77, 131, 115, 167-168.

[4] Nehama, *History of the Jews of Salonika*, 115, 301.

[5] See Lisa Pine, "Gender and Holocaust Victims: A Reappraisal," in: *Journal of Jewish Identities* 1/2 (2008), 121-141, here 124-125.

[6] See Rena Molho, *Οι Εβραίοι της Θεσσαλονίκης, 1856-1919: Μια Ιδιαίτερη Κοινότητα [The Jews of Thessaloniki, 1856-1919: A Special Community]* (Themelio: Thessaloniki 2001), 152; John Megas, *Ενθύμιον από τη Ζωή της Εβραϊκής Κοινότητας - Θεσσαλονίκη 1897-1917 [Souvenir from the Life of the Jewish Community - Thessaloniki 1897-1917]* (Capon: Athens 1993), 5.

In spite of a crisis in the 17-18th centuries,[7] the Jewish Community rose to prominence again from the middle of the 19th to the early 20th century, with the modernisation of Thessaloniki and the arrival of the liberal, French-based Jewish organisation, "Alliance Israélite Universelle" [A.I.U.] in the years 1873-1910).[8] It is worth noting that with the assistance of the A.I.U., which held the woman to be "Equal to the man, (as) his partner in life",[9] and in cooperation with female figures from the bourgeoisie and the community institutions, the position of the Jewish woman was redefined. Women's activities were expanded into the public sphere, particularly in education and social welfare, and the first women's faculties, professional training centres, and girls' schools were established. In some of these, women held administrative positions. Some examples include the remarkable work done by women at a private Jewish school for girls (1867), a vocational school for housekeeping (*Atelier de jeunes filles*), the Aboav orphanage for girls (1925), the "300 Ladies" association, and the Allians schools. Also of importance was the establishment of the first organised philanthropic associations,[10] focusing on training young girls.[11] In 1935, the first all-female community organisation, Vizo, was established, the social and charitable activity of which continues today.[12]

During these crucial years, which witnessed the annexation of the city to the Greek state (1912-1922), Jewish identity was redefined along the twin axes of national and religious identity – Greek and Jewish – as the result of the official recognition of the Jewish Community by the Greek state (1920).[13] The Jewish

---

7   See Albert Nar, *Κείμενα επί Ακτής Θαλάσσης [Texts on Sea Coast]* (University Studio Press/ Ekfrasi: Thessaloniki 1997), 87; Albert Nar, "Κοινωνική Οργάνωση και Δραστηριότητες της Εβραϊκής Κοινότητας Θεσσαλονίκης" ["Community Organization and Activity of the Jewish Community of Thessaloniki,"] in: Ioannis Chasiotis (ed.), *Θεσσαλονίκη, Ιστορία και Πολιτισμός [Thessaloniki, History and Culture]* (Paratiritis: Thessaloniki 1997), Α΄, 266-295, here 278-279. See further, Kostas Moskof, *Θεσσαλονίκη: 1700-1912, Τομή της μεταπρατικής Πόλης [Thessaloniki: 1700-1912, Section of a Resale City]* (Stohastis: Athens 1978), 139.
8   R. Molho, *The Jews of Thessaloniki*, 82, 150-151, 186, 190, 214-215, 217, 219.
9   R. Molho, *The Jews of Thessaloniki*, 151.
10   Philanthropic organisations such as Bienfaisance (1895), Tifereth, and Association des Anciennes Élèves de l' Alliance (1909); See R. Molho, *The Jews of Thessaloniki*, 177; Michael Molho, *In Memoriam* (Jewish Community of Thessaloniki: Thessaloniki 1976), 29-30.
11   See R. Molho, *The Jews of Thessaloniki*, 108-109, 146-154, 175-178.
12   Unpublished interviews with Jewish women, members of the Jewish community in Thessaloniki, May-July 2015.
13   See Efi Amilitou, Dimitra Toulatou (eds.), *Εβραίοι και Χριστιανοί στη Νεότερη Ελλάδα [Jews and Christians in Modern Greece]*, Bernard Pierron, George Saratsiotis (trans.) (Polis: Athens 2004), 80, 92, 94, 101, 137, 139, 145-146, 148, 150-153.

population had been the majority in the multiethnic society of Thessaloniki until the arrival of the refugees from Asia Minor (1922-23). In 1944 – following the outbreak of World War II, the invasion of German troops (1941-44), and the adoption of the Nuremberg race laws by the Nazi regime (2 August 1943) – within just six months, the vast majority of the Jewish population (around 96%, or fifty six thousand) was expelled and eventually disappeared.[14] Thereafter, the centre of Greek Jewry shifted to the capital of Athens, and the Jewish presence in Thessaloniki was reduced to a mere one thousand people.[15]

After the war, within the Jewish community but also in the broader local community of Thessaloniki, Jewish women survivors tried to rebound amidst complete social disorganisation and poverty. On the one hand, those female Greek Jewish refugees who survived the concentration camps, "thought about and longed for one thing only – returning home[…] But what is home?" they wondered.[16] On the other hand, the Greek Jewish women who were rescued were suspended in a shattered postwar community, attempting to reconstruct it either through volunteer work with youth or by getting married and starting families. Admittedly, the majority of the Jewish population was dominated by a strong shift towards the ideal of marriage as the only way toward personal stability and reintegration into society. Jewish women would say, characteristically,

> The two of us were the first brides who wore white wedding dresses. The ones before us were married even in robes[…] Until then, marriages were done two or three at a time[…] They were getting married to start a new life with a partner[…and] in order to endure their loneliness and unbearable grief.[17]

In conclusion, it is clear that the postwar Jewish female identity, under pressure from historical and social developments, has been shaped or negotiated not in terms of communal identity, but in terms of personal survival.

---

[14] M. Molho, *In Memoriam*, 351.
[15] They were later renamed Displaced Persons (DPs). For a reconstruction of the identity of women DPs, see Margarete Feinstein, "Jewish Women Survivors in the Displaced Persons Camps of Occupied Germany: Transmitters of the Past, Caretakers of the Present, and Builders of the Future," in: *Shofar: An Interdisciplinary Journal of Jewish Studies* 24/4 (2006), 67-89.
[16] Rika Benveniste, *Those Who Survived* (Polis: Athens 2014), 349 [in Greek: *Αυτοί που επέζησαν*].
[17] Nina Benroubi, *Μια Ζωή Γλυκιά και Πικρή [A life Sweet and Bitter]* (Modern Horizons: Athens 2004), 205-206 (my translation from Greek). See also Erika Kounio Amarilio, Frangiski Ampatzopoulou (eds.), *Πενήντα Χρόνια Μετά [Fifty Years Later]* (Paratiritis: Thessaloniki 1995), 158.

The Role of Jewish Women in the Contemporary Jewish Community in Thessaloniki: On the Margins or Not?[18]

The Religious Sphere – Synagogue

In the contemporary Jewish community in Thessaloniki, the concept of the religious sphere is identified with the word "synagogue". The religious structure is understood as a part of communal life, without completely coinciding with it. The religious element, in other words, is real, but clearly secondary, inasmuch as the synagogue, as the place of worship, does not represent for its members the whole of communal existence, but rather only a part of it: while they would never eschew it, they also do not consider it the foremost element of their collective unity.[19]

In today's Jewish community in Thessaloniki, Jewish women, even though they enjoy, according to rabbinical teachings, equality with men in worship and religious life, are nevertheless not able to exercise any liturgical or priestly office. Women – who, unlike men, are free from the vast majority of religious commandments (*Mitzvot*) – are limited to participation and supplication of the divine.[20] Even though women's religiosity is visibly weakened,[21] they make their presence clearly felt with their mass arrival on Friday evening, that is to say, at the lighting of the candles and the Saturday morning service, as well as on the major Jewish holidays. Unlike many other religious groups,[22] men often outnumber women, perhaps due to the requirement that at least ten adult men (*Minian*), not women, participate in the service. For their part, active female members describe the religious part of their lives in remarks regarding the individual level, such as "I feel proud to be born a Jew[...] It makes me stronger," and "I will defend my religious identity." At the collective level

---

[18] Title based on the book by Natalie Zemon Davis, *Women on the Margins: Three Seventeenth Century Lives* (Harvad University Press: Cambridge, Massachusetts 1997).

[19] See Maria Sidiropoulou, Θρησκεία και Ταυτότητα στην Εβραϊκή Κοινότητα Θεσσαλονίκης *[Religion and Identity in the Jewish Community of Thessaloniki]* (Master's Thesis) (Faculty of Theology – School of Theology A.U.TH.: Thessaloniki 2015), 86-89.

[20] Unpublished interview with the Thessaloniki Jewish Community Rabbi, 17 October 2013.

[21] The trends of religiosity are not universal. While women exhibit high levels of inclusivity in the synagogue in Ultra-Orthodox Jewish communities, in non-Ultra-Orthodox ones the levels are lower. For further, see, Paul Sullins, "Gender and Religiousness: Deconstructing Universality, Constructing Complexity", in: *American Journal of Sociology* 112/3 (2006), 838-880, here 849-851.

[22] For inquiries regarding the differences of gender and religious practice see Grace Davie, Κοινωνιολογία της Θρησκείας *[Sociology of Religion]*, Euaggelia Liliou, Niki Papageorgiou (trans.) (Critiki: Athens 2010), 360-367.

however, they note that "the role of religion has waned[...] We remember it only in times of need."[23]

In the synagogue, the rabbi has the highest institutional post, the religious leader, surrounded by male-dominated hierarchical positions such as that of the cantor (Hazan). The female roles are informal, silent, and non-institutional, but nevertheless important, since they contribute significantly and in various ways to the transmission of Jewish tradition. Jewish women, even if they are secular, socially networked, and integrated into local society, have never renounced their traditional role; in the synagogue, they are voluntarily entrusted with strengthening the Jewish element of the remaining members' identity. They offer valuable assistance with the liturgical and practical needs at the daily sacred services and immediately after their conclusion at the blessing (Kiddush), as well as in sacred ceremonies (marriage, circumcision, bar- and bat-mitzvah, memorials), always keeping the dietary regulations (Kosher).[24]

In sum, within the realm of the synagogue, one can easily observe the informal yet traditional female presence and active engagement as a unifying element and cultural conveyor of their religious, Judaic heritage.

The Communal Sphere: Collective Actions by Women

Undoubtedly, in the field of contemporary social reality and modern society, the role of the female sex is often understood as fixed and given. On a practical level, however, the enjoyment of this status quo is due to the endless struggles of women's movements, which began in the United States and Europe. Human rights for women, their entrance into the labor force, and the securing of their civil rights led to the improvement of women's position, inasmuch as, from the inertia of the pre-modern period, women have come to assume a tangible role and now share in public benefits. These reforms have also impacted the religious sphere, where women have claimed equal participation in the administrative, institutional positions of their respective bodies.[25]

In the early 1960's in the United States, just after the beginning of the second feminist movement, Jewish women seeking equality became the institutional

---

[23] Unpublished interviews with Jewish women, members of the Jewish community in Thessaloniki, May-July 2015 (Here and henceforth, my translation from Greek).

[24] Ibid.

[25] See Ioannis Petrou, Κοινωνιολογία [Sociology] (Vanias: Thessaloniki 2007), 295-300.

transformers of communal and public Judaism.[26] In other words, they began to actively occupy themselves with communal Judaic life, concentrating on aspects of their religious, ceremonial, ritual, and educational life, inside and outside of both their synagogue and their community, in the social and public sphere. Decades later, this activist wave of multi-faceted and impressive Jewish communal activity reached Europe through Westernised Jewish women, in the form of collective, charitable, and cultural initiatives.[27]

Indeed, in Thessaloniki, the individualistic aspect of Jewish, religious faith, in connection with the prevailing anthropocentric, communal forms of activity, shifted the centre of attention from the religious arena to the communal and cultural one. In a communal context of coexistence, what then is the role of the Jewish women of Thessaloniki? Is it institutional or non-institutional? Are they the clear protagonists of communal life, or its unsung heroines? Are there organised groups that represent only women's perspective? If so, what are the areas of activity of the women in Jewish communal life? What is their goal, and what impact do they have?

Nowadays, the aim of the Jewish community in Thessaloniki is, primarily, to serve the needs of its members at the communal, extra-communal, and social levels of life, and secondarily, to maintain and reshape their ethno-religious and ethno-cultural identity. Communal operations are founded within a secular rather than a religious system and run mainly by institutional community personnel, but also by decision making bodies such as committees and councils, in which women also participate in institutional capacities. The community is seen as a multivalent centre with a multifaceted character, the most important task of which is to strengthen the sense of belonging, solidarity, and cohesion of its members. Few are the members who completely identify with the community; others regard it as part of their lives; and nearly everyone perceives it as a reference point in difficult times.[28]

The contemporary Jewish females of Thessaloniki may not have as radical a presence as other Jewish women of the West. In the United States, Europe, and to a lesser extent Israel, various trends among Jewish women, such as

---

[26] For an autobiography of a Jewish woman in the United States after 1960, see Rebecca Walker, *Black, White and Jewish* (Riverhead Books: New York 2002).

[27] See Sylvia Barack Fishman, "Women's Transformations of Public Judaism: Religiosity, Egalitarianism, and the Symbolic Power of Changing Gender Roles", in: *Studies in Contemporary Jewry* 17 (2001), 131-155.

[28] Sidiropoulou, *Religion and Identity*, 78-85.

"secular" (*Hiloni*), "traditionalist" (*Masorti*), "religious" (*Dati*), and even "ultra-orthodox" (*Haredi*) are taking shape in both conservative and reform environments. At the same time, one finds fundamentalist voices within their communities, focusing on biblical reforms of the sacred law or on feminist, charitable, and religious groups and movements (some including women rabbis and others not).[29]

In contrast, the Jewish women of Thessaloniki are embedded in value-systems shaped by earlier structures. Thus, despite living in modern society, they are characterised by a unique community dynamic. These Jewish women, either through their religious space – namely, the synagogue – as mentioned above, or through communal action,[30] are convinced of the unbroken cultural unity of their Sephardic tradition and thus try "To be the editors[...] of Judaism to their children, and to make memories for them."[31]

Women's contribution to the communal arena takes place both formally and informally. Their formal contribution is manifested in staffing communal positions, such as community council and communal organisations. At the same time, however, the core of women's interest lies in many informal and

---

[29] For the United States, see Charlotte Elisheva Fonrobert, "Gender Identity in Halakhic Discourse," in: *Jewish Women's Archive* (2009). (http://jwa.org/encyclopedia/article/gender-identity-in-halakhic-discourse, 14 October 2015); Lauren Markoe, "Women Rabbis are Forging a Path Outside Denominational Judaism," in: *Religion News Service* (2015). (http://www.religionnews.com/2015/04/08/women-rabbis-forging-path-outside-denominational-judaism, 14 October 2015). For Europe, see Paula Hyman, "Gender and the Shaping of Modern Jewish Identities," in: *Jewish Social Studies* 8/2-3 (2002), 153-161; Chia Longman, "'Not Us, but You Have Changed!' Discourses on Difference and Belonging among Haredi Women," in: *Social Compass* 54/1 (2007), 77-95. For Israel, see Yaacov Yadgar, "Gender, Religion, and Feminism: The Case of Jewish Israeli Traditionalists," in: *Journal for the Scientific Study of Religion* 45/3 (2006), 353-370; Menachem Friedman, *The Haredi (Ultra-Orthodox) Society – Sources, Trends and Processes* (The Jerusalem Institute for Israel Studies: Jerusalem 1991). For Jewish Arab Feminist activist organisations, see Ruth Halperin Kaddari, Yaacov Yadgar, "Between Universal Feminism and Particular Nationalism: Politics, Religion and Gender (in) equality in Israel," in: *Third World Quarterly* 31/6 (2010), 905-920, here 913-915, 917. For a review of Jewish biblical issues, see Blu Greenberg, "Female Sexuality and Bodily Functions in the Jewish Tradition," in: Jeanne Becher (ed.), *Women, Religion and Sexuality* (WCC Publications: Geneva 1990), 1-44.

[30] For such surveys, see Harriet Hartman, Moshe Hartman, "Jewish Identity and the Secular Achievements of American Jewish Men and Women," in: *Journal for the Scientific Study of Religion* 50/1 (2011), 133-153.

[31] Sylvia Barack Fishman, Daniel Parmer, *The Gender Imbalance in American Jewish Life* (Brandeis University – Maurice and Marilyn Cohen Center for Modern Jewish Studies – Hadassah Brandeis Institute: Massachusetts 2008), 75.

non-institutional levels of Jewish life, such as the area of religion, dietary habits (*Kosher*), education, building relationships with Jewish youth around Greece, and finally, offering charity and social work. More specifically, the voluntary female contribution takes place both inside and outside the community, in frames such as a youth camp run by female members of the Jewish Youth of Greece [J.Y.G.]; a Jewish school providing catechism and information on the Jewish religion; communal charitable organisations and initiatives; the "Greece Israel" association; a Jewish choir; events for show-casing Sephardic music and cuisine; and, finally, commemorations of the Jewish Genocide.[32]

Furthermore, two entirely female charitable associations, the longstanding Vizo and the newer Ziv, are tasked with the preservation and conservation of Jewish cultural heritage. Women, approximately over seventy years of age, participate in Vizo, while women over twenty eight are involved in Ziv. The institutional structure of the two organisations is composed of one president, one treasurer, one secretary, and of course Jewish females as members. Their missions are philanthropic, such as supporting the poor or "those who have substantial needs" inside and outside the community (as in greater Thessaloniki), as well as Israel. It is therefore clear that, while these women's organisations are Jewish, their sphere of activity is multidimensional, since it includes the whole social fabric of the city.[33]

Despite these women's obvious and varied activities, they voice the belief that "we could have more members, and we could do more both inside and outside the community." The majority of young women involved participate in the events organised by J.Y.G., while the majority of older women, roughly between forty and seventy five, is entrusted with the preservation of customs, tradition, and Jewish cultural heritage.[34]

It may thus be concluded that women, with their communal activities, are the ethno-cultural forwarders and carriers of Jewish, Sephardic heritage, since they are the ones disseminating and transmitting the torch of their tradition to younger and future generations.

---

[32] Unpublished interviews with Jewish women, members of the Jewish community in Thessaloniki, May-July 2015.
[33] Ibid.
[34] Ibid.

Mapping a Female Jewish Identity: Self-Consciousness and Self-Determination

It is commonplace that in the contemporary realm of late modernity, notable and paradoxical circumstances can suddenly change the identities of communal subjects involved. This is in combination with general socio-politico-economic reforms. In other words, in urban living, the demands of the times may mutate and replace former traditional components of the identity construction with individualistic actions of a collective nature and a "local culture."[35]

This section examines the contemporary identity of Jewish women, with the Jewish community of Thessaloniki as the case in point. Under what conditions do Jewish women operate today, in both the communal and broader social realm? And how is their identity defined?

To answer this, one must first determine the components of modern, Jewish female identity. One is her direct and indirect roots: the elements of religion and ethnicity, namely Jewish religious identity, on the one hand, and the more recent Judaeo-Spanish or Sephardic roots from the Iberian Peninsula on the other hand. At the same time, a decisive role in female self-definition is played by tradition, manners, and customs, as regarding Jewish holidays for instance, by the Sephardi language (Judezmo or Ladino), and by the recent traumatic event of the Holocaust.[36]

A second component is these women's self-definition. The current research has made clear that the Jewish women of Thessaloniki see themselves today as having a dual identity, determined by their ethno-religious and national roots. The majority express their Greek citizenship and their Judaic faith by referring to themselves as "Greek Jews," or, to a lesser extent, as "Jewish Greek," or "Greek, non-religious Jews." The terms of their Greekness and Jewishness are therefore fully incorporated and reflected within their female self-understanding. The only instances in which individuals declare first their religious affiliation – with an obvious intent to defend it – and only second their national affiliation are when individuals of other faiths from outside the community ask about their religious identity. This happens, for instance, when others – usually Greek Orthodox Christians – assume that these Jewish women

---

[35] See Christos Tsironis, *Globalization and Local Communities* (Vanias: Thessaloniki 2007), 74-76 .

[36] Unpublished interviews with Jewish women, members of the Jewish community in Thessaloniki, May-July 2015.

are themselves also Orthodox Christians, or when they ask why they have non-Christian names.[37]

Generally speaking, Jewish women appear integrated into the Greek social network and environment. All seem to have developed friendly interpersonal relationships with members of other faiths, people from outside the community as well as secular co-citizens, while a considerable portion have contracted mixed marriages, which may be seen as an indication of their smooth integration into Thessalonian society. The vast majority of Jewish women interviewed believe that their Greek identity is inextricably tied to their religious one. In several cases, the only difficulty lies in the identification of Greekness with Orthodox Christianity, particularly among the younger generations, where one observes an obvious and strong connection with the modern state of Israel.[38]

Nevertheless, there is a strong sense of belonging to the local community of Thessaloniki. This may be explained by the fact that the women's dynamic activities often make them ambassadors of good will. They communicate in various ways with those outside their community in terms of reconciliation and a genuine desire for fellowship. In fact, this good will is often given institutional approval, with the recognition of their local, municipal, and private contributions to society.[39] It is worth noting that modern women researchers studying Ultra-Orthodox, Jewish female issues insist on discussing matters of women's identities outside the borders of their communal existence, in order to open them up and aid in the success of their communal activities as agents of their tradition.[40]

In conclusion, the Jewish female identity is able to maintain an active dialogue with the present. Preserving national (Greek) characteristics, ethno-local, and religious (Judaic) traits, women shape their identity both inside and outside the communal grid through cultural activities that promote their female Sephardic cultural basis, as well as through charitable acts. The purpose of this philanthropy, as they themselves – as Greek Jews – describe it, is "the common good (which springs) from our inner world to the outer world."[41]

---

[37] Ibid.
[38] Ibid.
[39] Ibid.
[40] See Chia Longman, Gila Schnitzer, "At Home in the Diaspora: Judaism, Gender and Globalization," in: Erik Eynikel, Aggeliki Ziaka (eds.), *Religion and Conflict* (Harptree Publishing: London 2011), 307-318, here 316.
[41] Ibid.

Of course, the transmission of their Jewish cultural tradition to younger generations is particularly important to these women. Today, the Greek Sephardim Jewish women act as the cultural transmitters, the last guardians, and the custodians of their Sephardic-Jewish ethno-religious heritage in the Greek reality of Thessaloniki. As they themselves have noted, "it is the favorite part of my life, which I want to pass on to my children, and that is why we are all trying to preserve that which could be lost."[42]

Conclusion

This overview of Jewish women's presence and identity has allowed us to draw the following conclusions within two spatio-temporal and socio-political frameworks: the earlier, traditional world of pre-modern society and communal Jewish female identity on the one hand, and the later, current world, which is defined by the gradual, highly innovative emergence of the Jewish woman and her transition into the public sphere.

In the modern era, always faced with the danger of community members completely assimilating in the broader culture, the primary goal of Jewish women's active and multifaceted presence and their communal and social contributions, is the transmission of their Jewish cultural tradition to the younger generations. With the exception of the two wholly-female institutions mentioned above, female identity and activity – unlike that of men – largely operates in an informal communal way; it is not institutionally recognised by its religious or communal leaders, and behaves in a way that vacillates between tradition and modernity.

Thessaloniki, due to its geopolitical position, has functioned as a crossroad of many people and many religions. In particular, the Jewish presence reached its apogee during the Ottoman period (15th-20th Century). Over the past hundred years, after the official annexation of Thessaloniki to the Greek state, the identity of the Jews changed. Despite the numerical weakness of the old ethno-religious Jewish community during its annihilation in the years 1941-44, today, once again, Jews claim a place in the city life. This paper will focus on the contemporary Jewish female presence in Thessaloniki. On the one hand, Jewish women have their own role contributing in various ways to the maintenance, transmission, and reproduction of their particular ethnoreligious identity. On the other hand, they negotiate their active role in the modern Greek society. In other words, the author investigates the ways

---

[42] Ibid.

in which Jewish women negotiate between tradition and modernity, between their own traditional and modern identity.

Thessaloniki war historisch betrachtet aufgrund seiner geopolitischen Lage immer Treffpunkt von Menschen und Religionen. Dabei erreichte die jüdische Präsenz ihren Höhepunkt während der osmanischen Zeit vom 15. bis zum 20. Jahrhundert. Im Laufe des letzten Jahrhunderts und nach der offiziellen Aufnahme von Thessaloniki in den griechischen Staat, änderte sich die Identität der Juden. Die alte ethno-religiöse jüdische Gemeinde ist heute noch lebendig. Dies trotz ihrer zahlenmäßigen Redizierung durch ihre Vernichtung in der Zeit von 1941-44. Heute sind Menschen jüdischen Glaubens stark im Stadtleben wahrnehmnbar. Der vorliegende Artikel widmet sich den Frauen unter ihnen. Jüdinnen widmen sich einerseits der Erhaltung, der Übertragung und die Ausgestaltung ihrer besonderen ethnisch-religiösen Identität, und andererseits leben sie ihre aktive Rolle in der zeitgenössischen griechischen Gesellschaft. Die Autorin untersucht die Art und Weise, in welcher die jüdischen Frauen in Thessaloniki zwischen Tradition und Moderne ihre Identität verhandeln und leben.

Maria Ch. Sidiropoulou is a PhD Candidate at the School of Theology of the Faculty of Theology, Aristotle University of Thessaloniki, specialising in Sociology of Religion. Her Master's Thesis (2015) deals with the role of religion and identity in the Jewish community in Thessaloniki.

Journal of the European Society of Women in Theological Research 24 (2016) 203-214.
doi: 10.2143/ESWTR.24.0.3170035

Elena Volkova

Every Son's Mother: Human Rights Mariology

There are about a thousand different types of Virgin Mary icons in Russia (in Russian she is called *Bogoroditsa* – "the one who gives birth to God"), around 250 of them are believed to be miraculous. As Orlando Figes states, from a comparative perspective:

> At the core of the Russian faith is a distinctive stress on motherhood which never really took root in the West. Where the Catholic tradition stressed Mary's purity, the Russian Church emphasized her divine motherhood – the *bogoroditsa* – which practically assumed the status of the Trinity in the Russian religious consciousness.[1]

Mikhail Epstein writes that "the feminine and specifically maternal basis of Russian civilisation has been grasped by many Russian poets and philosophers".[2] The first Russian philosophy was that of Sophiology developed by Vladimir Solovyov – a teaching of Divine Sophia, metaphysical femininity (Mother/Wisdom/Love) and soul of the world. Solovyov, like Leo Tolstoy but in his own meta-feminist way, wanted to build a bridge between orthodoxia and orthopraxia – religious dogmas and social practices. He believed that Divine Sophia could heal the world.

The first sand for many years only sactive grassroots organisation in the post-Soviet Russia of the 1990s was the Committee of Soldiers'grassroo (since 1998 – The Union of Committees of Soldiers' Mothers [UCSM]), founded in order to protect conscripts from illegal recruiting companies and military hazing, and to provide human rights consultation and education as well as shelter to victims of *dedovshchina* – "a system in which senior soldiers produce merciless abuse, haze, torture, and force recruits to perform

---

[1] Orlando Figes, *Natasha's Dance: A Cultural History of Russia* (Picador: New York 2003), 321 (emphasis in the original).

[2] Mikhail Epstein, *After the Future: The Paradoxes of Postmodernism and Contemporary Russian Culture* (University of Massachusetts Press: Amherst 1995), 177.

menial tasks".[3] In 2010 the committee reported 2,000 deaths from hazing, while Russia'n Defence Ministry declared only 14. Anna Colin Lebedev states that

> at the beginning of the 1990's when the Soviet regime collapsed, these movements were seen as the main actors of social and political change and as the only institutions able to oppose the return of the monopolistic control by the State of the society and to guarantee the democratisation of society.[4]

Starting in August 2014, Soldiers' Mothers began revealing that many Russian soldiers had been fighting in Ukraine. The Head of Committee, Valentina Melnikova, said that between 10,000-15,000 Russian troops had been sent over the border. Her research was based on information received from mothers and wives of servicemen.[5] Ella Polyakova, head of the Saint Petersburg branch of UCSM, demanded an official investigation having received information about 100 Russian soldiers allegedly killed and 300 wounded in Ukraine. Soon after that her branch was labelled "foreign agent," despite the fact that Soldiers' Mothers no longer received any foreign funding.[6] A controversial "Foreign Agents Law" was adopted in Russia in 2012, according to which NGOs that engage in political activities and receive any foreign funding, need to register as "foreign agents". Those who fail to register may face hefty fines or be closed down, while their leaders may be jailed for up to two years.

---

[3] Lindsay Fincher, "Enemies Within the Ranks: Human Rights Abuses in the Russian Army," 25 April 2002, 2. (http://www.lindsayfincher.com/papers/PSC167paper.pdf, 5 September 2015)

[4] Anna Colin Lebedev, "Rethinking the Place of Personal Concerns in the Analysis of Collective Action: The Case of the Committee of Soldiers' Mothers of Russia," 4. (http://blogs.helsinki.fi/understanding-russianness/files/2009/10/Colin_Lebedev.doc, 15 June 2015). See also Elena Zdravomyslova, "Peaceful Initiatives: the Soldiers'Mothers Movement in Russia," in: I. Breines, D. Gierycs, B. Reardon (eds.) *Towards a Women's Agenda for a Culture of Peace* (UNESCO: Paris 1999), 165-180.

[5] "Thousands of Russian soldiers sent to Ukraine, say rights groups," in: *The Guardian*, (1 September 2014). (http://www.theguardian.com/world/2014/sep/01/russian-soldiers-ukraine-rights-groups, 2 December 2014)

[6] Helen Womack, "#IndexAwards2015: Campaigning nominee Soldiers' Mothers," in: *Index on Censorship*, 5 March 2015. (https://www.indexoncensorship.org/2015/03/indexawards2015-campaigning-nominee-soldiers-mothers, 2 September 2015)

Mother of Seven

Four months earlier, in April 2014, Svetlana Davydova, mother of seven, called the Ukrainian Embassy in Moscow to warn the Ukrainian government that Russian troops might be sent to the Eastern Ukraine. Svetlana called the Embassy because she noticed that a military base, located near her home, looked unusually empty and overheard a man from that base talking over the cell phone about a group of servicemen going on "business trip," an expression used at that time for troops sent to Ukraine. She believed that such invasion would threaten peace in Europe and human rights for life and peace, and tried to protect the territorial integrity of Ukraine and human lives in both countries. Svetlana was arrested in January 2015 on high treason charges at her home town of Vyazma, Smolensk region, and brought to Moscow to an FSB "Lefortovo" detention prison.

Several public campaigns were launched to get Svetlana Davydova released from pre-trial detention. An Orthodox priest, Vyacheslav Vinnikov, compared Svetlana to Theotokos with many infants. What if she didn't have any children, or had just one, as each of the Pussy Riot activists, Nadezhda Tolokonnikova and Maria Alyokhina, had? What would have happened if she had been a man? Would she avoid trial? Probably not. The campaign in her defence gathered so many voices mostly because she was a breastfeeding mother and a mother of many children. It was her motherhood, first and foremost, that projected authority for solidarity and mercy. People were concerned about her children, particularly the two month old Kassandra, more than about Svetlana as an anti-war activist: 48% of Russians approved of her being arrested.

Besides, a treason trial would have inevitably raised an issue of Russian troops fighting in Ukraine. To avoid further scandal, the state dropped all charges against Svetlana Davydova.

Human rights activist Yuri Samodurov (twice charged with "inciting religious and social hatred" for organising art exhibitions at Andrei Sakharov Center)[7] asked me to help write an English text to nominate Svetlana for the Václav Havel Human Rights Prize as a heroine who protested against the Russian military invasion of Ukraine. Evgeny Ikhlov compared her to the writer and pacifist Carl Von Ossietzky, who in 1929 warned the League of Nations that Germany was secretly restoring its military in violation of the Treaty of

---

[7] Yuri Samodurov and Andrei Yerofeyev condemned to a fine for "inciting national and religious hatred". (https://www.fidh.org/en/region/europe-central-asia/russia/Yuri-Samodurov-and-Andrei, 3 April 2015)

Versailles. Ossietzky had been sentenced for treason, and later, in 1935, awarded the Nobel Peace Prize.

In September 2015, the third Vačlav Havel Prize was given to the Russian oldest human rights activist Ludmila Alekseeva, a founding member of the Moscow Helsinki group, who last year took part in several anti-war projects.

Saint George Killing the Dragon

While Russian activists first tried to prevent the war and later protested against it, Nadiya Savchenko, a pilot of the Ukrainian Ground Forces, had to defend her country against the Russian troops.[8] President Petro Poroshenko awarded Nadiya the title "Hero of Ukraine": "Nadiya is the symbol of unbroken Ukrainian spirit and heroism, the symbol of the way one should defend and love Ukraine, the symbol of our victory."[9] She was also appointed a deputy of Ukraine and member of the Ukrainian delegation to the Parliamentary Assembly of the Council of Europe.

Savchenko is hailed as a national hero in Ukraine, seen both as a Christ-like figure – "Jesus in jail" – and as a Saint George killing the Dragon. On 1 March 2015, Patriarch Filaret of the Ukrainian Orthodox Church (Kiev Patriarchate) awarded Savchenko the Order of Saint George the Trophy-Bearer – "for fight against evil".[10]

Saint George killing the Dragon was previously a religious image associated with the Pussy Riot group, who on 21 February 2012 prayed to Holy Mary in the Cathedral of Christ the Saviour, asking her to drive Putin away. Now it is attributed to Nadiya Savchenko, who became a Ukrainian feminine symbol of hope and resistance – the role which Pussy Riot played in Russia (at least in the eyes of their supporters). In both cases, the Kremlin is believed to bring all these women to a show trial while Vladimir Putin is depicted as Dragon.

The dragon imagery used in Russian protest iconography and discourse is also borrowed from two literary texts. A popular image of "Putin the Python

---

[8] Nadiya Savchenko was captured in the Donbass area by pro-Russian separatists on 18 June 2014 and brought to Russia, where she was charged with killing two Russian journalists. There is evidence, however, that she was in captivity when those two men were killed. Russian authorities deny her status of a prisoner-of-war.

[9] http://www.ukrinform.net/rubric-politics/1821036-nadiya_savchenko_awarded_hero_of_ukraine_329471.html, 3 April 2015.

[10] "Patriarch Filaret confers the order on Nadia Savchenko 'for fight against evil'," 2 March 2015. (http://theology.in.ua/article_print.php?id=59293&name=national_religious_question&_lang=en&, 26 April 2015)

Kaa" came from *The Jungle Book* by Rudyard Kipling. The allusion had been provoked by Putin himself when he called protesters "Bandar-logs" (monkey-people). Another rich source is a satirical play from 1944 called "Dragon" (*Drakon*), by Evgeny Schwartz. Every year, a town sacrifices a girl to the Dragon without any resistance until Lancelot comes and slays a dragon (dictator), but fails to liberate human souls – "mute souls, deaf souls, chained souls, snitch souls, damned souls."[11] Courageous women like Nadezhda Tolokonnikova, Maria Alyokhina, and Nadiya Savchenko are seen both as sacrifices to the Dragon and knights who challenge him.

Faith, Hope, Love

Both the Ukrainian female name Nadiya and the Russian one Nadezhda mean "hope". A Ukrainian National Pavilion at the 56th International Art Exhibition – *La Bienalle di Venezia* (2015) was called "Hope" in honour of Nadiya Savchenko. The pavilion was opened when Savchenko was on hunger strike (which she kept for more than 80 days). Nadiya's sister's name is Vera, meaning "faith", while her mother's name is Maria. An icon of four female Byzantine martyrs associated with these names – Hope, Faith, Love, and their Mother Sophia – was also used as an iconic symbol of Pussy Riot: three young protest-martyrs with Virgin Mary as the Heavenly Mother instead of Sophia.

A Ukrainian female artist Zhanna Kadyrova, whose works were presented at the Bienalle, said about Ukraine:

> It is obvious that changes which take place in this country strongly affect its citizens. Still the main hopes are connected to the people. We observe how society is being transformed in extreme situations, when powerful resources of humanity are manifested in people – mutual aid, self-organization, unselfishness. Therefore, the hope of building a civil society remains.[12]

A Ukrainian "Open Group" presented a video wall installation called "Synonym for 'Wait'," composed of nine live-stream screens that showed nine front doors of the family homes of Ukrainian soldiers behind which their mothers and fathers, wives and children were waiting for them to come back.

---

[11] Evgeny Shwarz. *Dragon*. (trans. Yuri Machkasov). (http://a7sharp9.com/dragon.html, 12 October 2015)

[12] "'Hope!', Pavilion of Ukraine at the 56th International Art Exhibition – la Bienalle di Venezia". (http://pinchukartcentre.org/en/biennale2015/works/crowd_day, 5 July 2015)

On the opposite side of the wall there were photographs of the families' dinner tables. As long as no soldier returns, the artist goes without food:

> The work moves between presence, absence and anticipation. The performative act requires a test of endurance, which is a quality shared by the families, the soldiers and Ukrainian society as a whole. It expresses hope for the soldiers' return and an end to this conflict. Through its simple and honest form, this work deals with people and their fears. It reveals the helplessness of people drawn into a violent conflict while suggesting the hopes that allow them to find new ways of making life go on.[13]

Visiting the pavilion, one could meet Anton Varga – an artist who had not eaten for 27 days, at the time, and see women on the screens opening those doors, most of whom looked like mothers.

The Ukrainian Committee of Soldiers' Mothers was among the first NGOs to publish a list of casualties of the Russian-Ukrainian war. They would organise street protests demanding Russian authorities to stop the war, bring their sons home, reveal the number of casualties, give all the soldiers military status, and pay pensions to those who lost their relatives. On both sides of the conflict, Soldiers' Mothers made very much the same demands which proved the mothers' proximity being based on common values of human life and rights.

Church of Mothers

Much more has been written about Soldiers' Mothers in the West than in Russia. Anna Colin Lebedev observes that

> Since the middle of the 1990's, about a dozen of researchers have studied the Committee of Soldiers' Mothers' activities [...] Two doctoral dissertations and a great number of articles are dedicated to the movement. This interest can be explained by the great visibility of the Committee since the war in Chechnya and by the lack of active social movements on Russian public scene during the same period. The Committee is mostly analysed from three conceptual standpoints: the research on civil society in Russia, the viewpoint of gender studies and the frame theory approach.[14]

Motherhood and human rights? "While most analysts note the double reference of the Committee's action, human rights and motherhood, understanding the combination of the two is a challenge for the researchers". Feminine but

---

[13] Ibid.
[14] Colin Lebedev, "Rethinking the Place," 4.

not feminist? Modern but pre-modern? Based on proximity engagement but without any familial corruption? "Mother taking part in her son's identity"? The maternal aspect of the organisation seems to present a number of para- doxes for scholars in social studies.[15]

Let us consider the issue of the NGO's religious identity. A mother protect- ing her child is certainly an image which in the Russian religious culture refers to the Orthodox icon of Virgin Mary with Jesus the infant. Icon-like pictures of a mother holding a baby are used by both supporters and opponents of the UCSM (opponents label Soldiers' Mothers as "foreign agents" or blame them as "traitors").

In her research on the Saint Petersburg branch of the UCSM, Russian scholar Elena Zdravomyslova observes that its emblem – a candle with crossed rays – is a Christian symbol, and the organisation itself functions as a church- like community. Well-educated and experienced leaders preach human rights to newcomers. Through consulting and teaching, "strong mothers" are shaping a new type of "responsible motherhood" to transform "week mothers" into legal self-confident defenders of their sons:

> Activists of this organization believe that Christian values laid a foundation for the development of the human rights mentality, that a Christian idea of motherhood is their major symbol. Leaders declare their religious beliefs in public. However their faith can be better identified as ecumenical than that of the traditional Orthodoxy. It is no mere chance that the office was sanctified in the 1990s by the clergy of the Lutheran, Catholic, Orthodox and American Protestant churches. When women meet there they light a candle in the corner; there are icons on the walls – those of Virgin Mary and Saint Francis of Assisi, the former being another cult figure of the organization. There is also the text of a "Mother's Prayer" on the wall calling upon the Mother of God to save one's son.[16]

These church-like female community members, who often have to defend their sons against the state authorities, can be easily contrasted with the highly patriarchal Russian Orthodox Church which has become an ideological depart- ment of the Russian government.

---

[15] Ibid., 5.

[16] Elena Zdravomyslova, "Politika identichnosti pravozashchitnoi organizatzii 'Soldatskie materi Sankt-Peterburga'," in: *Prava cheloveka v Rosii* (http://www.hro.org/node/6569, 5 August 2015). My translation from Russian.

Mothers of Beslan: Massacre of Innocents

The grassroots nongovernmental organisation Mothers of Beslan was founded in 2005 in response to the lack of negotiation and proper investigation, as well as the excessive force used by security services during the 2004 North Ossetian Beslan school siege. A group of terrorists seized Beslan school No. 1 on 1 September 2004, holding over 1200 people hostage for three days. 336 hostages, including 186 children, died.[17]

In 2007, the NGO, some members of which were highly critical of President Putin as the one responsible for covering up the circumstances of the siege and the excessive force used by the military, split into two groups. The new organisation was named Voice of Beslan Russian Public Organisation of Terror Act Victims. The Co-chair Ella Kesaeva claimed that the state wanted to divide and discredit them.[18]

On 2 July 2015, the European Court of Human Rights declared admissible complaints of about 400 applicants against Russia's violations of their right to life before, during and after the siege. Ella said before the hearing: *"The decision of the European Court* is necessary for people to have hope, to set a precedent for the future".[19]

Beslan mothers wear mostly black clothes and cover their heads with scarves. Many of them go to church. The cemetery where the victims of the siege were buried is called "The City of Angels." The mothers look very much like a monastic sisterhood but some of them firmly resist any collective religious identity: firstly, because there were both Christians and Muslims among hostages; secondly, because they want to preserve the school ruins as a sacred space. In 2007, they refused the offer of the Russian Orthodox Church to build a church on the place of the tragedy. "According to Ella Kesaeva, certain representatives of Orthodox Church are lobbying erection of their temple.' Signatures are now

---

[17] http://www.pravdabeslana.ru/english.htm, 1 April 2015.

[18] http://www.golosbeslana.ru, 4 April 2015; "Court Orders Beslan Mothers to Disband," in: *The Moscow Times*, 21 December 2007. (http://www.themoscowtimes.com/article.php?id=351533, 5 April 2014); "Russian Federation: Ongoing judicial proceedings and defamation campaign against members of the Voice of Beslan," in: *World Organization Against Torture,* 22 April 2008. (http://www.omct.org/human-rights-defenders/urgent-interventions/russia/2008/04/d19274, 3 May 2015)

[19] "European Court takes steps towards securing justice for victims of Beslan School Siege," in: *European Human Rights Advocacy Centre,* 2 July 2015. (http://www.ehrac.org.uk/news/european-court-takes-steps-towards-securing-justice-for-victims-of-beslan-school-siege, 3 September 2015)

being gathered in Beslan in support of this project. The victims view it as another act of confrontation and think that such issues are not for voting, since nobody should advocate one's faith by referring to the tragedy."[20]

Church on Blood

In March 1881, the Russian emperor Alexander II was assassinated in the centre of Saint Petersburg. In 1907, under Nicholas II, a church was completed on the site which is known as the Church of the Saviour on (Spilled) Blood (*Khram Spasa na krovi*). In July 1918, Nicholas II, his family and household were shot by Bolsheviks in Yekaterinburg. In July 2003, under Putin, a church was completed on the site which was called the Church on Blood in Honour of All Saints Resplendent in the Russian Land.

This Orthodox "Church on Blood" tradition has so far been only about members of the royal family. However, the mothers' NGOs in question were also "built on blood," meaning they emerged out of deaths caused in military service, the massacre in Beslan, or deadly threats to their children. The ruins of the Beslan school may be seen as a church preserved to commemorate victims of both terrorist attack and state violence. Persecuted by the state authorities, Voice of Beslan members demanded an international investigation of the siege and are looking forward to bringing the Russian state to justice.

Martyrology of Human-Rights Defenders

Civil Rights experts report that

> Since 2000 the human rights situation worsened in Russia and has greatly deterio-rated since Putin was reinstalled as President of Russia in 2012. State repression over the past few years became more sophisticated as legislation was adopted to discredit and/or attack human rights defenders [...] Prominent opposition leaders have been arrested on spuriously formulated charges. One of the most vocal critics of Putin, politician Boris Nemtsov, was shot dead in February 2015. The investigation into his murder leaves grave doubts regarding the impartiality and thoroughness of the investigation, the same that can be said regarding the silencing through murder of top government critics such journalist Anna Politkovskaya in 2006 and human rights defender Natalia Estemirova in 2009.[21]

---

[20] "Beslan residents are against erection of a temple in the place of the tragedy," in: *Caucasian Knot*, 17 May 2007. (http://eng.kavkaz-uzel.ru/articles/5830, 23 February 2015)

[21] "Human Rights in Russia," in: *Civil Rights Defenders*, 24 June 2015. (http://www.civilrights-defenders.org/country-reports/human-rights-in-russia, 15 July 2015)

When Anna Politkovskaya, an author of the book "Putin's Russia", who reported on abuses in Chechnya and corruption of power, was shot on Putin's birthday in the lift of her block of flats, a Russian Orthodox priest, Georgiy Chistyakov, commemorated her as a "civil martyr." The Russian list of women human-rights martyrs also includes Galina Starovoitova, shot in 1998, Natalia Estemirova, a leading human rights defenders in the North Caucasus, and Anastasia Baburova, a journalist, who investigated activities of Russian Neo-Nazi groups, both murdered in 2009.[22]

The Human-Rights Mary

A post-Soviet generation of women human-rights defenders introduced a new idea of both womanhood and motherhood. It has little to do with the traditional Theotokos as a sacred national symbol of the heavenly protector of Russia: it neither calls on mothers to sacrifice their sons "at the altar of their Fatherland" nor helps the army to conquer enemies of the Holy Russia or the so-called Russian World. On the contrary, the idea of the "responsible motherhood" assumes that women must defend civil rights of individuals as mothers would defend their own children.

The Human-Rights Mary would protest to Caiaphas and Pilate about Jesus having been arrested at night in violation of law, with no mandate or warrant issued and no charges read out in open court. She would claim that the witnesses were false, while no defence or evidence had ever been provided.

Clash of Maries

Glynn Cardy, a New Zealand pastor, stated that the conflict between the Pussy Riot group and the Russian Orthodox Church revealed a clash of two types of Christianity. In a sermon titled "The Power of a Prayer: Pussy Riot Tries the Church," he said that

> the Pussy Riot prayer [...] asks the fundamental, scandalous question about who owns God. Is God just a puppet toy belonging to the Church, a toy for the State to manipulate the strings and enhance its own power? Or is God a subversive power,

---

[22] "Russian Feminism Resources in memory of Galina Starovoitova". (http://www.lchr.org/a/3/ it/galina.html, 27 May, 2016); 2016); Politkovskaya, "A Life Lost in Pursuit of the Truth," Amnesty International, (http://www.amnestyusa.org/our-work/cases/russia-anna-politkovskaya, 27 May 2016); "Obituary: Natalia Estemirova," BBC News, 15 July 2009. (http://news.bbc. co.uk/2/hi/europe/8152648.stm, 27 May 2016); "Anastasia Baburova," The Economist, 5 February 2009. (http://www.economist.com/node/13055783, 27 May 2016)

out among the people, always working fearlessly to promote justice, mutuality, and equality? [...] Christian clowns, girls with guitars and foolish knitted hats, not men with guns, head a revolution against authoritarianism and the betrayal of the Church by its leaders. It was not just three women on trial. It was and is also Putin. It was and is also the Church. It is a way of exercising power that is on trial. It is the people's right to pray that is at stake. It is a clash of Gods. And it isn't over yet.[23]

The text of Pussy Rioters' punk-prayer may be interpreted as Mater Nostra, a feminist version of Pater Noster.[24] Thus, the contrast between the two different ideas of motherhood may be identified as a "clash of Maries", a feminine version of the given "clash of Gods." Behind this 'clash of Maries," one can find numerous growing conflicts – those between a new authoritarian political religion of the Post-Communist Orthodoxy and a civil religion of human rights, ecumenism and religious nationalism, pacifism and militarism, democracy and dictatorship, truth and propaganda, nonconformity and collaboration with the repressive regime.

In the post-Soviet Russia, mothers' NGOs and individual women activists transformed the traditional religious idea of the feminine and maternal. They introduced a civil type of the "responsible motherhood and sisterhood" which shaped a new image of Mother of God, namely, the Human-Rights Mary: the Mary that the Pussy Rioters prayed to in 2012. Religious images such as the Orthodox iconography of Theotokos and the infant Jesus, Saint George killing the Dragon, and a "Church on Blood" tradition, as well as connotations of the biblical stories of Herod and the Massacre of Innocents, the Sanhedrin Trial of Jesus, and Jesus in Jail, present a metaphorical reception of numerous political conflicts in and around Russia. These include the Beslan school siege, military hazing, lack of justice, political repressions, the invasion of Ukraine, casualties of the undeclared war, and many others. This "clash of Maries" points to a number of binary oppositions – those of a civil religion of human rights vs. the new authoritarian political religion of the Post-Communist Orthodoxy, ecumenism vs. religious nationalism, pacifism vs. militarism, democracy vs. dictatorship, and nonconformity vs. collaboration.

---

[23] Glynn Cardy, "The Power of a Prayer: Pussy Riot Tries the Church," sermon given 19 August 2012 at St Mathew-in-the-city: Auckland Aotearoa, New Zealand. (http://www.stmatthews.org.nz/?sid=97&to=Fergus%2BFreeman#!The-Power-of-a-Prayer-Pussy-Riot-Tries-the-Church/c11q0/i1ib1qya27, 4 November 2015)

[24] Elena Volkova, "Mater Nostra: The Anti-blasphemy Message of the Feminist Punk-Prayer," in: *Religion and Gender*, 4, 2 (2014), 202-208. (https://www.religionandgender.org/articles/abstract/10.18352/rg.9897, 2 November 2015)

Moderne Organisationen von Müttern und individuelle Aktivistinnen veränderten die traditionelle religiöse Idee von Femininität und Mutterschaft in postsowjetischen Russland. Sie haben ein säkulares bzw. kulturpolitisches Paradigma der verantwortlichen Mutter- und Schwesternschaft eingeführt. Daraus hat sich ein neues Image der Gottesgebärerin Maria entwickelt, zu der z.B. die Pussy Riot-Frauen 2012 gebetet haben. Religiose Bilder und wie z. B. orthodoxe Ikonographie der Mutter Gottes mit dem Christkind, der Heiliger Georg der Drachentöter, und Konnotationen der biblischen Geschichten über Herodes und das Massaker der Unschuldigen, über den Prozess Jesu und Jesu im Gefängnis widerspiegeln in dieser Interpretation politische Konflikte in und um Russland wie z.b. die Belagerung der Schule in Beslan Schikanen in den Streitkräften, politische Repressionen, der Einmarsch in die Ukraine usw. Dieser „Zusammenstoß von Marien" weißt auf einige Oppositionen hin – eine eine zivile Religion der Menschenrechte steht der neuen autoritären politischen Religion der postkommunistischen Orthodoxie gegenüber, der Ökumenismus dem religiösen Nationalismus, Pazifismus dem Militarismus, Demokratie der Diktatur und schließlich steht Nonkonformismus einem so genannten „Kollaborationismus".

En Rusia del período post-soviético la ONG de las madres y unas mujeres activistas transformaron la idea religiosa tradicional de lo femenino y lo maternal. Ellas introdujeron un entendimiento civil de la "maternidad y hermandad responsable " que dió forma a una nueva imagen de Madre de Dios – una María de los Derechos Humanos – a quien invocaron las de Pussy Riot en 2012. Las imágenes y connotaciones religiosas de la iconografía ortodoxa de la Madre de Dios y Jesús infante; San Jorge matando al Dragón, la tradición de la "iglesia a base de la sangre", tanto como las historias bíblicas de Herodes y la Masacre de los Inocentes, el Juicio de Jesús y Jesús en la Cárcel, presentan la recepción metafórica de numerosos conflictos políticos dentro y fuera de Rusia: la toma de la escuela en Beslán, "abuelismo" militar, falta de justicia, represión política, invasión en Ucrania, víctimas de la guerra no declarada, etc. Este "choque de Marías" indica una serie de oposiciones binarias: una nueva religión política autoritaria de la Ortodoxia post-comunista y una religión civil de los derechos humanos, el ecumenismo y nacionalismo religioso, pacifismo y militarismo, democracia y dictadura, inconformismo y colaboración.

Elena Volkova has a PhD in American Literature (1989) and Religion, Literature and Culture (2001). A professor at Moscow State University, she has taught courses in Comparative Literature and Culture, Religion and Literature, Bible and Culture. In 2011 she resigned from MSU in protest against ideological control. Nowadays she operates as an independent expert, blogger and researcher.

Journal of the European Society of Women in Theological Research 24 (2016) 215-222.
doi: 10.2143/ESWTR.24.0.3170036

BOOK REVIEWS – REZENSIONEN – RECENSIONES

Silvia Martínez Cano (eda.), *Mujeres dese el Vaticano II: memoria y esperanza*, Verbo Divino: Estella (Navarra), 2014, 156 p., ISBN:978-84-9945-985-1.

La conmemoración de los 50 años del concilio Vaticano II actualizó de nuevo el recuerdo de ese gran acontecimiento para la iglesia y volvió a decirnos que todavía había mucho por hacer, cambiar y construir en la vida cristiana de nuestro hoy si queremos responder con fidelidad al seguimiento de Jesús y a los retos que nuestro mundo contemporáneo nos presenta a comienzos del siglo XXI.

La Asociación de teólogas quiso también en sus jornadas anuales de 2013 agradecer, reflexionar y actualizar la memoria de este concilio, ya lejano pero aun necesario. Este libro, publicado en la Colección Aletheia que dirige la propia Asociación, recoge las aportaciones de las diferentes autoras y autores durante este encuentro cuyo objetivo fue, como recordaba Carmen Bernabé, presidenta de la ATE en su presentación de estas jornadas: "recordar el espíritu en el que fue convocado; mirar desde él los documentos para poder entender mejor lo que pretendieron, lo que significan hoy y hacia qué futuro señalan".

Las diversas perspectivas planteadas hicieron posible publicar un texto que permite acercarse a una visión plural, académica pero también experiencial de este acontecimiento que marco a una generación e inspiró a las que vinieron después. La pluralidad de voces que intervienen confluyen en el deseo de visibilizar la presencia y la acción de las mujeres, que como testigos no siempre visibilizados, vivieron y viven el camino eclesial iniciado por el Concilio.

El libro en su primera parte recoge distintas ponencias sobre lo que el Concilio supuso para la Iglesia y también los retos y esperanzas que todavía hoy suscita.

Juan Antonio Estrada en su estudio presenta las claves teológicas e históricas que pueden ayudar a comprender no solo la oportunidad de la convocatoria de este concilio en ese momento histórico, sino también las causas y consecuencias de sus pronunciamientos en las décadas siguientes. Él como testigo de aquella primavera eclesial refrenda con su experiencia lo que propone en su reflexión.

Pilar Yuste, como hija del Concilio, afronta la huella existencial y de pensamiento, que fundamentalmente la Gaudium et Spes, dejó en muchas mujeres inquietas y comprometidas de aquellos años y que se prolonga hoy en la memoria del camino recorrido en actualización de los signos de los tiempos y en el afrontamiento lucido y apasionado de los retos que una vez más son un kairos eclesial que necesita una continuación generacional para que los gozos y esperanzas que posibilitó el Concilio sigan impulsando los caminos del Reino en la vida de las mujeres.

Teresa Toldy nos sitúa con su reflexión en el nuevo paradigma que introdujo el concilio pero que no siempre pasó a la letra de sus textos. Desde ahí se pregunta por la capacidad de la Iglesia en la actualidad de mantener el espíritu del "aggiornamento" clave en el impulso conciliar y llevarlo más allá de la estética, haciéndolo cauce para mantener la fidelidad al Evangelio e instrumento de encuentro con los hombres y mujeres de nuestro tiempo. En esta clave reflexiona sobre el lugar y la palabra de las mujeres dentro de la Iglesia y los impedimentos y malos entendidos que "la cuestión de la mujeres" sigue produciendo al interior de la institución eclesial.

Dolores Aleixandre con su habitual perspicacia, nos invita a mantener una esperanza terca y una mirada lucida como miembros de la iglesia que nos ayude a ver las señales que el Concilio colgó en las ventanas y que nos siguen hablando e invitando a romper inercias, sacudir cansancios y proponer nuestro camino con humildad. A la vez nos propone descubrir las semillas que germinan en los textos conciliares y que poseen una gran capacidad de novedad provocación y vitalidad.

Por último, esa memoria pensada da paso a la memoria vivida. Rafael Aguirre, Marifé Ramos, Felisa Elizondo y Pilar Wirtz evocaron desde sus recuerdos personales, el impacto que en sus vidas, en su fe y en su modo de mirar a la iglesia, supuso el Concilio Vaticano II.

Rafael Aguirre evoca el impacto social y eclesial que supuso la celebración del Concilio, el ambiente y las diversas sensibilidades y movimientos que lo rodeaban e influyeron en la elaboración de sus textos. Sus palabras son testimonio de un momento privilegiado de la historia de la Iglesia que invitan al agradecimiento, pero también al compromiso de hacer posible una nueva etapa de recepción del Vaticano II.

Marifé Ramos tiende un puente entre sus vivencias juveniles en los primeros años del postconcilio y los retos y desafíos actuales. Sus evocaciones personales son iconos del impacto transformador que las líneas fuerza de la renovación conciliar produjo en las mujeres y hombres cristianos de aquellos años y que hoy necesitan seguir siendo profundizadas y actualizadas.

Felisa Elizondo recuerda la presencia de algunas mujeres en el Concilio, una presencia discreta y casi insignificante pero con un fuerte carácter testimonial. El despertar de la nueva conciencia feminista de aquellos años tuvo poco eco en los documentos conciliares y pero fueron las propias mujeres las que impulsaron su propia senda conciliar. Hoy sigue siendo un desafío para la Iglesia institucional incluir la realidad de las mujeres y sus desafíos en su presente y su futuro.

Pilar Wirtz desde su experiencia personal recorre los retos más significativos que la vida religiosa tuvo que afrontar en aquellos años postconciliares y como se fue encarnando ese despertar lucido, comprometido e estimulante que, con aciertos y errores, cambio significativamente el perfil de las religiosas y religiosos. El camino no fue fácil, pero el rescoldo de la hoguera luminosa del concilio ha mantenido las brasas encendidas y la esperanza ha hecho posible la permanencia.

La memoria vital y reflexiva que se recoge en este libro es sin duda estimulante y puede ayudar a las nuevas generaciones a hacer suyo un camino iniciado hace más de cincuenta años, pero todavía inconcluso. Puede además, incorporar nuevos datos a la historia eclesial y a pesar de los límites de cualquier palabra, provocar diálogos y encuentros. Este libro tienen también el valor de poner voz y mirada a muchas mujeres cuyas vidas se transformaron a raíz del Concilio y fueron parteras invisibles de su nacimiento. Ellas son también para las nuevas generaciones herencia de fe y esperanza.

Carme Soto Varela (Vigo – Galicia)

Sabine Dievenkorn, *La noticia del evangelio como traducción intercultural. Una teología sin imperativos en pos de un cristianismo inclusivo y de(s)colonial*, CEEP EDICIONES: Concepción, 2013, 318p., ISBN 978-956-8052-14-0.

Promoting the news of Gospel as an intercultural translation is a constant challenge. This is especially true in South America, where the majority of Christians actively participate in a congregation with authoritarian leadership and very rigid secular and ecclesiastical forms of conduct. In this sense, several paragraphs in Sabine Dievenkorn's *La noticia del evangelio como traducción intercultural* do not concord with the cultural and religious parameters of those who read it. While some of the themes are taboo for our Chilean idiosyncrasy, the author opens a few windows that allow in new rays of light through her questioning, reinterpretations of some biblical passages, and her own testimony and those of others, all of which may be taken as an invitation to a decolonizing Christianity that advances towards inclusivity. In spite of it being a difficult task, it advances thanks to the theological arguments proposed here, not as a final say but as a new possibility of participation in the Kingdom of God.

The richness of the book resides in the possibility of seeing the many distinct religious themes. Sabine Dievenkorn surprises us not only with her profound academic knowledge and her professional and cultural participation in other cultures, but also in her use of Chilean voices as an adequate compliment for her explanations, allowing her book to be read by a heterogeneous audience interested in the current religious themes.

The content allows us to identify both men and women's social roles, cultural and religious prejudice, and fundamentalisms and ideals with which we live every day. Sabine Dievenkorn shows us how we live our faith not only through theological arguments but through historic and idiomatic arguments as well, allowing for postures of support, questioning, and discrepancies.

Lovers of biblical references will find many parts of scripture in each chapter, the majority present in our collective unconsciousness and explained in a pastoral and a gender focused way. Those interested in learning more about ecclesiastic culture and interculturality will find testimonies about the happening in many different countries, to which Sabine Dievenkorn herself has been a generous contributor.

While the book naturally contributes to the social sciences, it is also a great contributor to practical theology. Each chapter can be worked with both independently and collectively. In this sense, it may support work in churches and various subgroups of regular participants, as well as those wishing to look into and study particular issues.

There is an innovative point of view discussing the pastor's conduct in accompanying those in need of his or her support, in light of the question posed by Jesus: "What do you want me to do for you?" Putting this as a requirement on the pastor leads to new responses and practices in the face of pain and crisis. The social differences between health, sickness, healing, and curing are then presented in this theological context.

The next chapters deal with biblical languages, theology, and gender. Here we discover that we are entwined in a hierarchical culture, patriarchal and exclusive, within which we operate daily through our languages. Sabine Dievenkorn proposes a biblical reading that promotes an outlook in which everyone is part of a just Kingdom, including the visualisation of women in many social contexts as a theological response taking gender into account.

Promoting an inclusive church in a decolonial context is thus a difficult task that requires the learning of a different usage of words, where, for instance, one may balance male and female power in a church where women are most oppressed. What is required is not only new languages, but also contemporary interpretations of the bible that do not contrast male and female power for believers, but rather allow and call churches, families, couples, friends, etc. to live a greater harmony with God

These new interreligious lectures, readings, and theological practices in social culture call upon themes that enrich our practice of faith and serve as constant references to how we should mark the way so that it always calls more men and women to church.

Cultivating a holistic theology, a liberating pedagogy, and an inclusive practice with the world each of us builds upon our own individual and social experience, is the key idea that reaffirms the entirety of the book and offers a different perspective for Christianity: one without imperatives. When people live with only one way of interpreting the scripture and a new way appears, it is bound to raise central questions and eventually lead to important changes.

Natalia Eva Salas Molina (Santiago de Chile – Chile)

Theresia Heimerl, *Andere Wesen: Frauen in der Kirche*, Styria: Wien/Graz/Klagenfurt, 2015, 173p., ISBN 978-3-222-13512-5.

Theresia Heimerl's book on women in the Catholic Church is a joy to read: it is witty, ironic, intelligent, critical, realistic, hopeful, generous. Heimerl analyzes official writings on women that have come forth from the magisterium (and as such have a certain authority without being infallible teachings), starting with *Pacem in terris* (1963) until the 2015 version of *Instrumentum laboris*, and reflects on how the Church's view on women has changed over time and what this means for women positioning themselves in the context of the Catholic Church. Quite apart from Heimerl's sharp, insightful interpretations, the book is thus also interesting as an overview of the (few) texts that have focused on women at all.

Two aspects of Heimerl's work are particularly noteworthy: first, her openly and deliberately subjective reading of these texts from the perspective of a woman, born after Vatican II and not just living with(in) the Church as a Catholic, but also working with it as a professor of theology and religious studies at an Austrian university. Thus, Heimerl describes her approach in this book as participant observation (8), an ethnographic approach that allows her to combine an outsider's view of the often strange rituals of the Catholic Church with an insider perspective on what life in the Church means for women (and men). Second, Heimerl consistently situates the texts she analyses in their social and cultural context, drawing in particular on the popular culture of the time (ranging from James Bond to David Bowie to The Simpsons) as an indicator of broader social attitudes. This enables her to trace both parallel developments in Church and society, and to point out the moments when the Church lags behind or – maybe surprisingly for some readers – is actually ahead of its times. Thus, according to Heimerl (152-155), in comparison to what was before, the acknowledgment of women's equal human rights and participation in public life in *Pacem in terris* has to be seen as a huge step forward, positioning the Church ahead of contemporaneous views of women's rights, even if it seems rather old-fashioned from our perspective today. While this head-start is lost with *Humanae vitae* in 1968 and the Church falls further and further behind, its fear of female autonomy and the loss of male power is increasingly shared by society, if the products of popular culture (and probably the larger part of the male population) from the 1980s can be seen as symptomatic. From the 1990s onward, developments in gender theory and social realities have again increased the asynchronicity between the Catholic view of womanhood and the social context by which it is framed, but the 2015 *Instrumentum laboris* has minimised their discrepancy as it sees, maybe for the first time, the world and the Church, and the role of women in it, in all their real plurality and complexity.

The book is organised chronologically with chapters on *Pacem in terris* and *Gaudium et spes*, *Humanae vitae*, *Inter insigniores*, *Familiaris consortio* and *Mulieris dignitatem*, *Ordinatio sacerdotalis*, *On the Collaboration of Men and Women in the Church and Society*, and the 2014 and 2015 versions of *Instrumentum laboris*, with a concluding chapter that summarises central themes and ends with a brief section on *"Und die Männer?"* (169). In between, there are three short chapters, one on the notion of *Wesen*, a rather versatile term that in German means both "being" and "essence", as an adjective (*wesentlich*) "relevant" or "important", and in its negative form (*Unwesen*) "trouble", and as such provides a nice hook for the discussion of the philosophical background to Catholic understandings of the essence of femininity and their political consequences; a second one that imagines an unlikely meeting between Thomas Aquinas and Judith Butler and offers a precise overview of these complex philosophical models and their influence on theories of gender; and a third one that briefly discusses the astonishing absence of women religious from the magisterial texts about women.

Moving from the 1960s towards the present, Heimerl notes the ever-increasing focus on the eternal and universal "essence" of womanhood, thought to be found in the role of a woman as wife and mother, with the associated suppression of the diversity of women's experiences and idealisation of marriage not just as the space of full expression of femininity, but also as the central metaphor for the relationship between God and the Church. Heimerl sees this development as a response to social changes that lead to greater independence of women and a threat to the male position of power, the attempt to return to an idealised past in which women were the "weak sex" that needed the protection of the strong male: *"Retro, aber aus der Distanz nicht ganz unromantisch"* (85). In a sense, then, these documents, purportedly speaking about "women" and their position in the Church, can be seen as an attempt to come to terms with changes in the understanding of "masculinity" and men's role in the Church and the world, as Heimerl discusses in particular in regard to *Ordinatio sacerdotalis*, the document that prohibits even the discussion of women's ordination. As Heimerl concludes, it is less interesting as a document on the biblical, historical, or theological arguments for or against women's ordination, but highly interesting for a discussion of the relationship between gender and power (95) – a topic that is, of course, taboo in polite theological conversation.

In the chapter on the most contemporary texts, the two versions of *Instrumentum laboris* produced in the context of the Synods on the Family held in 2014 and 2015, it becomes clear how much has changed over the years, at least in inner-Catholic discourses. The perception of women has moved from seeing them as *aiduitorium viri* (men's helpers) with a kind of secondary soul in pre-1963 theology, to full members of Church and society, first with equal human rights, then with a dignity of their own, which sounds nice but can create problems when dignity and rights are pitched against each other, and women's dignity becomes "woman"'s dignity, essentialising and generalising women's plural experiences. *Instrumentum laboris* takes things a large step further, especially in its 2015 version: it acknowledges the plurality of the Catholic Church today, and with it the plurality of family situations and women's experiences. Closely analysing the changes between the 2014 and 2015 versions, Heimerl shows how for once the Church has moved *"knapp unter der erlaubten Höchstgeschwindigkeit und für manche subjektive Wahrnehmung deutlich darüber"* (133). First of all, women are no longer a topic that requires special attention, but are finally fully a part of the reality of the Catholic Church and the public life of society, in the variety of their roles and positions. Given continued discrimination in patriarchal systems, the Church sees it as its responsibility to contribute to change by including women in decision making processes, and appreciating their importance and responsibility in the Church (134). No longer is the "essence" of femininity the central topic, and gender is no longer the evil responsible for all kinds of confusion on the individual, theological, and ethical level. While women are still primarily seen within their familial context, the document does no longer idealise family life, but instead acknowledges its risks and problems and the diverse forms it might take. The model of the family that it proposes is then not the bourgeois happy family (the father, mother, child, and dog we see smiling from advertisments), but the Holy Family – and this is, as Heimerl shows, a family that couldn't be any more different: a family that is far from perfect, with conflicts, an absent father, and a rebellious son.

Change no longer seems to be something to deny in order to (unsuccessfully) protect the status quo, but something that is acknowledged, accepted, and maybe – who knows? – even something to be welcomed (while this last view might not yet be explicit in the document, there's hope that the changes that have taken place may lead to that – the Spirit moves in unpredictable ways).

Heimerl's analysis is both clear-sightedly realistic, fair and hopeful: yes, the Church's views on women have led to suffering, have contributed to discrimination and inhibited women from fulfilling their potential as full members of the Church. The women who decided to turn their backs on this Church did so with good reason. But when read in their historical context, it is also clear that the documents are results of their times and particular philosophical and theological traditions, which at least helps to understand where they come from. For Heimerl, the recent changes – especially when seen on the background of this history – are promising, and thus she concludes, hopefully: *"Wer es als Frau bis jetzt in der Kirche ausgehalten hat, sollte bleiben, denn jetzt wird's erst richtig spannend"* (169).

With its wonderfully ironic style, critical analysis, and accessible explanations of complex theoretical and theological issues, this book addresses a broad audience, but offers new insights and ideas also to those who are specialised in the field of gender and theology.

Stefanie Knauss (Villanova – USA)

Journal of the European Society
of Women in Theological Research

All volumes of the Journal of the ESWTR can be ordered from Peeters Publishers, Bondgenotenlaan 153, B-3000 Leuven
Fax: +32 16 22 85 00; e-mail: order@peeters-leuven.be

The volumes of the Journal of the ESWTR are also available online at
http://poj.peeters-leuven.be